HEADHUNTER
One One

*The Vietnamese Memoir of a
Recon/Observation Pilot*

Vincent Capozzella
219th Aviation Company

EAGLE EDITIONS
2007

EAGLE EDITIONS
AN IMPRINT OF HERITAGE BOOKS, INC.

Books, CDs, and more—Worldwide

For our listing of thousands of titles see our website at
www.HeritageBooks.com

Published 2007 by
HERITAGE BOOKS, INC.
Publishing Division
65 East Main Street
Westminster, Maryland 21157-5026

Copyright © 2007 Vincent J. Capozzella

All rights reserved. No part of this book may be reproduced or transmitted in any form or by any means, electronic or mechanical, including photocopying, recording or by any information storage and retrieval system without written permission from the author, except for the inclusion of brief quotations in a review.

International Standard Book Number: 978-0-7884-4485-2

Contents

Acknowledgements	5
Preface	7
The Board and Vietnam	11
A Troubling Beginning	17
An Army Career	23
The 219th	39
Arriving in Vietnam	43
Pleiku	51
An Khe and Our Vietnamese Allies	57
The Routine	63
Bao Loc	67
A Tiger Hunt	83
Goodbye Lieutenant Trumball	91
Promotion and the Ace of Spades	97
Tea and Ms. Raye	103
Strange Customs	111
Special Forces	113
Ia Drang Valley	117
The Gonorrhea Fiasco	127
The Roadblock and the CIA	141
Dalat and Mistakes	145
R & R	159
Heads and Senseless Death	165
Missions on the Coast	171
The 25th Division	177
Flying for God and New Ways to Kill	185
Home and Lessons	191
Epilogue	199
Glossary	201

Acknowledgement

Headhunter One One is the factual story of Lieutenant Vincent J. Capozzella during his journey with the 219th Aviation Company during his one-year assignment in Vietnam from June 1965 to June 1966. All the individuals mentioned in this book are actual people who served with me although I have changed the names of many of the various characters with the notable exceptions of Major Robert A. Lust, commander of the 219th, Captain Ramon Leyda, my immediate supervisor, and close friends and comrades, Lieutenants Charles Kellum and Barry Taylor. The name changes are the result of poor memory and somewhat questionable behavior and activities which might bring discredit to their efforts during this difficult period.

Preface

The Vietnam War is a confusing history. The accessibility of previously classified documents has made it clear that the United States made both a strategic and tactical mistake in committing its troops to defend the shaky administration in South Vietnam. These mistakes led to America's withdrawal from South Vietnam and the eventual victory of the Communist North. Increasingly American veterans have become vocal in their denial of historical facts and maintain that civilians, who did not understand military concepts and restricted the U.S. forces from fighting properly, squandered victory. This stance does an injustice to the thousands of Americans who gave their lives and limbs to bring victory to the cause. These Americans fought under difficult circumstances and gave their best. Unfortunately this effort was not enough to overcome an enemy that fought with a tenacity that surprised both the U.S. administration and the military high command.

Americans are generally ignorant of the facts, that after the French surrender at Dienbienphu in 1954, the convening peace negotiations attended by representatives of France, China, the Soviet Union, the United States, Great Britain and Ho Chi Minh's Vietminh decided to divide Vietnam into two parts until the summer of 1956. At that time an election would be held to determine the future of the country. All participants signed the accord except the United States. America's political leaders realized that a nationwide election would unite North and South Vietnam under the leadership of communist Ho Chi Minh. Ho was easily the most popular Vietnamese and was considered the George Washington of his country after leading the revolution against the French. Very quietly the United States began to undercut the terms of the accord and gave both economic and military aid to South Vietnam with the understanding that the South would not submit to the nationwide election. It was believed that with the support of the United States that South Vietnam under the leadership of Ngo Dinh Diem would be the building block to stop the eventual takeover of Southeast Asia by the communists or as called by the U.S. government, the Domino Theory. President Diem's regime proved to be unsatisfactory to President Kennedy and the South Vietnamese military assassinated Diem in 1963 with the possible approval or at least support from the CIA. This assassination led to an increase in military support for the South and to a massive increase in American fighting forces by Presidents Johnson and Nixon.

This book is not a history of this war but rather a glimpse into the day-to-day happenings involving one American and those soldiers with him. It is not a glorification of a war which was in reality a hot, dirty, and terribly tragic fight nor is it a condemnation of a situation that should never have happened.

In truth, I went to South Vietnam with all the eagerness of a young untried warrior convinced in the purity and justification of my mission to stop the hated Viet Cong and their puppet masters from North Vietnam. After a year in country, I returned to the United States with a disillusionment of our efforts to win the war, the willingness of our South Vietnamese allies and the lack of support from the American people. After leaving the military it took many years and reading to come to the understanding and conclusion that the American people were mislead and our leaders had sent its young men and women into a situation which was not winnable in the context of commitment and support.

Like most Americans, I did not initially have a very favorable impression of the fighting qualities of the Viet Cong or "VC" as the fighting men labeled them. My impression was that these were a people lacking in sophisticated weapons and military training. Their leaders were probably peasants like themselves with no leadership skills. I also assumed that most of the VC were pressed into the war and had no true commitment to defeat the South and to fight the American military. True, the French Foreign Legion had been defeated by the Viet Minh. Yet most American fighting men and our leaders did not have a very high opinion of the French forces. All of these concepts were fostered by first the John F. Kennedy administration and then the Lyndon Johnson and Richard Nixon administrations. President Johnson referred to Vietnam as that "damn little pissant country" and his feeling was shared by most of the Army's officer corps. Unfortunately for thousands of Americans who gave their lives for this cause, none of these concepts were true. In reality, our enemy was eager to fight the American invader. Their leaders understood an insurgency that was to be fought in a jungle terrain that neutralized much of our industrial advantages and their forces were hardened professionals that had fought years against first, the Japanese, and then, the French.

I had been trained, first as an infantry enlisted man and then as a 90-day wonder from the U.S. Army's Officer Training Program. By the time I had completed my training I had accepted all our country's theories and beliefs about the Vietnamese. I was convinced that our cause was just and we would prevail with superior weapons, training and fighting spirit. I failed perhaps like most of the American leadership, to read any of the history of the French involvement in Indochina that included Vietnam, and neither did any of my instructors. Yes, the French defeat in their war against Ho Chi Minh's Vietminh was briefly discussed but was easily explained away. Our reasoning was that the French have been militarily soft since their horrible casualties from World War I and II and consequently lacked the espirit de corps to effectively wage war against any enemy. In addition, the French lacked our resources particularly in aircraft and armor vehicles. History has shown that perhaps the French did lack our resources in terms of equipment but they certainly did not lack in courage and willingness to fight the enemy.

In the early 1960's I as most Americans believed what my country's leaders were telling us about the cruelty and inhumanity of the enemy. The oriental people were not held in the highest esteem by either the American government or the American military. In the last twenty years, the United States had withstood the Japanese in World War II who gained an initial advantage because of their sneak attack on December 7, 1941 but fell to the skill of the American soldier. During the Korean War, again the United States had withstood a sneak attack by the North Koreans and then an attack by the Communist Chinese who were able to force a stalemate based on their use of millions of massed troops flung into battle without any concern for life. Now, again the Orientals under the concept of World Communism were challenging the United States in what we saw as a life or death struggle for world leadership. Americans were told that the people of South Vietnam were freedom loving people whose only desire was to be allowed to exist in peace and were being overwhelmed by an enemy supported by both Communist China and the Soviet Union. It was our duty as the caretaker of freedom to assist the South Vietnamese in their quest for freedom and democracy. Inveritably, leaders always attempt to inspire their own people. They argue, that those countries we are about to help, are freedom-loving people starving for the right to vote and elect their leaders. While this concept has a natural appeal to Americans, it was not necessarily true or even close to being accurate in South Vietnam.

My tour of duty in Vietnam would test all these concepts and preconceived theories concerning the VC and South Vietnam. I was totally convinced that the South was being attacked by a great magnitude of enemies and valiantly holding their own. I was also convinced that the United States military would prevail and defeat these small, ill equipped peasants. I would certainly have labeled myself as a right-wing American who classified all those who disagreed with our Vietnam policy as being dangerously close to treasonous.

Presidents Johnson and Kennedy had convinced us of the threat of the communist conspiracy to roll over this part of the world and to strip the United States of its allies. They called it the Domino Theory. The theory implied that the North Vietnamese communist supported by their masters the Soviet Union and Red China would invade one country after another until all of the Far East was under their control. I was still young enough to believe this rhetoric and much like later day soldiers, who would also embrace exaggerations from our government, was ready and willing to put my life on the line to stop the red menace.

President Lyndon B. Johnson had decided in late 1964 on the advice of Defense Secretary Robert McNamara and National Security Council Chief McGeorge Bundy to begin the build-up of American military personnel to assist the South Vietnamese Armed Forces (ARVN). This decision was made in spite of the evidence that indicated that the North Vietnamese would be difficult or impossible to defeat. In 1963 the U.S. military had staged a war game code named Sigma I. It concluded that at least 500,000 American troops would be needed to have any chance to defeat the VC and its ally, the North Vietnamese. I was part of that 500,000 increase although I was not privy to the decision or its misgivings. To make matters worst, in response to Air Force Chief of Staff Curtis Lemay's boast, that we could "bomb North Vietnam to the stone age", another war game was held in 1964 code named

Sigma II. This exercise concluded that it was impossible to defeat North Vietnam with air power and like Hitler's Germany and the Japanese in World War II, its people would merely carry on through the hardship. Yet, President Johnson ordered the bombing of North Vietnam using the pretext that two American destroyers, the Maddox and C. Turner Joy, had been attacked without provocation in international waters in the Gulf of Tonkin. This incident was a mistake on the part of the ships' crews and although the incident was quickly clarified, the president decided to mislead Congress and obtained their support for the air war. Unfortunately neither Congress nor I was aware that the President's advisors were already dubious as to our chances for success or the legitimacy of the call to arms. Like many young men and women in 1965, I was more than ready to fight for my country and was totally convinced as to the righteousness of the endeavor.

Chapter One – The Board and Vietnam

I had been back from my tour of duty in Vietnam for over a year. It was late fall of 1967 and I was again assigned to Fort Rucker, Alabama. My military counselor told me in the first month after returning to the U.S. in June 1966 that I would receive my orders for the second tour of duty in Vietnam within one and a half years. To make matters even worst, I would be returning to combat as a section commander and pilot of a group of attack helicopters called the Cobra. The thought of having to learn how to fly this new aircraft and of leading a bunch of young, untrained pilots in Vietnam did not give me a good feeling as to my chances of surviving another tour. In addition, I had come to the conclusion that, when the war was over, I and my fellow pilots would no longer be needed and would find ourselves without jobs and futures after giving our country some of our best young years. I decided to secure my Army career by applying for what was called a "Regular Army Commission." I was a Reserve Officer in the Army and could be discarded by the Army when I was no longer of any use. "Regular Army Commissions" are given to top graduates of a college Army ROTC program and to all West Point graduates. I could obtain one only by application and the odds of success are very low.

Regardless, I was standing in front of the Army Board, which would determine my fate as to the commission. The room was situated like a miniature courtroom with the judges sitting behind an extended podium. They were at least two feet above me while I was allowed to sit on a chair facing them with no other furniture near me. As usual it was a sunny day and the light shined through the windows like a spotlight. Perhaps the light would beacon a new direction for my military career.

There were five officers on the Board and I didn't know any of them. The head of the Board was Colonel James Francis who had a look of being quite annoyed at having to chair a hearing that had little hope of success. Two other officers held ranks of Lieutenant Colonel while the last two were a major and a captain. I was relieved to see that all five men were like myselfme wearing the wings of an Army pilot. Although all the board members had more decorations than me, I took some delight in knowing that none had a Vietnamese campaign ribbon nor any medals or decorations for combat. I wondered whether my awards would impress or merely antagonize them. I also realized that people who have never flown in combat couldn't understand the fear, exhilaration and satisfaction from that experience. Unfortunately, the other four Board members also had the same disgusted or bored look on their faces. I saluted the Board and hoped for the best.

"Sit down Captain Capozzella, "Colonel Francis said.

I was relieved that he at least knew my name and pronounced Capozzella correctly. Perhaps things were not as bad as I thought.

He continued, "As you know this Board's objective is to interview you and make a recommendation to higher authorities as to you fitness to hold a

Regular Army Commission. We do not have the authority to approve or disapprove this action but can only make a recommendation. Do you understand, Captain Capozzella?"

"Yes Sir." I replied in my most snappy voice. I had decided to keep the answers as brief as possible so that I didn't put my foot in my mouth as I have been prone to do in the past.

"Your Army record speaks for itself and I might add that after a shaky start as an officer you did distinguish yourself in Vietnam as a combat pilot. Consequently we're not interested in your past record but rather your views about the Army and the war."

I could feel a cold sweat break out under my armpits. I really didn't want to talk about the war. It wasn't that I had some deep-seated revulsion to talk about death but rather my disgust about how the war was proceeding and the waste of the year I had spent there already. I silently told myself, that whatever they asked,, I had to play the game. In interviews such as this one, it was always better to tell the decision makers what they wanted to hear rather than your own views even if it meant lying. People already have preconceived notions of events even though the only news they have is second hand. They simply choose to believe what they want as long as it conforms to their beliefs. I realized that military personnel tend to believe their work is important and they must succeed. The Vietnam War was the only war at the moment and the military needed to show the civilian world that we could be successful. Consequently they had already determined the war could be won and could be won through the swift and massive application of airpower. The improvement of the helicopter and the remarkable durability of the Huey (UH-1) convinced them that success could be achieved by mobility. Just as a cavalry unit could move more quickly than infantry, the United States Army's fleet of helicopters gave us an advantage over the enemy that lacked airpower and mobility. Therefore once the military decided that he had an advantage of movement and obviously weapons, our forces had to succeed. What the military failed to realize was that our troops had a decided advantage in movement to a battlefield; we were merely transporting them to areas where the enemy was already established and didn't need swift movement. Also the jungle negated the advantage of mobility since the enemy could move unseen below the thick canopy. If one has never walked in a jungle or flown over it, you cannot understand the difficulty in implementing your advantage.

This panel wanted me to tell them that at least in 1966 the United States was winning the war. They knew this fact to be true since the body counts by our troops already confirmed this belief. If they understood the reality of the body count theory, than perhaps they would not have been as confident. But they were never in Vietnam. The board needed me to confirm their belief the war was being won primarily through the use of aircraft. They needed me to say the soldiers serving in Vietnam were all the best we could field since the United States had the best trained and supplied army the world has ever seen. They needed me to say the soldiers were all gallant and ready to give their lives for the cause of freedom. They needed me to say our South Vietnamese allies were adequate and were willing to fight alongside American troops without flinching. Unfortunately their beliefs were totally wrong. Yet I was trying to condition myself to tell them what they wanted to hear and what they believed to be the truth. I felt like a prostitute who simply said whatever her client wanted to hear. The feeling of being dirty was most evident as I sat before these gentlemen who knew nothing about what they were presumed to know.

"Now Captain, how do you think the war is going in Vietnam," asked Colonel Francis? "We would like your perspective as to the Army's progress in bringing the war to a successful conclusion although we are also aware that you can only speak from the vantage point of a small section of the war."

The question was so fundamental and straightforward that I was completely taken off guard. Why couldn't they ask questions dealing with the Army's role or achievements in Vietnam? Their question went to the heart of the matter and was asking me whether the U.S. was winning the war and whether the Army was contributing to that success. Obviously they expected me to say, the war was slowly being won, that it was just a matter of time before we neutralize the enemy and the Army, particularly Army Aviation, was making a tremendous difference toward that adjective. I just couldn't do it.

For some unknown reason, I decided to go for the quick kill and tell them what I really thought. "Sir, I don't see how bombing an enemy from 30,000 feet can win a war. The Army taught me victory could only be achieved by defeating the enemy's ground forces and taking over their areas of control. Right now, all we're doing is making large craters in the jungle."

Immediately I could see from the look of shock and doubt on the faces of the board members that I had made a terrible mistake. Quickly I scanned the uniforms of the Board members and realized that although they were all Army pilots, none of them were from the infantry branch as I was. The infantry is taught that victory is achieved when the enemy's ground forces are destroyed or neutralized but this action can only be accomplished by one's own ground forces supported by air power. They obviously were not buying my attempt to teach them the fundamentals of military doctrine. The average person in the military believes that his job is the more important or at least one of the top two most important jobs. It is difficult to convince military minds that the job at hand is to win and winning can only truly be accomplished with defeating the enemy's forces and will to resist. World War II should have taught everyone that Germany was defeated when the allied armies swarmed over all of Germany and their ground forces were either destroyed or captured. There is no question that air power assisted this victory but the Nazis would have continued to fight no matter how many bombs were dropped from the skies. The second problem of my answer to the board was to imply that we were not winning. Every military mind looks at every bright spot of war and magnetizes that achieve even though the majority of the data is negative. The military has difficulty in accepting the fact they are not winning. I just told the board we were not winning.

I had made the mistake that I had told myself not to make. I shouldn't have answered the question in this manner but I really couldn't help myself. The answer was the truth. A further survey of the officers on the Board also revealed that none of them were wearing the Air Medal or Vietnam Service Medal. The lack of these medals meant that none of them had served in Vietnam and therefore knew only the information coming from the Johnson administration, the Army and the still pro-war news agencies. Sure I had seen the war first hand for over a year but that meant nothing to these men.

Colonel Francis seemed at a loss for words. After a few seconds that seemed like an hour, he said, "Are you trying to tell this Board that we are losing the war?"

"No sir, we're not losing the war but I don't think we are winning it either. This war is going to require the United States to fight the VC in the jungle and perhaps eventually on the ground in the North. I just don't see us making that kind of commitment. The administration and the military are trying to minimize the ground losses through the extensive use of airpower, which in reality is effective but not going to give us victory."

"So, you don't believe that the air forces of the combined military services can achieve success," asked Colonel Francis?

"Sir, our air power will not be denied success. However, in my mind air power is intended to be one of the numerous methods to achieve victory and not the main and only means."

"I'm glad to see that you have a strategic grasp of the situation. Yet our information tends to indicate our bombing efforts are inflicting horrendous numbers of casualties and destruction of equipment against the enemy."

"That is true, Sir. Yet the enemy continues to successfully recruit replacements and the equipment we are destroying tends to be minor such as bicycles used to carry supplies from the north along the Ho Chi Minh trail to the south."

"Bicycles," asked Francis?

"Yes Sir," I replied. Now I knew I was speaking for a losing cause. These men didn't even know that the main vehicle used by the VC to bring supplies from the north was a bicycle.

"Well, Captain Capozzella, what do you think of the proposed Tet ceasefire that is being proposed by some of our politicians?"

Tet was a period of time in Vietnam given to observing their religious background and culture and had been marked in the previous three years by a reduction in Vietcong military action. The question had some historical irony since the Vietcong and North Vietnamese troops would on January 31, 1968 launch their Tet offensive thereby shifting American support against the war.

Since I probably had already botched the interview, I would give answers that reflected my true conviction. "Sir, if we are ever going to end the war, eventually we must sit down with the enemy to discuss issues relating to the conflict. Without direct dialog between them and us, the war will simply go on indefinitely. Since I have made my position clear on what I see as a lack of commitment by both the military and the public, I believe some type of honorable peace would be the most logical choice open to us."

Again the look of disbelief by the members. Lt. Colonel Turner then spoke for the first time. "Do you see any negative affect of a ceasefire?"

"Yes Sir, during a pause in combat operations against the enemy, they obviously will have the opportunity to regroup and to resupply their units."

"And you believe this is a gamble our forces should take when the war is going against the North?"

I quickly replied, "Sir, without face-to-face dialog, the war will just simply continue to go on."

"Captain Capozzella, your answers really imply we are losing the war," countered Colonel Francis?

"No Sir, I didn't mean to imply that conclusion; I just don't think that the tactics we are using are going to win the war. The best we will achieve if we continue the present activity, in my opinion, is a stalemate."

"And you have a crystal ball indicating this conclusion," interrupted the previously silent Captain at the far right of the Board?

The blood rushed to my face as I turned to the Captain. "The Vietminh fought first, the Japanese and then the French for almost fifteen years without any sign of a let down. I don't think the American people are going to support a war that could last that long without positive signs of victory."

Lt. Colonel Turner responded, "Our kill ratios against the Cong and North Vietnamese are fantastic. The enemy can't continue to fight with those kind of loses."

"Sir, I can only say that those numbers are misleading and not very accurate. Kill ratios also don't take into account the recruitment by the VC of family and friends of those people we have killed who want revenge. For every VC we kill, I believe the enemy is recruiting at least one or more additional recruits." I realized the interview had broken down into a debate between myself and the Board, which would inevitably mean my rejection.

At last Colonel Francis spoke up, "Well, Captain Capozzella, we thank you for you responses to our questions and the Army will shortly notify you as to the status of your request for a RA Commission." The Board then stood up and departed the room.

I knew I had failed in my quest to secure my future in the Army. In one short 20-minute span, I had changed the direction of my life and knew my future lay outside the military. I continued sitting in the interview room thinking back to Vietnam and the events that would polarize my views of the war eventually leading to my failure to play the game. My thoughts drifted back.

I remember feeling a hot gust of wind blow across my face as I looked out over the large airfield at Travis Air Force Base in California. We really couldn't see much of the Air Force base since we had just walked down the ramp of a C-130 four-engine troop and cargo plane. The plane was parked on the tarmac in front of a large military hanger and was being refueled for the next leg of our journey to Vietnam. I stood with a small group of Army officers awaiting our flight across the Pacific Ocean to join in the fight against the communist invasion of Vietnam. This trip was my first visit to California and I had hoped to have a day or two of leisure to see the area before continuing my mission. However, this hope was not to become reality and I stayed at Travis for only one hour. My observations of California were limited to looking over a small wire fence at an empty field of grass.

Along with a group of other would-be patriots, I boarded our C-130 for the flight to Vietnam in June 1965 with a great deal of excitement and apprehension. Our unit the 219th Aviation Company was composed of only 6 staff, 24 pilots and 20 aircraft mechanics and support personnel. The pilots held a rank between 2nd Lieutenant and Captain and were all volunteers. The war had not reached the point when most personnel going to Vietnam were primarily draftees and reluctant participants. As I looked around at the other pilots and ground personnel I was filled with amazement and admiration for our determination. Most of them had a lean hard look about them. Thousands of groups like our own would be making the same journey over the coming years although our group was slightly different from later groups in terms of our ages and dedication. Most of the pilots were experienced pilots with three or four years of military flying and all were on this mission because they wanted to be here. The majority of the pilots were between 25 and 30 years old and none had any combat experience prior to this tour of duty. Our attitude was one of excitement, confidence and determination to defeat this enemy. I differed only in the fact that I was one of the lowest ranking pilots and had only limited flying experience.

Our mission was "search and destroy" by air. The planes used were outdated and slow observation aircraft without benefit of armaments. Once the enemy was located we were to call either air strikes or artillery against the targets.

The 219th was formed just two months earlier as a result of someone's imagination and belief that the Vietcong could be observed and neutralized from the air. Apparently this person or persons had never had to deal with a guerrilla style war and had no conception of the reality of the dense jungle in Vietnam. Our command chose as our call sign "Headhunter" and I was assigned Headhunter 11 with the call sign of Headhunter One One.

I knew few of the personnel in the unit with the exception of one pilot from my flight class. All the men wore the typical somewhat heavy green fatigues that we had starched so that they fit like a board over our bodies. When we experienced the heat and humidity of Vietnam, those fatigues would literally soak our perspiration and show lines of starch and body salt stains. The pilots all had the stern look of determination and I wondered how the Vietcong would be able to stand up to America's best.

Chapter 2 – A Troubling Beginning

At the time I had been married for a little over a year to my college sweetheart with a daughter born five days before the flight to Vietnam. I was born and raised in Utica, New York in a lower middle class environment. I come from a close-knit Italian family in a city with a large Italian community. As in most Italian families during that time of American history, my grandmother on my mother's side of the family was the hub and glue that kept us a tight knit family. We would meet as a family at my grandmother's apartment once or twice a month. The usual activity was eating some of my grandmother's famous Italian pasta and playing penny ante poker. My family called me "Vinny." I really disliked this nickname and so once established away from home at college, I adopted "Vince" that has stayed with me throughout life with the exception of occasional visits to see my relatives.

My father's side of the family was much less friendly and probably could be described as dysfunctional. My grandfather had been sent to jail in the late 1920's for the murder of his wife's lover. According to the bits and pieces I learned, he had learned of the adulterous relationship when he caught his wife in bed with the other man. My grandfather was only about 5'2" tall but built like a fireplug. He killed the man and was sent to prison for over five years. I always wondered why he just didn't simply walk up to the bed and thank the man for giving him the opportunity to get rid of this dreadful woman. Unfortunately my grandmother was also built like a fireplug since she appeared to be 5' tall and 5' wide. She was an unloving type of person. When my grandfather returned from prison, she sentenced him to live in the basement of their home. By day he worked for a railroad repairing lines in the summer and removing snow from around the switches and buildings in the winter. After work and on weekends he would spend his time pressing grapes and making wine in a large wood vat of about 6' diameter. While he was pressing the grapes, he would drink last years wine from another vat of the same dimensions. I thought he was far happier and better off than living upstairs in the main portion of the house with his wife. My grandmother often wore pants. They were quite unusual for this time period and quite comical considering her size. She worked during the summer as the foreman of itinerant black workers recruited from the south. The workers picked vegetables planted in fields near Utica and lived in a long complex of wood shanties that were owned by my grandmother. She also owned and operated a small grocery and liquor store located next to the shanties. In all probability, the workers ate and drank all their wages and left the summer work with very little in their pockets.

Raised in this kind of environment it was easy to understand that it would have a distinct affect upon my father. He worked as a mailman with the U.S. Post Office while my mother worked as a supervisor in a cloth mill that made children clothes. My relationship with my father was poor since he was quick to lose his temper and an alcoholic. Fortunately any abuse he administered was verbal and not physical but was enough to strain our relationship and cause me to drift away from my most immediate family members. I cannot blame my father alone for our ruptured relationship since my commitment to serious life style was slow to develop.

In grammar school and high school I was a typical nerd who did enough school work to receive a B average. Although I had many friends both male and female, my love life left much to be desired. I had a number of crushes but usually was not very successful although my one major attribute was my ability to dance the popular dances such as the jitterbug. I really never matured as an athlete in high school although my height of slightly less than 5'7" did not provide me with natural advantages in football or basketball. In baseball I really couldn't hit a fastball and lacked a good glove. Track was out of the question since I was terribly slow.

As a result of the sputnik scare that America was losing the race to space because of disinterest in engineering and sciences, schools began the push for students to major in related fields. I was caught up in this movement and went to college as a chemical engineer major. This choice was a tragic mistake since I had neither the desire nor the ability to handle this curriculum.

In 1962 I flunked out of college after four years of study in what I liked to describe as majoring in girl chasing. The release from the constant badgering from my father became evident in the dedication to academic studies and the realization that I was finally free although my financial support was from my parents. With the exception of Christmas break, I remained at college even during other holidays while my life centered on drinking and dating as many girls as possible. College was for me one continuous party and I did not dwell on my immediate future or the world's problems. My dismissal from Clarkson College at Potsdam, New York for poor grades had seen the final break between my father and me. In the summer of 1962, I had returned home with few opinions as to what to do with my life. I felt like a loser. I was one of the few members of my close family including my aunts, uncles and cousins who had gone to college. They were initially very proud of me although my failures made me feel embarrassed.

My high school and college friends were all graduated and moving on to career employment while I had few options. I took a job with the Post Office in Utica which unfortunately was also where my father worked. I attempted to go back to college for my final year but realized that I would have to do it on my own with my own finances. In 1962, there was little financial support from the federal government and school loans would require the signature of a working adult. Turning to my father was not an option and so I turned to the only other person available. My on and off again girlfriend, Carmela Casale, from high school and college, had just graduated from college. I had known Carmela since grammar school and had fallen in love with her at an early age. She had developed into a very beautiful young lady with dark complexion and deep brown eyes. Our relationship was strange since I pursued her throughout high school with only marginal success. Her family was fairly well off financially and she decided to attend Russell Sage College in Upstate

New York. The college had a reputation of being a snobby women's college for rich young ladies. My college had an excellent scholastic reputation as an engineering college and as a hockey power. Once free of my father I was totally infatuated with the college freedom and life style. Although I was considered somewhat of a geek in high school, I suddenly found myself being able to successfully pursue any of the women at college. I wondered why I had not the same degree of success in high school and particularly with Carmela. However, each summer I had returned to my relationship with Carmela. I found that if I did not pursue her as rigorously as before and treated her less sincere, the closer our relationship seemed to grow. To be honest I was not considering any permanent relationship with either her or my girlfriend from college who would eventually become my wife. Since Carmela's father was fairly wealthy and I reasoned that perhaps with my relationship with his daughter being as close as it was, that perhaps he would be the adult to sign my college loan papers. I called Carmela about two weeks after my return to Utica from college. I realized that I would have to convince Carmela of my idea before making the pitch to her father. I phoned her in the evening although I had yet to see her.

Carmela answered the phone. "Hi, how are you doing?" I asked.

"I expected you to call me before now," she answered in a somewhat agitated tone. "I've been home for almost a week and no word from you."

"Well," I hesitated, "I've been trying to deal with flunking out."

Carmela responded, "I can imagine. One our friends called me to let me know of your problem." I could picture her ordeal in trying to tell her parents that her sometime boyfriend was a failure. Somehow I couldn't imagine that her parents would be very happy with her relationship with me. It didn't help that I had very little contact with her parents although they had known me for at least ten years. I had never had a conversation with her father that lasted over a minute or two. I had serious doubts that they held me in very high esteem. At the time it was probably a fairly accurate assessment based on performance.

"Listen. You know my father. I can't stand to be living here and I have to come to some plan for my future." I said and hoped that she didn't pick up on my mistake of referring to my future instead perhaps on our future.

"What do you plan to do?" she asked. "I assumed you would try to get a job somewhere and get your degree in night school."

"I've been thinking all week about my problem and what to do and I've decided to return to school perhaps at Oswego State Teacher's College for my final year."

"Do you want to be a teacher?" she asked.

"I don't care what kind of degree I get as long as I graduate and from what I've read, I can probably get accepted easy enough and it doesn't have that difficult a reputation. It's also nearby and logistically it would be easier than going to a school far from Utica."

"What can I do?"

"If I can get accepted I will need to borrow the money to return to school. I checked with a local bank and they said a loan was possible if I had a responsible adult with good credit who was willing to co-sign the loan. I'm not even going to consider asking my parents since they've done enough already and I'm on my father's shit list."

"Who do you think would be willing to sign for the loan?"

Now we were getting to the heart of the matter and for a moment I hesitated. Finally I said, "Do you think your father would be willing to co-sign?"

There was a brief pause but she responded, "I think he would be willing to sign if we had a commitment for our future together." The response caught me off guard and I didn't know if she was suggesting an immediate commitment such as marriage.

Surely I had always considered marrying her and thought that our marriage was a good possibility. We had never discussed getting married throughout the long courtship and it was one of those things that I took for granted. I was also aware that during our college years that Carmela had boyfriends during the college period but didn't know how serious they were. I also was concentrating on the problem that I faced at that moment and marriage had not entered my mind. The easy response would have been to consent to a marriage or at least engagement to obtain the loan and eventual college degree. Yet I couldn't deceive a person I had known and cared for all these years. I responded, "Frankly Carmy, you're not part of my plans at this moment and all I want is your help. You know how I feel about you but I can only deal with the college problem first." I knew immediately that I had made a serious mistake but had been truthful.

There was a ten second pause and Carmela hung up the phone. I never saw or talked to her again and heard that she had married her college boyfriend about two months later. It was possible that her marriage to this other suitor was already being planned or that she was in a hurry to begin life as a housewife. I never knew or discovered the answer. I accepted the rupture of our relationship without much mourning since I had not given my future much thought at this point in life.

The failure to secure support for my college loan doomed any return to college and forced me to look for permanent employment. My work in the Post Office did not improve my relationship with my father as by then I had given up on any attempt to become his buddy. Every night I listened to his tirade about my failure and his disappointment in me. I listened to my father's complaining for a summer and sneaked off one day and enlisted in the Army. To this day, I don't really know what motivated me to enlist or to choose the Army. Perhaps it was the hype being discussed concerning President Kennedy's support for and the creation of the Army's Special Forces concept. I did realize that unless some change was made in my life that I was doomed to continue as a failure and remain somewhat dependant upon my father. That idea was totally repugnant to me and I snatched at the most available and cheap way out of my problem.

I enlisted in the Army in September 1962 and requested training to become a Green Beret in the Special Forces. I remember coming home and announcing the surprising news to my mother and father. My father was as usual agitated and went off on a tirade about being a loser and giving up a good job in the Post Office. His face turned red as he continued his attack. I said nothing in return since I had learned long before the foolishness of arguing with him in this condition. When he had exhausted himself, I simply stated that the papers had been signed and that I was leaving for basic training in a week.

All my relatives were informed about my departure with the exception of my grandfather. As an immigrant from Italy he had a natural distrust of government and the military. I remember when I joined the Boy Scouts and went to his home in my uniform. He became extremely distraught and insisted that after remaining in the Boy Scouts for a few years the military would come and take me forcibly to serve in the army.

My departure went seemingly unnoticed since all my friends were already at their new jobs across the country and I had no local girlfriend to say goodbye. I didn't bother to call my girlfriend at college since upon leaving the school we had said our farewells with the understanding that I would not be back and she had two more years of schooling before she graduated. I doubted that I would ever see her again.

Chapter 3 – An Army Career

Although I was 22 years old when I stepped on the bus heading for Georgia, I was very excited and apprehensive. This was truly the first time that I would be totally on my own. Most of the recruits on the bus were white although when we stopped in New York City, a number of black men boarded the bus also destined for training at Fort Gordon. I had never thought of my relationship with black men before entering the Army. In my high school in Utica, there were at most only five or six black students of over four hundred in my class. Although I had been raised in a city that had many ethnic groups, the main groups were Americans of Italian and Polish decent. Two of the black students were in my homeroom and I was certainly friendly with them but not necessarily close. I never considered myself to be prejudiced although I had never given the concept much thought. The same situation was evident at college where there were only a handful of black students and none of which were friends. My training company at Fort Gordon was filled with approximately 40-50% black men who were predominately from the New York City and Newark, New Jersey area. They tended to act much differently then did the black students I had met in high school and college and frankly I didn't like their attitude. I stayed away from them and actually grew to dislike them as a group. It is difficult to recall my feelings at this point since within a year, two of my closest friends would be black men from New York City.

At Fort Gordon we all took tests to see where in the Army we would be best suited. I expected to score high on the tests. They were comparatively easy. When I was called to talk with a counselor as to where I would be assigned, he advised me that I had one of the highest scores in the group. I was thinking that I would be selected for intelligence or an administrative job of some type and was surprised when he advised me that I would be placed in the infantry. I always had considered the infantry the place where they sent the losers or at least the mentally slowest soldiers. Perhaps they were right but I didn't ask for an explanation or argue about the selection since I assumed that I would need to be infantry for the Green Berets. The counselor advised, that after basic training, I would be staying at Fort Gordon for advanced training in what was called "heavy weapons infantry." I completed my eight-week basic training course without any difficulty and actually enjoyed the atmosphere. I looked forward to the next eight weeks of training in the heavy weapons program.

The training in this area was also quite enjoyable as we learned to use the 82mm and 4.2" mortars and the 105mm recoilless anti-tank rifle mounted on a jeep. There was a good deal of rivalry in this program as we were always in competition for grades to be the top graduate. One other recruit, Mark Houseman was my closest competitor and although we became close friends during this period, I was quite pleased to nose him out for the top graduate spot. I began to picture myself using these weapons against the VC and looked forward to the time that I would be going for more training for the Special Forces. In never dawned on me or mentioned by the instructors, that generally most of the weapons with the exception of the 82mm mortar were not suited for jungle warfare.

All of the graduates were given assignments throughout the world and I was surprised when I was advised that I would be staying temporarily at Fort Gordon. I was pleased and quite proud of myself when I was given the temporary rank of corporal while I worked with new recruits and became the battalion commander's driver. While settling into these duties, I took every test available for different schooling including a test to attend Officer Candidate School. My battalion commander told me, while I was driving him to a function, that I had scored very high on this test and would probably be selected soon to become an officer. I felt like I was beginning to redeem my reputation as a loser.

By the end of January, 1963 I received my orders to attend Officer Candidate School in Fort Benning, Georgia and looked forward to becoming an officer as a way to show my family that I was not a total failure. I arrived at Fort Benning, Georgia in February 1963 after a short visit home with my parents. My father had a completely different attitude concerning my military career and was very pleased that I was going to OCS. He even went out of his way to pay for tailoring of my uniforms so that I would look as good as possible. When I returned to Fort Benning, I began six months of training that was the most difficult experience of my life.

There were 50 students in my class with two officers as counselors. The training would last for six months. During World War II, many future soldiers went to OCS and due to the immediate needs of the country were graduated in ninety days and was the reason why OCS graduates were always called somewhat mockingly, '90 day wonders'. My class was a mixture of about twenty-five experienced enlisted men, twelve college graduates and the remaining enlisted personnel with some limited military experience. I was in this last group. The training was not academically difficult although the physical portion was somewhat challenging. Fortunately I excelled in the academics and was able to maintain myself in the physical requirements. My weakest portion of my training was in military knowledge such as marching leadership.

OCS had a strange method of evaluating students, which as my class showed was quite counter-productive. The academic grades were maintained but used only to dismiss students. Students with satisfactory academic grades were not secure in remaining in the school since the school's primary objective was military leadership of a more fundamental nature. The Army also did not yet have a great need for junior grade officers at this time and therefore were committed to graduating a number between 50-75% of those students in attendance. In order to determine the strength of student's leadership ability, the class was required to grade fellow students from one to forty-nine with the strongest getting the lowest number. Unbeknown to me, at least initially, the experienced soldiers got together and pooled their selections so as to keep themselves at the top of the grading and to eliminate the college graduates. The experienced soldiers disliked the college graduates perhaps because they felt a little inferior to them academically and also because they had the least amount of military experience. In all honesty, the experienced soldiers were naturally the best in marching and Army know-how but were at the bottom of the class academically. The first rating was finished after the sixth week and I was very pleased that I ranked 26th of the 50 classmates. Although I would have preferred to be higher, I realized I had limited Army experience and the rating was probably fair in terms of that training being evaluated. The bottom twelve students were all the college graduates and the counselors announced that the class would be reduced by twelve. They were eliminated from the program. I thought the list was strange and the Army foolish to eliminate the only college graduates in the class. I said nothing since I remained in training.

My two roommates in the school became my closest friends. They were Jim Boyd and Clarence Cook. We worked well as a team and were one of only two rooms to have all graduate from OCS. We were required to spit-shine our floors every day and to fold all our clothing in certain predetermined ways. At dinner we ate at large rectangular tables with upper classmen who made it mandatory that every bite of food was placed in our mouths by movements of 90-degree angles and every bite was chewed a definite number of times.

None of us walked on our floor. The marks left by our shoes on the floor would have required time in the morning to maintain the shine. Consequently we climbed from one bed and dresser to the next to sit at our desks or lie in our beds. The instructors would inspect our room every morning and delighted in walking into the room and spinning on their toes leaving a round scratch mark on the tile. I decided to fool the inspectors by making the surface of our floor so hard that they would be unable to leave marks. I recalled from bowling that the bowling lanes had a hard bright shine that was obtained by merely applying a liquid. My father obtained a can of this liquid from a bowling lane in Utica and sent it to me. My roommates and I applied the liquid and to our surprise turned the bright floor into a cloudy appearance. Naturally we failed our inspection the next morning and we spent the following evening scrapping the film off the floor with razor blades and then spit shinning the floor again. My roommates were not happy with my idea but we continued to work together for the common cause of becoming officers.

OCS was the first experience in my life that I began to have doubts as to my abilities. Certainly I had already failed academically from college but I felt my failure was simply my lack of applying myself and perhaps my immaturity. Now competing against other soldiers I realized that I had limitations as to military knowledge. I knew it was unlikely that I would have attained enough military know-how in less than a year to compete against men who had been soldiers for over four or five years. Academically they would have difficulty competing against me. My doubt was in regard to my leadership ability. I had never been asked to show leadership prior to this experience and I began to doubt if I could rise to the occasion. I decided to just continue to give my best and take my chances. The only time I really began to have confidence was in the fourth week. The instructors decided to push the class to the limit of its physical stamina. They took us out to the parade ground and began to run at a fairly brisk pace. After three miles I was completely drained of my strength and out of breath. Of the fifty men only about twenty-five were still running. One of the instructors ran along side of me and yelled that I looked dead and I would not be able to keep up with the other men who were far bigger and stronger than I. At that moment I decided that I would die before I dropped out of the run. The class ran another three miles with seven more runners dropping out but I continued to run. It became obvious from their remarks that the instructors were surprised that I was still running and continuing only to see how long before I quit. I quickened my speed and ran to the head of the class and shouted, "We can do this all day." The other runners all yelled affirmative responses and the instructors called a halt to the run.

After three more weeks another evaluation was made and again the experienced soldiers got together to make their lists. By now I was aware that they were subverting the selection process but said nothing and tried to avoid antagonizing the ringleaders. Again I was ranked 26th in the class of now 38 students and again the counselors announced that the bottom twelve students were eliminated from the class. Although I was pleased that I remained in training, I was now the last ranked member of the class and any further evaluations would see me eliminated. There was little I could do to change the ranking and accepted my eventual elimination. Just prior to the eighteenth week there was the final evaluation. This evaluation placed me 26th in the class of 26 candidates. I was so certain that I was the next washout from the OCS class that I experienced a dream where I was eliminated from the training. The dream was so real that for the next two days I wasn't sure if I had been eliminated. I was surprised but ecstatic when the counselors announced that there would be no further cuts, as the war in Vietnam was demanding more infantry officers. I had made it and did exact a small measure of satisfaction when I graduated at the top of my class in the academic area. Prior to graduation I applied for both Airborne and Ranger Training. Apparently I still believed in volunteering although OCS had taken some of my enthusiasm away.

After graduation I was sent to Airborne Training and surprisingly made my mandatory five parachute jumps to receive my airborne wings. The first time that I was ever in an airplane was my first scheduled parachute jump. The airborne training was a mixture of officers and enlisted personnel in a ratio of about 1 to 5. As an officer I was selected as the "stick commander". This designation basically meant I was the first person to stand in the door of the plane when jumping. As I approached the open door of the plane on my first jump and first plane ride, I placed both hands on the edge of the door I learned inward so as not to be sucked out or inadvertently fall from the plane. Over the door were two lights. The red light for remaining in the plane and the green light to jump. The crew chief in charge of the jump said something to me. I couldn't understand what he said.

I turned to him and said, "What?"

"When you see the light turn green it means we're over the drop zone, jump," as he pointed to the green and red bulbs over the side door of the plane. I looked at the lights which showed an illuminated red light and realized it was not yet time to jump.

The crew chief again said something to me. I could not hear him due to the roar of the engines and rush of the air. When I turned to ask again what he had said, the green light came on. Instead of waiting for my reaction to jump he placed his foot in my back and gave a firm push that propelled me into space. A parachutist is supposed to count to five and if the parachute, which is activated by a static line attached to the inside of the plane does not deploy, he is to pull the reserve parachute. Instead I held my breath for about thirty seconds with my eyes tightly closed and when I eventually looked up, I was grateful that the chute had deployed without any help from me.

The Airborne training was conducted by experienced enlisted personnel who took great pleasure in telling officers, especially 90 day wonders, to "drop and give me fifty" when ordering us to do pushups at the slightest infraction or failure. I don't mind stating that I was a terrible parachutist. My body was always tight with fear and consequently could not really execute the landings with any sense of confidence or style. However, I was still determined to prove my father wrong and to become an accomplished military warrior. I had emerged from basic training and Officer Candidate School with a firm belief that I was virtually invincible. It was this training that again started to give me doubts as to my ability to handle any military situation.

By the time I had graduated from Airborne School with the required five jumps, I vowed to never jump from a plane again, as the landings seem to be getting harder and harder. They teach you to make a three point landing when hitting the ground. Landings are called "PLF's" for Parachute Landing Fall's. It requires the jumper to land on the feet, then twist to the side hitting the soft part of the legs and then the side of the rib cage. My three point landings always were feet, ass and head. I had no wish to emerge from my military duty with severe brain damage. I can truly say that I was a terrible parachutist. I was very fortunate in airborne training in not being eliminated from the program. Prior to our first jump we would practice our PLF's on a six-foot platform. Time and again I attempted the PLF with only minimal success. I overheard the head instructor tell one of his subordinate to get rid of one of the students which was me. The subordinate got confused and picked out another 2nd Lieutenant who was also a weak student and informed him that he was out of the class although he could restart with the next class. With the reprieve I was able to complete the required five jumps and get my parachute wings.

Prior to attending Airborne Training I had requested Ranger School training but was told that all the classes were filled with graduates from West

Point. I was determined to show my family and friends that I was capable of succeeding at even the most difficult of training and experience. However, once I finished the airborne training, I was notified that an opening existed and I could attend the Ranger School. This training had a reputation of being one of the most difficult to complete. By now I was basically exhausted from all the combat type training and schools and declined the opportunity. My decision probably saved my life. Yet I still craved the opportunity to do something special and consequently applied for pilot training.

Before being selected for Flight School, I was sent to Fort Leonard Wood, Missouri as the Executive Officer of a Basic Training Company. This assignment would indirectly have a great influence on my career in the Army. Fort Leonard Wood is situated in the middle of the state with very limited recreational opportunities and those assigned there often called it the "armpit of the Army". I was not really enthusiastic about my assignment since dealing with the new recruits was often like babysitting for either whiners or discipline problems. I did my daily duties and attempted to be a tough disciplinarian but really found the job boring. Although I believed my attitude for my assignment was adequate, my battalion commander had a different prospective of my work performance. One day I was called into his office and told to report to Basic Training Company B as both their Commanding Officer and Executive Officer were not available for duty. The company would be involved in training for the day and an officer was required to be present during all training phases. Upon arrival at Company B, I met Sergeant First Class George Smith, a tall black man who looked as though he had a number of years experience in the Army. Since it had been hammered into our brains while at OCS, that officers were far better off to leave the day-to-day operations with senior enlisted men, I gave Sergeant Smith authority that I would regret for the next five years.

"Sergeant Smith, proceed with the training that is scheduled and I'll accompany the unit as its necessary officer but I don't feel qualified to interfere with the training. You have the training schedule and we will simply follow it," I said.

"OK, sir." Sgt. Smith responded with a slight expression of smugness.

Already I was regretting this decision but I really had no knowledge of the unit's training plan since none was available before my arrival a few minutes earlier. Giving my authority to a sergeant was not in keeping with my personality but lacking the knowledge of the situation I shied away from antagonizing the senior enlisted man who had the knowledge. However, I should have realized that the people with the advice about allowing senior enlisted men to handle day-to-day operations were all senior enlisted men with no desire to place themselves under the command of new lieutenants.

Company B marched off to our training assignments. I was told the training consisted of bayonet training, hand-to-hand combat and classes on biological warfare. The men in the training company were all raw recruits who knew very little about the Army. While at bayonet training at approximately 11:00 am, our unit was visited by an Inspector General.

Evaluation Team followed within minutes by an Army Inspection Team. Both of these groups randomly would visit units to inspect their training effectiveness. The chances of being inspected by either team were probably 1000 to 1 and to be hit by two with no connection to each other within the same hour was astronomical. Unfortunately, Sergeant Smith had misread the training assignment and the unit was at the wrong location doing the wrong training at the wrong time. Naturally the inspection teams gave the unit a poor grade. In all honesty I didn't realize the seriousness of the situation and shrugged off Sgt. Smith's incompetence as an unfortunate but understandable mistake.

Upon my arrival back at Battalion Headquarters, I was called into the office of Major Stewart Lamont. His office was situated within one of those hastily erected rectangular wood structures built two or three feet off the ground on cement pillars during World War II. They were always cold and drafty in the winter months and hot in the summer.

As Battalion Commander, Major Lamont looked like a worn out officer who at his age should have held higher rank or been sent to a home for old soldiers. He was bald with a face that looked at least ten years older than his forty years. Obviously my opinion of him was not much different than his opinion of me. He had few ribbons on his uniforms and I thought he had never served in any responsible command assignment. Training assignments were filled primarily with new young lieutenants or senior officers who were not going to be promoted and would soon retire. The look on his face indicated that he was flushed with anger and hatred.

Before I could make any statement he yelled: "Why did you do this to me? Do you realize that the inspection teams will write a report criticizing both the battalion and me?"

I then proceeded to tell him that I had allowed Sergeant Smith to take the men to their training and he had chosen the wrong training. Lamont interrupted me. "Were you in charge?"

I replied, "Yes."

"Your stupidity has probably cost me my next promotion, Lieutenant. I will fuck you if it is the last thing I ever do. Now get out."

"Sir, I ...."

"Get the hell out of here, now Lieutenant."

I quickly retreated from his office. I really wasn't that concerned as I had already received my orders to report to pilot training and didn't believe there was very much that he could do to get back at me. How wrong I was. I would find out later the extent to which this vindictive man would go. However, I learned a lesson that I have taken with me throughout my life ever since this incident. If you are in command or have the responsibility to make a decision in which your reputation or career is dependant, make your own decision. I saw nothing wrong with getting advice from those around me but the final decision would be mine. I would rather have suffered the consequences of a mistake if the decision were my own decision. Also, I decided that I would take command of any situation where I was the ranking person or when there was hesitancy by the ranking person to make a decision.

When my Company Commander, 1st Lieutenant Dave Crisp submitted my evaluation report prior to my departure for Fort Rucker's Aviation School, Major Lamont refused to accept it until it was significantly lowered. Lt. Crisp admitted to me that he was under pressure to agree to Lamont's demand or face a similar low evaluation. Consequently the evaluation was changed from an average report to an extremely low evaluation. Lamont submitted a written endorsement in which he stated:

"He (Capozzella) appeared to be spiritless with a minimum amount of interest and motivation. He habitually neglected to prepare himself for the days duties. When he was alone with the company in the field, he was uninformed on the disposition of personnel and details of what the unit was doing."

I really couldn't dispute some of the facts since based on at least that one day's performance, I had failed to perform the duty required of me. When given the report, I still didn't anticipate any difficulties with my career and was relieved that I would soon be out from under Lamont's authority. I later learned that he retired within a year still at the rank of Major. This information made me feel warm inside.

Since there was little social life at Fort Leonard Wood, I returned back to my college to visit with friends before reporting for pilot training. I contacted my college roommate, Bryan Eddy, who was still finishing his last year at Clarkson College and told him to arrange a date for me. He contacted my last college sweetheart and arranged for me to date her when I arrived. She was also finishing her last year at an adjacent school, Potsdam State Teachers College that unfortunately for my own academic endeavors was filled primarily with young women. The ratio of women to men including my all male college was approximately 3 to 1 and when you factored in the fact that most of the men at my college were total social nerds, the ratio rose to a substantial 8 to 1. It was in my third year of college that I met the woman, Barbara Emperor, who would become my closest companion and friend for over the remainder of my life. Being from the small village of Saranac Lake, New York that is only a stones throw away from Lake Placid where the Winter Olympics were twice held and being the only daughter of a very conservative couple, it was expected that Barbara would also be shy and conservative. Her personality and outlook were far from this upbringing. I have always jested that she was the wildest girl I dated in college. Fortunately the wildness was merely an adventurous and accommodating spirit that enjoyed life and would be my main support in the years ahead.

My visit back to Potsdam resulted in a promise of engagement with Barbara. I had planned to milk the engagement to the limit of endurance. However, Barbara proved much too clever for this situation and when told that I could not afford an engagement ring, she successfully obtained the diamonds from both her mother and grandmother's rings to have a ring prepared. Even with a ring on her finger I still felt safe from marriage, as I was still in the Army many hundreds of miles away. I continued to believe that I was the smartest of this couple.

In January of 1965, I received a phone call from my mother. "Vinny, I just received a phone call from a girl in Saranac Lake that you are getting married in June. Is this true?"

The announcement hit me like a sledgehammer and I really didn't know what to say. Finally I just accepted the situation and said, "I guess so."

I then proceeded to tell my mother about this girl from Saranac Lake. I certainly was filled with mixed emotions and didn't really know if Barbara was the person, I wanted for my wife but I allowed the situation to continue. Faith then intervened when I was told that my Flight School was to begin in June. I then pulled the last remaining ace from my hand and advised everyone that I would be leaving for Flight School at the end of May and therefore could not be married in June. Barbara was again too clever for this turn of events and announced the wedding was being moved up to May 24th. I accepted the change and marveled at her determination. We were married in Saranac Lake, New York in May and we returned to Potsdam for a three-day honeymoon while she completed her final exams. Surprisingly she received her best grades ever. The marriage took on some unpleasant immediate results as I was forced to sell my fairly new MG sport car in order to purchase a new sedan to carry all the wedding gifts and luggage for two. With my new wife as a companion I reported for pilot training at Fort Rucker, Alabama.

Fort Rucker would be home for two of the next three years of duty remaining in my Army career. It was an old base in terms of buildings. The Army was trying to upgrade it and had christened the base the home of "The Army Aviation School". Fort Rucker would supply the vast majority of Army pilots for both helicopter and fixed wing aircraft that would serve in Vietnam.

It was there that I met the two pilots I would have my most unusual adventures both in the air and on the ground, Charlie Kellum and Barry Taylor. Two more different individuals never walked on the face of the Earth. Kellum was a short, stocky, white, Texan who was married and had a great sense of humor. In the air he would prove to be both capable and steady. Taylor was the opposite of Kellum in almost every aspect. He was a black man from New York City who was single, terribly horny, and a pilot of questionable capability. Taylor had been with me in Officer Candidate School and Airborne Training at Fort Benning, Georgia the previous year. We had become good friends and I found him to be a great source of enjoyment and bewilderment. He was a product of a rough neighborhood although he wasn't a particularly tough individual and had a jovial personality but lacked common sense.

At Airborne Training, Taylor had an incident on our final jump. It was a typical day in Georgia with the sky clear and a slight breeze from the southwest. I was one of the lead jumpers and had successfully landed. As I watched Taylor's plane approach the landing zone he jumped and his parachute deployed in a 'Mae West'. This situation is caused when one of the parachute lines gets caught on the top of the chute and creates two small side-by-side chutes looking like a bra. Unfortunately the two small chutes do not have the same lift and floating capacity as the regular chute.

The Airborne School usually has an instructor at the drop site with a powerful megaphone to talk to jumpers that might be experiencing difficulty. I doubted that a jumper in trouble would take much notice from someone on the ground even if he could hear him clearly. Needless to say, the instructor noticed Taylor and his Mae West and yelled, "You with the Mae West, pull your reserve chute and throw it with the wind."

Basically, Taylor was suppose to pull the reserve that is attached to his front belt but not let it deploy until he grabs the edges of the chute and throws it with the wind so that it deploys without become tangled with his already deployed main chute. Taylor may have heard the instructor or at least acted as our training required and pulled the reserve chute, grabbed the edges of the chute and then threw it not with the wind but into the wind. The chute immediately flew back at him encasing him in the chute looking like a mummy and also spiraled around the main chute causing even less lift.

The instructor yelled, "You with the Mae West, pull in your reserve chute back and redeploy it."

By this time it was obvious that Taylor's efforts to redeploy the reserve chute could not be done in time as he descended at twice the speed of the other chutes. All I could see was a person covered with his chute frantically kicking and grabbing the chute from the inside.

As Taylor rapidly approached the ground, the instructor yelled his final instruction, "You with the Mae West, prepare to make a good PLF."

Taylor hit the ground like a bag of garbage thrown from a three-story building. He landed 200 yards from where I was watching. All I could see upon impact was a small cloud of dust much like the Wily Coyote cartoons when the coyote is propelled off a high cliff and plunges to the valley floor below, landing in a cloud of dust. I ran to Taylor. As I approached, he was already getting off the ground without a broken bone or a scratch but was as pale as a very black complexion black man could look.

"Barry are you OK," I asked?

He merely looked at me and said with a face without the slightest glimmer of emotion, "Sure but it was certainly a great ride." We both laughed and hugged each other while the instructors looked on in amusement. I must say without the least hesitation that Taylor was lucky but extremely accident-prone.

Being stationed in Alabama during this time period was especially difficult for blacks as the civil rights movement was beginning to create shock waves across the country. Governor George Wallace was still a segregationalist who called Blacks "nigrows" on television probably as a compromise between "niggers" and the generally accepted term for that period "Negroes."

Taylor drove a new white Bonneville convertible. The vehicle was as large as a boat and certain to draw attention from local rednecks. I often joked with him and said, "Barry, someday a white lynch mob is going to hang your black ass over that huge white car."

Taylor merely laughed and replied, "Never happen because I'm an Army officer."

Unfortunately being an Army officer had little impact on many of the southern rednecks. One day Taylor was riding through one of the small Alabama towns when the police stopped him. Their interest was drawn to the large car by the fact that Taylor was wearing his flight helmet with the convertible top down. The police mistook him for a civil rights protester and marcher equipped with helmet for combat with law enforcement. Fortunately Taylor was able to contact the military base and military spokesmen were able to obtain his release from the police with the threat to send a company of soldiers to the town to force his freedom. He later explained that he was wearing his helmet to show the people he was a pilot.

My wife accompanied me to Fort Rucker where we were able to obtain an apartment near the base, as the base housing was full. The apartment was cozy but like many of the dwellings in Alabama was infested with what the locals call "water bugs". As a Yankee, I called them cockroaches although they were twice the size of the typical northern roach. When the lights of the apartment were turned off at night, these sneaky creatures would scurry out of the woodwork and take over the apartment, particularly the kitchen. The landlords did order spraying once a month. This action only seemed to increase their numbers. However, the apartment became a meeting and partying place for the pilot trainees and we enjoyed it immensely.

Barbara was able to obtain a job as a schoolteacher at the local grammar school. The school was an all white school in Skipperville, Alabama within tem miles of the Army base. The school system was segregated but was touted as being equal in quality between the all white and all black schools. However, Barb's school was fairly new with a large grass covered field and play ground while the school for the black children was an old, decaying, building with numerous broken windows and a small dirt playground with a broken, dilapidated swing set. It was difficult for she and I to accept this way of life, which was obviously so prejudicial to the black community, when many of our friends were black couples. Surprisingly we really didn't discuss the situation other than to joke about it. It seemed that Vietnam was a bigger issue for us with the knowledge that most of us would probably soon me in the fight.

While at Fort Rucker, Barbara and I were happy to learn that we were expecting our first child in the summer of 1965.

Pilot training was a torment for me. We initially learned how to fly in the Army's old and reliable L-19. The plane was originally designed and built by Cessna in the early 1950's and allowed for one pilot with a second tandem seat for a passenger or an instructor since the seat was equipped with a floor mounted stick to control the plane and a speed control. The plane was very rugged and slow with a high wing strut construction and a straight spring landing wheels which were not retractable.

The majority of the instructors were civilian pilots. My instructor was an old potbelly pilot named Gus Helton. Gus had the habit of getting excited whenever I made a mistake, which seemed to be often. The more Gus yelled the worst I flew. I was able to complete my solo flight in 12 hours a fairly good time but continued to have difficulty to even complete coordinated turns with Gus in the back seat. I hated to report each day for flying because of my inability to please my instructor. Due to the bad weather in Alabama during these months, the flights were often cancelled and I was usually thrilled.

When a pilot trainee has trouble, the first thing that the pilot training program does is to change instructors. This was fortunate for me since my next instructor, Tye Barlow, another old pilot, was very easy going. He took me up for a check ride and after the ride announced, "You're OK Lieutenant. Keep flying solo for the next few days and I'll get back to you." His attitude and demeanor probably saved my flying career and I began to progress smoothly and with renewed confidence.

It was during pilot training that I began to realize what an excellent pilot I was becoming. I had a tendency to be reckless and careless but always had the "luck" to get out of most situations. Shortly after I was reassigned to Tye as my instructor, I was flying alone over the Alabama countryside. Unexpectedly, the engine began to sputter and quit. This plane was equipped with two fuel tanks and emergency procedure required an immediate shift in fuel tank selection, switching on the auxiliary fuel pump and an emergency call explaining the situation. I was flying at only 1000' above the ground and had only a short time to make the emergency call.

Trying to show no fear in my voice I radioed, "Fort Rucker Control, this is Gold 23, my engine has quit and I am going down around twenty miles to the southwest of the field."

"Gold 23 this is Fort Rucker Control, please wait while we give landing instructions to another plane."

Apparently the control had not understood my first call or didn't recognize the emergency. "Fort Rucker Control this is Gold 23, declaring an emergency. I am going down twenty miles southwest of field."

"Gold 23 this is Fort Rucker Control please state the emergency?"

By this time I was just above the ground and I had no further time to reply and doubted that the transmission would be heard. I had selected a large grassy field as my touch down point and made a perfect 'dead stick landing' without the aid of my now silent engine. My biggest fear since I had absolutely no knowledge of planes or engines was that the plane would shortly burst into flames. Being an avid reader of both WWI and WWII books about pilots in combat, a burning aircraft was my biggest fear.

The plane came to a controlled stop and moments later I jumped from the cockpit and ran from the plane. I then noticed that running in the opposite direction was a herd of large pigs. They gathered under and around the aircraft as if the plane was their mother. I stood there looking at the plane expecting a large explosion. There was no indication of smoke, fire or explosion and I got my nerve back. After a few minutes I walked back to the plane and turned all the instruments off but was still too frightened to sit in the suspect aircraft for a period long enough to again radio the airfield. In any case I had really no idea as to my location other than a general direction and distance.

I noticed a small wooden shack made of pieces of old wood and sheet metal but boasted a TV antenna on the roof. The building was typical at least on the outside of a poor black farmer's home. Clad in my flight suit and carrying my flight helmet, I walked to the front door and knocked. From the front door my plane could clearly be seen only 100 feet from the house. The door opened and a small middle-aged black woman clad in a worn dress appeared. She had a clear view of the plane but took no unusual interest in it being parked in her field. I noticed a large color TV playing before three children and a grown man. The TV surprised me since few families could at that time afford a color TV especially a family as impoverished as this one.

Calmly and without any apparent surprise, the woman said, "Well what can I do for you boy?"

"Sorry to bother you, but I just landed my plane in your field and need to call the Army base immediately." I assumed that she had not seen the plane and in the excitement of the moment forgot that my clothes indicated my status as a pilot. "I'm an Army pilot from Fort Rucker."

"Sorry boy but we don't have a phone," she said as she closed the door in my face.

She had made no other offer to help and closed the door to probably return to the TV. Although somewhat upset, I realized that a phone was my biggest concern and not the amenities of a social get-together. Helmet in hand I began walking down the dirt road in the general direction of the field. Within an hour I was picked up by a military truck that had been sent out from the field to look for the wreckage and I was driven back to the field. Apparently another plane had radioed my location and even before returning to the base, a repair crew had arrived at the plane's location. The repair crew radioed that the plane had no visible damage and I had made a most difficult landing without aid of engine. This emergency was made doubly difficult by my limited flying experience. The instructors were full of praise and at least for the next few hours I was dubbed a hero. Next came a phone call from the onsite inspectors who reported that the engine had quit because I had run out of fuel in one tank with a full alternate gas tank available. My changing the fuel indicator had come with not enough time for the fuel to reach the engine and restart. Because of that incident, I was given in good nature the "Award of the Jackass" by the instructors and made the brunt of many jokes by my classmates.

This incident was really quite rewarding since I never again failed to check and double-check my gas tanks selection. Unfortunately, the L-19 did not have a fuel capacity indicator. This fact meant the fuel must be monitored by flying time. I got into the habit of changing from one tank to the other after one hour and then back after two hours in the second tank. Since the tanks only held about two hours of fuel in each tank, this procedure enable me to know that on the second transfer I should begin to watch my time for a return to an airfield for more fuel.

Interestingly, my flight class had five Iranian officers attempting to learn the basics of flying. At that time, Iran with the Shah as its leader was the United States' strongest ally in the Middle East. Although they were our allies and therefore our country gave them as much military training as possible, the Iranians were the worst pilots imaginable. The program was not allowed to flunk any of them and they continued to fly regardless of their ability or improvement. I knew from that moment that the United States would never have to be concerned with Arab pilots from the Middle East for many decades ever being able to compete for dominance over the skies of that region regardless of their equipment.

Although the Iranians were generally incompetent as pilots, they did have as a group a great sense of humor. One of the Iranians was being harassed by his instructor over some type of mistake when he grabbed the control stick and pushed the stick forward. The pilot yelled: "We die for Allah!"

The plane when into a steep dive which the instructor sitting behind the student was unable to overcome since the Iranian pilot was holding the stick forward with all his strength. As the plane approached the ground, the Iranian pulled back on the stick and the plane leveled off at a few hundred feet above the trees. The Iranian said with a smug expression, "I fooled you, didn't I?" Needless to say the instructor was replaced with a more accommodating individual who wouldn't yell at the Iranian.

I liked the Iranians because they were always fun at parties. They also had something that the rest of the flight class didn't have – a liquor quota. The U.S. government allowed each Iranian to purchase a case of liquor a month without any tax. The reason for this generosity escapes me but I and some of the other American pilots took advantage of the Iranians' good luck. Since they seldom were able to drink a whole case of liquor in a month, they often purchased liquor for their American classmates. I was able to obtain two cases of Chavez Regal scotch at $3 per bottle. This price was a great deal. I never drank scotch but Barbara liked it very much. I was strictly a beer drinker in those days.

The main part of the flight training was to learn to land on small dirt roads or landing strips with short limited fields. The instructors would deploy a rope over the tops of two tall poles separated by about fifty feet at the beginning of one of these short landing fields. We would be expected to land over the top of the rope but close enough to allow ourselves enough room to bring the plane to a stop. A number of pilots landed with too little room to stop and wiped out their planes in the woods adjacent to the field. The only way to accomplish the feat for this short landing was to bring the plane into the landing with a nose up attitude on the verge of a stall with sufficient power to continue to fly but still have the plane descend to the earth. The plane would have a ground speed of somewhere between 40-60 MPH and needed little runway to come to a complete stop. The disadvantage of this landing for an incompetent pilot could be disastrous with the plane falling to earth like a rock if it stalled. I became quite adept at this technique. This training would be of a great benefit in the landing sites I would encounter in Vietnam. Although I never attempted the feat, I thought I could land my plane perpendicular to a paved runway in only 40 to 50 feet.

The first part of our training in the L-19 concentrated primarily on short field landings, low-level flying and dead reckoning navigation. The L-19's were not equipped for instrument flying and pilots would have to learn to navigate by computing the effect of wind, the compass and sight of ground landmarks. I never dreamed that this expertise would be my primary method of flying and staying alive in the next year. By now I was beginning to enjoy flying and was disappointed when the flying would be cancelled due to inclement weather. I felt as though I had finally found my niche in the military. I began to look forward to each new learning experience.

The second phase of flight school was navigation by instruments. We learned to fly the DeHavilland "Beaver", a plane designed for service in the Artic and which was an extremely capable cold weather aircraft. It was equipped with a large radial engine and could hold two pilots (side by side) and four passengers. I loved the Beaver since it was heavy, easy to fly and very forgiving. In addition to learning to fly by instruments the students also had to endure the flight simulator. This training forced us to strictly use our instruments since you could not look out the window to stabilize your flight. At first I hated the flight simulator since I almost always had difficulty in pleasing the instructors. At some point, however, I began to see the simulator as merely a game pitting the instructor against the student. The instructors took great enjoyment from disabling some of the instruments to force us to use other instruments as a back up. I would look forward to having instruments becoming inoperable and enjoyed the pleasure of being able to fly and navigate on as few instruments as possible. For instance, if the rate of climb and decent instrument was disabled, the pilot could determine whether he was climbing or diving by his airspeed. I was able to successfully complete this part of my training with no difficulty and also to take and past the test for a civilian commercial pilot's license.

My friend, Taylor's prowess as a pilot was always a question in my mind. After obtaining our flight wings, Taylor and I were flying together in the Beaver aircraft. This plane was weather equipped and required a pilot and co-pilot.

I was the pilot for the flight with Taylor as the co-pilot. We had flown to an airfield in northern Florida. The field boasted a restaurant with great Mexican food. On the way back to Fort Rucker we inadvertently flew into a terrible storm and it took all my physical ability to keep the plane in the air.

I told Taylor, "I'll fly the plane and you take over the radio and instruments. Just keep us on course and I'll try to keep her straight and level."

Taylor agreed to maintain radio contact with Flight Control and handle the IFR equipment while I maintained direct flying control. I could hear the ground Flight Control advise Taylor to maintain 8,000 feet and to follow the flight path we had earlier submitted. Taylor told me, "Turn to a 245 degree heading." I immediately turned to 245 degrees from our current heading of 270 degrees.

The Flight Controller said, "Army 4176, you are drifting off your flight plan, please make the necessary correction."

Taylor advised me, "Turn to 230 degrees heading." I made the correction although now I was doing my own calculations in my head. The original flight was for us to fly a 270-degree heading to return to Fort Rucker. Assuming there was a strong wind associated with the storm blowing from the north, we would have to turn the nose of the plane slightly into the wind to maintain a ground direction of 270 degrees. Yet a 5 degree adjustment to the south was a massive correction in the wrong direction and not very likely to keep us on a flight path. A proper shift would require a correction to the north not the south. I assumed the wind must have shifted at our current altitude.

Again, the Flight Controller advised that we were off our flight path and Taylor suggested a more radical change in direction to intercept the flight path. Finally the Controller advised that we were off his screen and had no idea where we were located. I then became alarmed and took full measure of the flight instruments while still battling the storm. I discovered that Taylor had compensated for our intersection with the flight path in a 180-degree opposite direction. I took control of contact with Flight Control, turned the plane in the opposite direction and was able to get back to the flight path in about 30 minutes and arrive safely back to station. Obviously from that period onward I was suspect of his flying ability but still remained the best of friends.

Chapter 4 – The 219th

Upon graduation from pilot training at the beginning of April 1965 we received our orders. Most of the pilots including myself volunteered for duty in Vietnam although I doubt if my assignment was influenced by my enthusiasm. I was disappointed that I was placed for assignment in the OV-1 Cessna "Birddog". I had hoped to get one of the more sophisticated aircraft such as the twin engine 'Mohawk'. The plane was used as both a close ground support and observation plane. I was probably lucky to not get the Mohawk as the pilots in Vietnam soon began calling the plane "the widow maker". The Mohawk had two engines. They were slanted slightly up from their wings and had the unfortunate habit of twisting on its back and slamming into the ground if it lost an engine on take off. Yet the plane was the most sophisticated aircraft the Army possessed and I wanted to fly it. These wasn't a chance in the world I could get the plane as the pilots assigned to it were either very experienced or had a great deal of contacts with the Army high command.

I was assigned to the 219th Aviation Company. It was a new unit being sent to Vietnam. Two other sister units, the 220th and 221st Aviation Companies were also created for assignment to Vietnam. Taylor was placed in the 220th while Kellum was placed with me in the 219th and we were transferred to Fort Hood, Texas for organization. I did not see or hear from Taylor until our paths again crossed in Vietnam. The 220th would operate in what was designated as 3rd Corp and 4th Corp areas to the south, east and slightly north of Saigon, while the 219th would operate in the 2nd Corp and central highlands, and the 221st would operate in 1st Corp or the area just south of the division between North and South Vietnam. At the time the central highlands were considered the most active in terms of enemy activity.

Although my wife, Barbara had accompanied me to Fort Rucker for the pilot training, we decided that she would return to her parents' home in Saranac Lake, New York since my stay at Fort Rucker would be only for a month. In addition, she was due to have our first child in July.

My assignment to Fort Hood was uneventful other than learning to fly the new model of the L-19 Cessna. This model now designated the OV-1 had a variable pitch propeller that gave it the capacity to fly at the incredible cruising speed of about 105 MPH. Our mission was the brainchild of some high ranking Army officer who thought that these slow moving aircraft would be more capable of spotting a hidden enemy, especially an enemy in the jungle. Apparently no thought was given to the fact that a slow moving aircraft that was capable of spotting a hidden soldier would be easy pickings for the enemy's guns. The concept was to assign one or two planes in various locations across Vietnam and to fly daily reconnaissance missions to look for enemy movement and changes in the terrain. A change might indicate their presence. The OV-1 was a very reliable plane equipped to handle a pilot and one passenger or spotter in a seat directly behind the pilot. The plane was somewhat flimsy and had little instrumentation other than basic flight indicators. The only instrument for indicating directional assistance was a radio directional needle that pointed the general way to a commercial radio station but did not include distance and did not include any instrument indicating locations of airports. Of course radio stations in Vietnam were almost non-existent other than the Saigon station.

Our unit met with instructors who were suppose to advise us as to what to expect in Vietnam. The advisors were all Special Forces personnel who could only talk about small unit tactics and training of the South Vietnamese. In the summer of 1965, the United States had only a small number of military personnel in Vietnam and other than pilots they were all assigned to train the ARVN. A number of helicopter units were there to assist the ARVN as well as both World War II propeller fighters and also jet fighters. Not one pilot from either the Army or Air Force ever came to Fort Hood to advise us as to what to expect and give us some advice. Our unit would discover the do's and don'ts of flying in South Vietnam, the old tried and true method of trial and error. Surprisingly none of the pilots ever expressed any concern for our lack of knowledge since we never doubted the outcome or our success.

The OV-1 was not armed with any weapons but did have eight rocket connections for firing four smoke rockets from either wing to mark the enemy when they were located. Not once during our training or organizational period did we ever fly the OV-1 with rocket launchers or fire the rocket to develop accuracy. We were only told that because of our slow speed and lack or protection on the skin of the plane that it was advised that we fly at either 1500 feet or tree top level. This altitude would still give us the ability to observe enemy movement and perhaps not be hit by small arms fire. One of the pilots asked if the enemy had weapons larger than small arms what the recommended altitude was. The instructor said, "I wouldn't fly at that height if I was you." This limited instruction was the extent of our training for what would eventually be the test of our lives.

It was at Fort Hood that I developed my fear and respect for Mother Nature. Kellum and I had flown to a commercial airport in southern Texas to have a lunch at a place known to Kellum during his college days. We were each flying an OV-1 when we started to fly into a line of storm clouds. The OV-1's were not equipped for flying IFR (Instrument Flight Rules) in poor weather conditions and did not have the size or stability to tackle this type of weather. On our flight back to Fort Hood, we followed a major highway heading in that direction. Our altitudes crept lower and lower in driving wind and rain until we were barely 100 feet above the highway which already was a violation of FAA regulations. Our view to the front was completely obscured and I could no longer see to our rear. Our altitude was already below FAA minimums although this fact didn't faze me, as I was more concerned with just surviving the situation.

Finally I radioed Kellum, "Charlie, I'm going to take my chances and land on the highway. There are thunderstorms ahead of us that are driving us lower and lower. We're already below flight limits."

"I don't care about the limits right now and if you land, they'll take your wings for that."

"Better that then getting killed in this crap," I replied.

"OK, but I'm going on."

"Suit yourself but at this altitude and weather you'll likely get killed." I turned my plane 180 degrees

As I lined up for my approach to the highway choosing to land with the traffic and hoping that the drivers would see my plane before crashing into it, I noticed to my side of the road a small airfield with two small planes sitting on the parking apron.

I radioed Kellum, "Charlie there's an airport here, come back."

He returned and we both landed safely and sat out the passing storm. We never repeated the story to the other pilots but I learned to make every attempt to stay clear of weather if at all possible in the future. Poor weather was my one true fear and I hoped that I would never have to deal with it in Vietnam. Since I was unfamiliar and lacked knowledge of the weather in the central highlands, my hopes were quite ridiculous. Flying in South Vietnam was often a pilot's worst nightmare. This episode in Texas was the first of many moments of out and out fear that I experienced in my flying career.

The Fort Hood organization was to shake the confidence in many of the pilots but certainly not the enthusiasm for our upcoming adventure. Our commander Major Robert A. Lust left much to be desired in terms of leadership or the ability to meet our needs. He was a pleasant officer with no special experience although he had been a pilot for a number of years. He was middle age but looked terribly out of shape for the oncoming ordeal. Like many officers hurled into command in combat situations, he lacked the inner authority to overcome difficult problems or the fortitude to stand up for his men when faced with superiors who lacked flying capability and knowledge. The Executive Officer, Captain William "Bill" Beach was an able officer who was more interested in his personal flying duties than those of being second in command. Both Kellum and I were placed under Section Leader, Captain Ramon Leyva. He was a man of modest looks with a good heart. He would be my protector from our own command and outsiders on more than one occasion. Leyva and I got along well together from the start and fortunately for me had a good sense of humor.

Kellum and I often talked about the upcoming situation although our interests primarily centered upon staying alive. We were so naïve about combat that at one time we decided to purchase small derringers and tie them around our necks to hang behind our backs. We felt we would be able to have a final weapon of defense if the Vietcong ever faced us with capture. Although this fanciful idea looking back was quite idiotic, I thought it held great promise at the time. Perhaps bowing to common sense, neither Kellum nor I attempted to buy the weapons

It was obvious that the 219th and its sister units were created on a spur of the moment decision by someone far, far away with no combat experience in Vietnam. Without the ability or experience to mark targets our efforts would not be very productive. Most issues such as living quarters, spare parts, and personal weapons, coordination with support and combat personnel, and locations of airfields were left to our local commander to resolve. Major Lust's response to this problem was basically to ignore the issue and hope for the best. He had been promised support for our unit when we arrived in Vietnam but in reality the unit was being sent there with no substantial plan. The locations for our home base and satellite bases were known but not much more regarding support were know.

Our destination for our home base in Vietnam was to be a place called Pleiku in the Central Highlands. Frankly, I had never heard of Pleiku although at that time I was familiar with only the names of the large cities. Fortunately as my curiosity grew I found that newspaper accounts during the current phase of the war were primarily centered on the central highlands. Kellum and I looked up the recent war news about Pleiku and discovered that three months earlier the Vietcong had overrun the base during a surprise night attack but that the airfield was quickly taken back by our own troops. Of course this knowledge did little to alleviate our worries. However, my immediate concern was the coming birth of my first child. My wife went into labor and delivered my daughter, Dana, one month prematurely. I was able to obtain emergency orders to rush back to New York to see my wife and daughter on May 30th. The visit was one of joy and some anxiety but I was too excited about my daughter. I could stay only two nights and was back at Fort Hood by June 3, 1965.

Chapter 5 – Arriving in Vietnam

We began our trip to Vietnam on June 5, 1965. Most of us assumed that we would be traveling to Vietnam on one of the large passenger jets that were being leased by our government. When advised that our trip would be by Air Force C-130's, there was disappointment. This plane is very safe and large but leaves a lot to be desired in terms of speed and comfort. As anticipated the C-130's provided for our flight overseas were terribly uncomfortable since we were required to sit on webbed seats for the three day flight. We stopped for a few hours for refueling in Hawaii, Wake Island, the Philippines and finally Tan Son Nhut Airport in Saigon. In Hawaii, we were allowed to go to the main airport facility were I ate my first fresh pineapple. All I can recall about the stop was that we were given two hours to walk around the commercial airport terminal before reboarding.

Our landing at Wake Island was a surprise since I expected a small tropical island with lots of coconut trees and a small airfield. Instead the island was even smaller than I expected and quite devoid of vegetation. It was basically a barren rock covered spot with airport runway that ran from one end of the island to the other end. I could only dream about the heroic defense of the U.S. Marines to hold this piece of real estate against incredible odds during World War II. The island still had deteriorating concrete blockhouses. They were built by either the U.S. or Japan but were now terribly outdated and unusable for defense.

I had not brought any reading material for the trip but we were all provided with a pamphlet regarding Vietnam including its history, religion, main centers of population and customs of the people. The information included 'do's' and 'don'ts' most of which I found later to be either erroneous or certainly biased. I recalled watching numerous WWII movies were the characters were also issue information about the inhabitants of the locations where our troops were invading. These pamphlets were also usually quite inaccurate.

It seemed as though we would never arrive in Vietnam and our excitement grew as we observed our first sight of the Vietnamese coastline. The sight did not dampen my enthusiasm. I saw a lush green landscape dotted with water covered rice fields adjacent to the coast extending usually one or two miles inland where the terrain became quite mountainous and covered with a thick jungle. Small villages lined the coastline and everything looked quite peaceful without any evidence of war. The first view of Saigon from the air was a surprise since I had not expected to see a city as large as the one now sprawled before my view. All around the city were the typical water covered rice fields and numerous rivers flowing in every direction in and out of the city.

Upon debarking from the aircraft at Saigon, our first reaction was the intense heat blast that met us. I don't think I have ever felt that much heat combined with the high humidity before this exposure. The view, that struck me as being different from anywhere else I had been, was the immense brightness and glare. The field was enormous and extremely busy with aircraft of every size and use. I saw sleek F-105's and even WWII vintage Navy Corsairs all parked in well-spaced sand bagged bunkers. The runway had at least twelve large commercial jets awaiting takeoff while on a parallel runway I could see combat aircraft taking off for missions somewhere in Vietnam.

I expected to see a glimpse of some jungle on the outskirts of the field but saw only flat land. This flat land was primarily the rice fields I saw from the sky. They were fed by the numerous rivers and tributaries in the Mekong Delta. The main sight was the hundreds of soldiers boarding and debarking from every conceivable type of aircraft.

Our arrival preceded the large commitment of troops authorized by President Lyndon Johnson that would take place in about four months. At the time of our arrival the war was still being waged by handfuls of Special Forces units and MACV advisors to South Vietnamese units. There were probably fewer than 50-60,000 American personnel in Vietnam. The build up of American troops would swell our ranks to over 200,000 personnel by December and nearly 400,000 before I returned to the States. The number of soldiers was quite immaterial since I don't think any number of soldiers would have been successful certainly within the framework of our tactics and strategy. I would not come to this opinion for at least another 12 months. At this time there was no doubt that we would be successful. If someone had asked me as for the length of time before the war would be won, I would have estimated between 24-30 months.

We were transported to a tent city somewhere close to the Tan Son Nhut Airport where we stayed two uneventful nights. It seemed that there was no transportation for our journey to Pleiku Airfield and apparently no plans made for our deployment. Major Lust was in favor of loading us into three or four trucks and travel Highway 14 through central Vietnam directly from Saigon to Pleiku. I overheard a transportation officer question Major Lust. The Lieutenant was of slight built and dressed like us in starched fatigues. I doubted by his look and demeanor that he had ever ventured much further than a few hundred feet from his billets and office at the airfield.

"You want to transport your men to Pleiku in trucks?" The sound of his voice was full of incredible disbelief.

Lust answered, "Sure, we can probably get everyone there with a few three quarter ton trucks and a jeep. It would also help our security if the Army would assign a tank or two to accompany us or provide armed personnel carriers instead of trucks. Unfortunately our unit doesn't have any vehicles assigned to us in Saigon and we will need to have some made available. Is there a problem? "

"Sir, there are no drivers available for this trip and I don't have the authority to loan you any vehicles."

"Listen Lieutenant, my men will handle the driving if you can provide a guide and some of these trucks I see parked in your area."

"Sir, what will you do for support, I mean do you have weapons?"

"The men have 45's," Lust returned.

"Sir, do you realize that most of the roads heading north are controlled by the VC?"

"Oh, I didn't realize things were that bad here." Lust paused and continued. "Well, is it possible to obtain some armored personnel carriers and fight our way through.through?"

The transport officer had a bewildered and shocked look on his face. "Sir, we don't even send tanks up that road."

Lust had a rejected look on his face but finally brightened as he responded, "I guess we'll have to wait for some other type of transport or link up with a large convoy going north. I assume you can at least handle that assignment?"

The transportation officer said, "Sir there are no large or small convoys of any size that travel on these roads."

Apparently the transportation officer finally discouraged Lust from this idea and further talk of a convoy was not raised again. Thankfully someone, possible Major Lust, secured another C-130 to transport us by air to Pleiku. One can only wonder why Pleiku wasn't our first stop instead of Saigon. It seems that almost all the troops from the States throughout the war were first transported to Saigon before arriving at their final destination. This ritual had no purpose since nothing other than sitting in a tent for two days was accomplished although the first feeling of disillusionment crept into my thoughts. It was becoming obvious that the war was not being run as smoothly as I thought it would.

To make matters worst, the pilots had all been issued a .45 caliber Browning semi-automatic pistol when we left Fort Hood but neither the enlisted personnel nor the pilots were issued a M-16 rifle with or without ammunition. However, for safety reasons while in transport to Vietnam, no ammunition was issued for the .45 and no one in command gave the supply of ammunition any further thought. After all, we were headed to a combat zone. It was probably overflowing with ammunition of all calibers. After arrival it became apparent that none of the units in Saigon were authorized to supply us with anything except lodging in tent city and food. Some of the more creative officers went out scrounging on a trading mission and returned with enough .45 caliber ammunition so that each man was issued one round. I felt like Don Knotts as the inept deputy sheriff on the Andy Griffith Show. I wasn't sure if the round was intended to be fired at the enemy or to commit suicide.

We heard over the Armed Forces radio in Saigon that President Johnson had just authorized the use of American troops in direct combat if requested by the South Vietnamese Army. The request was a pure sham since the ARVN were already becoming desperate even before the emergence of North Vietnamese units. Yet the president's announcement meant that the United States would truly be fighting the hated communists. I thought the decision was justified and it was merely a question when enough American troops were in Vietnam before the war would be over. Victory was now assured. The

219th was one of the first units in the country and we all expected to see plenty of combat once we could get away from Saigon.

Meanwhile at tent city we were allowed to go into the main city of Saigon. Our command cautioned us to stay in the downtown area and not to be lured into other areas of the city. We were also allowed to wear our sidearm on these visits although our supply of ammunition obviously was limited. This rule of allowing side arms would change in two months with the American buildup of personnel. The majority of the pilots and the enlisted men decided it was safer to remain on the post. About four of us took a taxi to the center of the city. It was filled with GI's of every conceivable rank while the streets were crowded with Vietnamese riding either a bicycle with standard peddles or a bicycle with a small engine that turned the front wheel. This engine was situated in front of the handlebars and once the rider began to turn the pedals of the bicycle they would rotate the engine down by hand onto the tire. The small gasoline engine with start and propel the rider at a speed of less than 15 MPH. I admired the ingenuity of this device and secretly dreamed of marketing them in the States.

The setting of Saigon did not surprise me. It had the appearance of what I thought an oriental city should look like although it was perhaps more sleazy than I expected. The streets were ringed with shops of every type attempting to lure Americans into them for a sale. Besides the well-lit bars that were the majority of the establishments, the other businesses were primarily clothing and souvenir stores. I always regretted not taking advantage of these two initial days in Saigon prior to the military build-up and the accompanying skyrocket of prices. Many exotic items were for sale at reasonable prices. I haggled with one shop owner over the price of a tiger skin with head for $125. I really wanted to purchase it but decided to wait until I was situated and would then purchase one on another trip to Saigon. By the time I was able to come back to Saigon in September, the price had already climbed to $500 for the skin. Other unusual items were made of elephant skin and included wallets, briefcases and women's purses. I eventually bought an elephant hide brief case. It was nice looking but very heavy and not put together with the best workmanship. I even had the opportunity to purchase an elephant tusk for a few hundred dollars but decided against the item because of its size and weight.

Kellum and I visited a number of bars and in every bar prostitutes attempting to turn a trick approached us. I learned that my nickname was really "Cheap Charlie" since I would always haggle with them at a price that was far below what they would accept. When they would be unable to get me to raise my price sufficiently for a contract, the prostitutes would walk away proclaiming that I was Cheap Charlie. I enjoyed the haggling but was honestly too frighten of venereal diseases and desire to maintain my marriage vows to even consider such a relationship.

While most establishments were willing to accept American money, it was obviously in our best interest to exchange our currency for Vietnamese money. We had been warned at the airfield not to exchange our money on the streets since this activity was against military regulations. There was one place at the airport that exchanged money but the rate was approximately 125 piastas for each dollar. We were already acquainted with the situation to realize that we could get somewhere near 200-250 piastas for a dollar on the streets. While walking, Kellum and I were approached after nightfall by two men offering to exchange our dollars for piastas.

The leader of the two men said, "My name is Hoang and I give you good deal for American dollars. You will not get a better deal from anyone on the street."

As he smiled I noticed a mouth full of rotten teeth and breath that was stronger than any I could recall ever experiencing. Hoang was wearing the typical Vietnamese dress of black silk pajamas and shower slippers. The other fellow looked as bad although he seemed to be the stronger of the two men. Neither man was an imposing physical specimen but I imagined that they were probably caring some type of concealed weapon such as a knife. Kellum was hesitant about dealing with the two men but I insisted.

"What kind of exchange can you give me," I asked?

Hoang replied, "200 piastas for each dollar."

"Sorry not enough. I can get better than that at the base," I lied.

"I give you 250 piastas per dollar."

"Nope. It's not worth the effort for less than 275 piastas." I doubted that he would agree to that price but since I had nothing to lose I could take a tough position.

Surprisingly, Hoang replied, "OK, but you must exchange at least $200 American dollars."

"Alright," I said as I quickly calculated in my head that this would amount to 55,000 piastas.

Hoang said, "We make exchange in that alley,' as he pointed to a small alley off the main street. It was quite dark in the alley and I immediately began to have serious doubts as to their honesty and motives. He continued, "Only you in the alley not the other guy," as he pointed to Kellum.

Now I really was suspicious as to their true intentions. "Why do we have to make the exchange in the alley? Just count out the money and we will hand it to each other."

"Many police around and this is an illegal act we do. You would not be in trouble but we would be put in prison if caught." Hoang continued, "The alley or no deal."

"OK, but no tricks," I said.

"We go get the money," said Hoang. "You wait here and I will return with the money in the correct amount." The two Vietnamese departed into a nearly building to obviously obtain the money.

Kellum became concerned and said, "You're not going down that alley with them? There are two of them and that guy is the strangest looking person I have ever seen. Let's forget it and exchange the money on the post with someone we can trust."

Frankly I wasn't in fear of the two men as long as I had my .45. However, I realized that the exchange rate was a little high and therefore the two Vietnamese might be up to something. Also perhaps like most young men who go off to war, there were more serious things to fear than these men.

I told Kellum, "No. I'm going into the alley but if I'm not the first one out, stop them."

"Do what you want but I don't like it," Kellum responded. "By the way, keep them both in front of you and watch out for knives."

After about five minutes, Hoang and his partner emerged from the building and motioned me to join them. I walked into the alley with the two Vietnamese as I released the webbing that secured the .45 in the holster. At the end of the alley one of the men pulled out a large roll of Vietnamese bills and began counting the bills one at a time from his hand into the outstretched hand of the second man. I did not object to this setup since I wanted my hands free to reach for my pistol if I needed such action. I was convinced that there was something wrong and watched the counting of the bills very closely. They began with eight 1000 piasta notes and ten 500 piasta notes and then came this huge pile of 100, 50, 20, and 10 piasta notes. I realized that something was wrong since they had so many small denomination notes. It was the equivalent of a bank giving a customer a large pile of quarters, dimes and nickels for a $100 check. When they had finished counting the 55,000 piastas they handed the wad to me while I handed them two $100 bills. As they turned to leave I fanned the money and quickly realized that there was only one 1000-piasta note and no 500 piasta notes at the bottom of the pile. In an astonishing quick reaction, I pulled my .45 from the holster and yelled, "Hold it."

The two men stopped, turned and I could see from their faces they were astonished to see the .45 pointing at them. The leader said, "What's the matter?"

"You've cheated me. All the large notes are gone. I don't know how you did it but you cheated me."

"You make a mistake in the counting," he responded

"No, there's no mistake," as I kept the gun leveled at the two men. I was glad that I had managed by this time to secure a full clip of ammunition for the .45.

The man pulled the two American $100 bills from his pocket and offered them to me. "OK, no deal. Take the money back and we will forget it."

I took the bills they offered, putting them into my pocket and also put the piastas into my pocket.

Hoang yelled, "You give us back our piastas. We gave you the American dollars."

"Sorry, but I'm keeping these too."

"No! You're robbing us. That's our money." They cried.

As I waived the .45 pistol in their faces, I asked. "Do you want to argue with this gun or shall I also call the police?" I could see a look of despair and knew I would have no trouble with them. I backed down the alley feeling good about by righteous aggression and the fact that I had gotten about $50 worth of piastas from two crooks who had probably swindled thousands of dollars from unsuspecting GI's. I still cannot understand how they were able to palm the large bills from the pile with me watching at such a close distance and obviously aware that something similar would take place.

On the second night in town, Kellum and I continued our bar hopping. The beauty of the young Vietnamese women astonished me. Most had well-rounded figures although their busts were small. They had very small wastes and nice shaped hips. Their figures were highlighted by their tight fitting tops that split below the waste on each side and draped the back pajama style pants they wore. Most of the women wore either all back clothing or a mixture of black and while. Colorful clothing was the exception rather than the rule. The women had attractive dark skin coloring and needed no makeup. All the Vietnamese were short with the women averaging about 5 feet tall and the men 5'4". In many of the bars, women singers would wear traditional western style dresses and hairstyles. I felt it made them look cheap. It was almost comical to hear them sing popular American songs in English but with heavy accents.

Many of the Vietnamese men were in military clothing. At one bar it was obvious that the clientele was primarily Vietnamese nationals with a high number of military types. One group was dressed in green fatigues and red berets with insignias indicating they were Rangers. They tended to strut about and were quite boisterous and arrogant when they talked to the other soldiers in the bar. One of the Rangers and a regular Army of the Republic of Vietnam (ARVN) soldier became involved in an argument over a cocktail hostess at the bar. The Ranger appeared to pull rank and the soldier left the bar. Kellum and I decided to leave before any further problems. As we left the bar we observed the ARVN soldier approach the front door of the bar and throw a grenade into the establishment and quickly run down the street. The grenade went off and there was considerable damage and obvious loss of life. Kellum and I didn't wait to see the outcome and left the area. I began to realize how little life seemed to mean in this place.

The two evenings in Saigon were adventuresome since this was the first time that either Kellum or I visited a foreign country. It was a much-needed prelude before the more vigorous schedule that we would be subjected in the coming months.

Chapter 6 - Pleiku

Finally, transportation inland was arranged and we flew from Saigon to Pleiku, a trip of about 250 miles. The C-130 followed the coast for a short period of time before veering to the west and over the highland mountains. The mountains were modest in size resembling the height of the Adirondacks in upstate New York but covered with dense jungle foliage. Few openings in this landscape were visible and only occasional dirt roads dotted this picturesque scene. I wondered how we would ever be able to locate an enemy in this terrain. I also realized that a mistake of running out of gas and setting down in a field would be completely out of the question.

As we emerged from the mountains, the landscape changed significantly. Cultivated fields and lush foliage were more common. With the exception of the coastal area, no cities or villages were observed although an occasional grass hut could be seen on the hillsides. As we approached Pleiku, the airfield was adjacent to a modest sized city. The airfield and city looked as though they had been scraped into the landscape with nothing but red loose clay and dust as a base. The city and airbase are situated in the Plateau du Kontum. This area has fairly level terrain and a minimum of thick jungle in the central part of the plateau. When the C-130 came to a halt and we ventured from the plane, it was obvious that there was no vegetation on the field and every propeller and gentle breeze would kick up a torment of red dust that covered men and equipment. This location would be my home for the next nine days.

Everything in the base was situated around the airfield. There was a small twenty foot high control tower surrounded by a number of metal sheds. They were large enough to house supplies and equipment but not the aircraft. There seemed to be about ten Huey helicopters, mostly B and C models parked along the field. There were three olive colored OV-1's with U.S. Army markings and two gray OV-1's with U.S. Air Force markings. These planes surprised me, as I didn't know the Air Force was flying anything as small and slow as these planes.

Instead of a concrete runway the landing area was dirt covered with a metal lattice. It obviously was intended to provide some grip to the larger aircraft landing at the field as well as to provide some protection from the constant mud. There was a large Quonset style building that served as our mess hall, bar, theatre, and gambling casino. Nearby were about fifteen large military style tents.

The 219th had twenty-four pilots assigned that included the commanding officer, an executive officer, an operations officer and three section leaders. Removing the administrative staff, this meant that only eighteen pilots would be used for the primary missions although the section leaders and operation officer also would fly some missions. This set up seemed to diminish as our tour in Vietnam continued. Most of the pilots including myself were extremely anxious and excited about getting to fly actual combat missions. To me it was like a dream come true. It wasn't as if I wasn't frightened. I was frightened but the adrenalin that flowed as I contemplated combat dampened my fear. I was like a boy who had been given his first toy gun and the opportunity to shoot the bad guys.

We were housed in one of the large tin and plywood buildings that held twenty bunks. A four-foot high line of sand bags surrounded each building and the tent floors were covered with wood. While the floors offered a degree of comfort from the red dust and the muddy monsoon weather, they also offered safety to an enemy that would emerge as we slept. The Vietnamese rat was my second greatest fear after the swiftly changing weather. These rats were of Herculean proportions and seemed to have little fear of man. Each night when I went to sleep I would take great pains to ensure that my mosquito netting was firmly tucked between my bedding and the canvas cot. Many times at night I could see the furry outline of a rat slither past and often they would literally claw at the underside of my cot. One of the pilots awoke to find a rat sitting on his stomach taking a bite from his flesh. The cure for rabies during this time period was 21 weekly shots of medicine painfully administered with a large hypodermic needle directly into one's bellybutton.

Rather than to tear up the wooden floor and to battle the underground inhabitants, our tent arranged to trade for a local Vietnamese style cat to do our killing. Most American cats would have been no match for rats of this size and number. The Vietnamese cat called a "city or sity cat" looked itself like an oversized rat. It had a pointed nose and its hair was irregular and lacked grooming. The cat ventured out of its sleep only at night and was a virtual killing machine. Its only drawback was that it prowled constantly at night over and around the cots constantly awakening us from our troubled sleep and lacked the civility we had grown to expect from cats in the States. This cat would discharge its waste products wherever he happened to be sitting at the moment even if on a rafter over one's cot. Within a few days, the tent's occupants felt safe enough to trade the cat to another tent in need of its services. It this way, the cat traveled from tent to tent staying long enough to accomplish its mission and to wear out its welcome.

The Pleiku Airfield housed the 52nd Aviation Battalion to which the 219th was assigned. With the exception of our three OV-1 Birddogs, the field belonged primarily to the Huey helicopter pilots. The UH-series Hueys, that were the workhorse of Army airpower, were parked the entire length of the one serviceable runway. About six CH-47 Chinook helicopters were also assigned to the field. Each day two or three larger aircraft such as the Air Force's C-130's and C-123's arrived bringing to the base its much needed supplies and replacement personnel.

The base was surrounded by two large sets of concertina razor wire and a system of trenches and bunkers. With the exception of only about three lookouts during the daylight hours this defensive perimeter was not defended. At night approximately ten to fifteen American soldiers and twenty to twenty-four ARVN with one or two American officers defended the perimeter. The officers included shifts by pilots who doubled during night hours as officer-of-the day and stood guard in one of the bunkers.

Just outside the main gate was the beginning of the city of Pleiku. Most buildings were mere shacks made of sheet medal although the more substantial building was made of cement block. Surprisingly there were few bars in Pleiku since most Americans drank on the base. Only a modest handful of prostitutes walked the streets although a whorehouse could probably easily be located if one wanted such recreation.

The streets were generally dirt although parts of the main street had cobblestones. The main gate was the only way to enter and leave the base with the exception of some small entrances used by patrols covering the perimeter. Personnel assigned to the base were allowed to leave at any time up to curfew beginning at 10 pm and ending at 5 am. Generally the guards ignored the steady stream of Americans and Vietnamese that passed through the main gate. Numerous American personnel were observed walking around Pleiku.

When one ventured outside the base, small children begging for money immediately beset you. On my second visit outside the base, a small child approached me begging for money to purchase sandals for his bare feet. Most of the Vietnamese in this area wore synthetic rubber shower clogs. Being slightly soft hearted I told him I would purchase a pair of clogs at one of the many store fronts that all sold this flimsy foot wear. Before taking a step another child who overheard my remark also asked for clogs. I agreed to his request and by time I reached the shop that was a mere 30 feet away I was accompanied by at least 15 children for whom I purchased a pair of clogs at a price of fifty cents each. I quickly departed the area before every child in the city was begging for something from me.

We discovered that our Birddogs were being sent to Vietnam on a small aircraft carrier and would be unloaded in a few days at Qui Nhon. The three Birddogs assigned to us at Pleiku were on loan from another unit. Most of the pilots eagerly pursued opportunities to fly during this first week. The assignments usually went to the section leaders and two or three of the senior pilots. Eventually I was given the opportunity on Day 3 to fly a twilight recognizance mission in the vicinity of Pleiku. The mission was uneventful but gave me the opportunity to observe close at hand the geography around the field. The landscape was grasslands and I could not see how an enemy could approach in a large unit size without being observed at least during the daylight hours. These grass fields extended for one or two miles in every direction and for about twenty miles to the east until one entered the mountain chain between the highlands and the costal region.

On my second flight of the fourth day in Pleiku, I flew to a small Special Forces camp at Plei Me. Our unit had finally been issued M-16 rifles. The weapons were carried in a makeshift rack in our planes. However, I wanted another weapon that I could carry on the plane and use against ground troops that I might encounter or as a backup weapon if I was forced down. The Special Forces camps were organized to support the local populace by training and arming villagers in the vicinity of these "A" camps. It was rumored that these camps were filled with weapons of every size and make and could be had with some creative bargaining. The camp I had chosen was 25 miles to the south of Pleiku and boasted an extremely small dirt airstrip. These camps traditionally had no communication with planes wanting to land unless one had knowledge of the radio frequency they were monitoring. I did not have the frequency but landed and was greeted by the commanding officer, Captain Blane Cooper and a sergeant.

Cooper was dressed in lightweight fatigues that showed a great deal of wear. He had a pleasant look to him and offered his hand before I could even think of a salute. "I'm Blane Cooper and this is Sergeant Cook."

"Vince Capozzella," I responded and I immediately offered my hand to the sergeant who seemed surprised by my friendliness.

"What can we do for you, Vince, or is this a social call. We don't generally get many social calls." Cooper continued.

"Let's call it a sight seeing visit to find out how well you Special Forces live." Cooper laughed as I turned back to my plane and reached inside to obtain two bottles of scotch that had been strapped to the back seat. They were Johnny Walker Red. I knew they were a good brand even though I never drank scotch.

Cooper's face lit up with a smile and he was obviously pleased by my offering and said, "Do you want to own the camp? Two bottles of scotch can get you just about anything we have."

I laughed and replied, "Frankly, our unit just arrived in country and we really have few supplies in the way of weapons. We've been issued the M-16 but I was hoping to possibly obtain another one as a backup piece in case of trouble."

Cooper smiled again and put his arm around my shoulder as he led me into the barbed wire perimeter. "Vince, you've come to the right place. The one thing beside Cong that we have in abundance is weapons."

He brought me to a grass hut. When I entered, I was surprised to see it was filled with weapons of every type imaginable. They were piled in the middle of the hut lying in a pyramid of tangled medal on the ground.

"Take your pick," he laughed.

I selected a "grease gun". I had observed this weapon many times in WWII movies. This weapon was solid medal with only one moving part and easy to disassemble. It shot a .45 caliber slug identical to my issued sidearm. The only drawback was its weight and the fact that the muzzle velocity of the bullet was much slower than newer weapons and consequently had less range. These drawbacks did not deter me, as I would be using the weapon primarily shooting from the cockpit window of my plane aiming downward or as a last ditch weapon if my plane was to be shot down over enemy territory. Cooper supplied me with ten clips for the weapon and enough ammunition to fill the clips that included tracer rounds. Tracer rounds were ammunition tipped with red phosphorous and glowed after being fired so that the shooter could see the path and strike of the bullets. I loaded my thirty round clips with every third round as a tracer.

Cooper then showed me the camp and we had a small lunch with a can of beer. I learned that the Special Forces units were extremely friendly and made every attempt to be on good terms with pilots for both close combat support and the resupply of items that were hard to obtain by normal means. These items included beer and bottles of alcohol. They were prohibited from being transported by air to these camps and meant that the camps could not get these items if not for pilots like myselfme. I never again went to an "A" camp without a case of beer or a couple bottles of booze.

I would probably have been better served if I had chosen some other type of weapon but the grease gun looked quite menacing and gave me extra confidence of my invincibility. As I said my farewell to Cooper and the other men of the camp, I could see in their faces a friendliness that had been missing by the other soldiers I had met since arriving in Vietnam. I also felt a moment of guilt as I looked around the camp and realized there was very little standing in the way of this camp being overrun by a determined enemy. My admiration for the Special Forces units that were assigned to these small camps never diminished throughout my tour of duty.

I returned to camp with my new weapon and never took another flight in Vietnam without my M-16 with six clips of 20 rounds each, my grease gun with ten clips of 30 rounds each and my .45 pistol with two clips. No one ever mentioned the grease gun or challenged my use of the gun from the air at ground targets. It never dawned on me or for that matter any of the other pilots that we needed permission to alter or modify our armament or planes to accomplish our mission. Most of us went to some unusual efforts in order to make our small observation planes into killing machines.

Life at Pleiku was quite monotonous during my short time there in June 1965. Each morning we awoke to either extremely low-lying clouds with rain or fog. That gave us a chance to stand for hours in front of a small vending wagon operated by the Army making fresh donuts. I was thrilled if I could obtain a couple of donuts and coffee for breakfast and felt very fortunate. If a plane was available, I flew a reconnaissance mission or hitched a ride in a Huey gun ship on a similar mission. Otherwise we lay around our tent or hutch as they were called.

The weather was extremely humid with temperatures in the high 90's. I sweated constantly. Unfortunately, my only uniforms were the green khaki shirts and pants that soldiers in the States wore for both summer and winter but were totally unacceptable for a jungle theatre of operations. I noticed that within a week in Vietnam that all the administrative staff and pilots who were close to the command were issued the new jungle fatigues of lightweight cotton polyester mix uniforms and jungle boots with air panels. Not being or wanting to be part of the inner circle, I was not issued the new uniforms. When I asked for them, I was told by the supply officer that only a small number of the uniforms were available although I noticed that he had an ample supply of such uniforms for his own use in the supply tent. Kellum was not issued the new uniforms either although he did receive them in about six months. I was never given an opportunity to get them and eventually I didn't really give a damn.

My uniforms were constantly damp and both uniforms and boots became mildewed. In order to keep the uniforms from completely rotting they were stored after washing and drying in a "hotbox" that was a large wooden clothes closet with a light bulb. It was kept constantly lit to create heat and drying capability.

Each tent was allowed to hire a "hutch maid" who would clean the tent and wash clothes. The clothes were washed by hand in a large open concrete pool of water and placed on a clothesline ringing the tent to dry. Often the clothes would be on the line for two or three days due to the intermittent rain that usually fell each morning and late afternoon. Our hutch maid was a small Vietnamese woman of about 25 years old. We called her Tam since we couldn't pronounce her given name. Each morning she and about 40 other Vietnamese workers would enter the airbase and other than giving their names were never checked for weapons. Fortunately while I was stationed at Pleiku, there were no incidents of sabotage. This activity would have been relatively easy to initiate.

Chapter 7 – An Khe and Our Vietnamese Allies

On Day 6, I was informed that Kellum and I were to participate in an operation at a place called An Khe that was located about 60 miles due east of Pleiku on Highway 19. An Khe was situated on a plateau surrounded by mountains separating the coastal plains and the central highlands. According to the briefing by Captain Leyva we were to take two planes and two crew chiefs and support the ARVN as they cleared the plateau and nearby areas of Vietcong personnel. An Khe was being cleared for the 1st Cavalry Division. This unit was arriving in Vietnam sometime in August. An Khe would be their home base. Naturally Kellum and I were excited by the first opportunity to begin combat flying and to be involved in an operation together although I wondered why the more highly placed pilots had not jumped on this opportunity.

Unfortunately the day prior to our move to An Khe, I was in the town of Pleiku and went to a local restaurant to sample the Vietnamese cuisine. The food was tasty but I had forgotten about the possibility of bacteria. It really didn't dawn on me that the water might be polluted. At the meal I had only a small drink of the water but that was enough to do a job on my internal organs. I awoke the next day with a severe case of diarrhea and cramps. Although I went to the medics for pills, I didn't notify my command as I wanted to do the mission assigned.

At 10 am I took off with my crew chief and with Kellum taking off thirty minutes later. The flight to An Khe was relatively easy as I only had to follow Highway 19. This route was the main and only road leading east from Pleiku. The road went directly to An Khe and ended at the costal city of Quin Nhon. The highway had a rich history in the annals of the French Indochina war against the Viet Ming. Apparently, a large French garrison was cut off from the coast and attempted to march via Highway 19 from Pleiku to Qui Nhon. The Viet Ming fought them all the way ambushing them every mile or so and then melting away into the jungle much like our minutemen did to the British enroute to Concord and Lexington at the start of the Revolutionary War. They say the French lost so many men that they were buried feet first in small four by four foot holes to conserve space along the road.

Eventually An Khe would become the largest hellicopter pad in the world to house the numerous UH-1 and CH-47 helicopters needed to make the First Cavalry Division a mobile unit. At this time there was only the one dirt airstrip, which like the Pleiku airfield was covered by heavy metal plates to support the larger aircraft such as the C-130. An Khe also had a Special Forces camp located in the vicinity of the field that I never had the opportunity to visit.

When I arrived over An Khe, I observed the airfield with one north-south runway. Most of the runways in Vietnam were dirt strips hacked into the jungle by the Japanese during their occupation of Vietnam in WWII. The runways were always built parallel to the coastline or north to south that was quite insane. The prevailing wind during the monsoon seasons was always from the east to west and during the dry season from west to east. This meant that most landings were crosswind landings and often extremely difficult. My luck continued and that day the wind was from the south. I didn't notice the windsock along the runway and assumed I would be facing a cross wind and the direction of landing was immaterial. I was watching the activity in and around the field. A C-130 was parked at the far end of the north entrance to the strip with a large fuel blather also lying on the runway adjacent to the C-130. It had just been unloaded and awaiting removal to another location. These fuel blathers were about ten feet by ten feet, constructed of heavy rubber material and filled with aviation fuel.

I started my approach to the field and decided to land from the south to the north as I assumed the C-130 had also landed since it was parked at the north end. I obviously intended to stop well before the fuel blather and C-130 since the strip was much longer than I needed for the Birddog. This approach placed the wind to my back. This situation was definitely not the desired landing setup. Since there was no tower giving instructions to incoming aircraft, I made my approach and landing. The wind propelled my plane further down the runway than anticipated and at a much faster landing speed than was necessary or prudent. I hit the breaks hard but the plane hurled down the runway toward the blather and C-130. I saw personnel running from the end of the runway away from the pending collision. I braked so hard the plane almost nose-dived into the landing area but stopped a mere ten feet from impact and possible catastrophe. Quickly I turned the plane 180 degrees and taxied to the other end of the field to put distance between myself and the irate personnel picking themselves off the dirt.

I reported to the commanding American liaison officer, Lieut. Colonel Frank Thompson. He advised me to set up our small two man tents adjacent to the runway for immediate action, if needed. All around were over one thousand ARVN troops in foxholes and tents. The only permanent buildings were the remains of an old mission church and adjacent building that housed the command center of the operation. It was our responsibility to fly continuous coverage in our two planes around An Khe so as to be able to alert our command about the approach of enemy troops, which were thought to be massing around An Khe. This would require Kellum and me to fly two three-hour shifts for the required twelve-hour coverage that was needed. We decided that we would alternate these shifts so as to fly one shift in the morning with a three-hour rest period and one shift in the afternoon.

Although my diarrhea continued throughout the night, the next morning I awoke and took the first three-hour shift. With the exception of beautiful scenery, the only troops I saw were the ARVN units moving into defensive positions. The shift did have its down side as I was unable to withstand the attack of the diarrhea and soiled my pants twice on each shift. Slightly embarrassing but other than the normal jokes, the mission went forward.

Although the scenery was quite beautiful, there was no evidence of any enemy troops or camps. The only troops were the ARVN units. They stayed within a half mile of the airfield although they certainly could have secured a much larger perimeter. Assuming the First Cavalry Division expected the area to be clear of any enemy forces, the ARVN would have to secure a perimeter of at least three to four miles from the field to acquire security. No attempt was made to move the troops far from the security of the main base. Since this was my first true contact with the ARVN, I was surprised by their inefficiency and lack of motivation.

Like most Americans, I had been led to believe by the Johnson administration that the ARVN were highly motivated combat veterans who needed only modern equipment to become a great fighting force. This propaganda by the American government was either misinformation provided by the military and embassy in Vietnam or an attempt to totally mislead the American public. It took a few months before I understood the lack of desire to win this war by the ARVN.

Vietnam was a civil war between the rural and predominately Hindu North led by Ho Chi Minh and the urban and predominately Catholic South led by Ngo Dinh Diem. The ARVN had difficulty deciding which side they should support and generally elected to sit on the side lines if they could. This decision meant American troops did not have a strong ally fighting with them. The strength and training of the ARVN did not matter in terms of their fighting ability and effectiveness. Almost always they did not fight and often chose to run or ignore a chance to become involved in combat. This decision was not limited to just the privates in their army but permeated throughout the entire chain of command.

At the evening intelligence meeting, Kellum and I were asked to give our assessment of the possible enemy movement. Kellum and I had discussed the day's missions and agreed that there was no evidence of enemy troops. I stood up and said, "Neither I nor Lieutenant Kellum observed any enemy troops or movement or any evidence they are near An Khe. We had a good look at the roads and trails in the vicinity of the base for ten to fifteen miles in each direction."

This report brought a swift reaction from Colonel Khang, the ARVN commander, who said in fairly good English, "My troops report over 2,000 Vietcong moving against us supported by tanks and artillery. I consider the report to be very accurate"

I responded, "We didn't see any indication of this activity, Colonel" as I attempted to be diplomatic.

The Colonel countered, "Perhaps you didn't fly low enough to observe them or didn't fly to the north where they are located."

Anger replaced my diplomacy as I responded. "Both Lieutenant Kellum and I flew often at tree top altitude and nothing was observed in every direction. I think I would have seen armored units on the trails or at least tracks."

"The Vietcong are masters of camouflage and sweep any track signs from the roads," he said. "I think my men have been fighting the Vietcong longed than you, Lieutenant, and they would be more aware of the capabilities of these devils."

I continued our defense, "There are no roads to the north capable of allowing the passage of tanks."

"Again, when you have been in my country longer Lieutenant you will be more appreciative of the capability of the enemy."

"Fine, tomorrow, Lieutenant Kellum and I will concentrate our surveillance to the north and perhaps our allies will move their defensive perimeter further to the north, also." My response had the desired effect as the ARVN colonel's face flushed with anger and he did not offer a counter although Colonel Thompson quickly spoke up in an attempt to diffuse the discussion.

"Fine, Lieutenants Capozzella and Kellum will focus their attention on the north in an attempt to assess the enemy situation in greater detail," Thompson said. "Will that should satisfy you, Colonel Khang?"

"That will be acceptable but I don't want some inexperienced American officers telling me something I know to be false," as he turned and walked out of the briefing.

Thompson turned to Kellum and I. "You both know what to do tomorrow. Give it your best shot and don't be afraid to tell it like it is regardless of Colonel Khang."

"Sir, I really could care less what the Colonel thinks or says but I will not be insulted," I responded. Kellum signaled his agreement.

The next day we again flew our two shifts and again did not observe any sign of an enemy. Again I was victimized by the diarrhea twice each mission. The nightly intelligence meeting was again marked by near hysteria from the ARVN commanders that we were about to be overrun by large Vietcong forces supported by numerous tanks.

Again we attempted to explain, "There is no evidence from the air of this development," I said.

The ARVN Colonel countered, "My troops report observing evidence of a large number of Vietcong personnel supported by tanks moving into positions to attack An Khe."

"Colonel, we flew our planes as close to the ground as possible and did not observe any sign of this type of enemy movement. I guarantee the enemy is not that close and there are no tanks," I protested. "Perhaps your troops should radio these reports while we are flying so that we can confirm and utilize air strikes."

Major Madsden was the American military adviser to the ARVN Colonel. He quickly interjected that he would personally give Kellum and I instructions for the next day's flight operations. The situation was again defused but I could only wonder about our allies' determination to fight the enemy. This mission was my first close encounter with ARVN troops and their leaders. I knew the ARVN were not as reliable as our own troops but I thought they would be as least as good as the Vietcong. My hope was not to be, as I never observed the ARVN and their leaders ever perform in an aggressive or courageous manner during my entire tour of duty in Vietnam.

As Kellum and I left the debriefing, Major Madsden said, "Look Lieutenant, keep flying your missions and give me your reports and I will handle the debriefings." It was obvious that Major Madsden didn't believe the ARVN reports any more than I did and was only attempting to save face for the ARVN colonel. Without us at the meetings the ARVN Colonel would be able to report any enemy movement he desired without challenge. However, we promised to take a closer look the following morning. Kellum and I went to sleep along the runway with the confidence that although the ARVN had the jitters, we were surrounded by a thousand friendly troops.

Morning came without the usual noise of constant movement. I realized that it was already 0730 am and we had not been awaken. As I exited the tent I was greeted by total silence. There was no sign of any ARVN personnel or any other person other than Kellum, the two crew chiefs and myself at the An Khe airfield. I walked quickly to the command center to find that it was completely empty. Our allies had silently pulled out in the night, obviously fleeing the onslaught of the imaginary Vietcong.

I woke Kellum, "Charlie, those bastards have left us here alone."

Kellum poked his head from the tent and said, "What are you talking about?"

"The bastards have left. There isn't anyone here."

"They have to be here. They're just down at the end of the runway."

"Charlie there is no one here except the four of us. I went to the command center and it's deserted. All the equipment is gone. Even the American advisors have left."

Kellum was finally alert and standing outside the tent giving the field a look. "I don't believe it. How could they leave without us hearing them?"

"Charlie, we have just seen the first real accomplishment by the ARVN. They were able to walk out on us without even waking us. You have to give them a hand for at least doing that correctly. Let's get the hell out of here."

We quickly threw our belongings in the rear of our planes and took off from the field and headed back to Pleiku. The tents were left alongside the airfield since they weren't ours anyway. I assumed the ARVN were heading by truck to the east toward Quin Nhon. This direction would force them to take a dangerous route through the mountains. Neither Kellum nor I were particularly interested in offering them air cover on their return to safety and we flew west toward Pleiku and home. Upon our return I explained the situation and was awarded with an at-a-boy from the operations officer. Three days later the 10th Air Assault Brigade arrived at An Khe without the assistance of the ARVN and established their base without any opposition from the Vietcong.

I had learned two important lessons during that first week. One, the ARVN are prone to exaggeration and will flee at the slightest hint of danger, and two, don't drink the native water. One of these lessons to my regret, I would ignore toward the end of my twelve month tour.

Chapter 8 – The Routine

With the exception of our flight missions, life at Pleiku was often boring. After flying, there was the opportunity to shower, have a drink at the Officer's Club, eat, and either gamble at the casino or watch a movie. Movies were at a premium and the movie reels were exchanged between bases one at a time very infrequently. The first movie I saw at Pleiku was <u>Becket</u> with Richard Burton and Peter O'Toole. It was a great movie, the first time I saw it but became somewhat less worthwhile after seeing it for three straight nights.

The club boasted an extensive gambling area with slot machines, a dice table and poker table. Slot machines had no interest and I quickly found that I had no ability with dice. My interest was drawn to the poker table. Frankly, I felt that I was a great poker player as I had been brought up since a small child watching and playing poker. Whenever my family got together with my aunts and uncles in Utica, New York, they always would play poker for hours. These get to-getters were held at least once or twice a month and provided me with extensive knowledge in poker. By the time I was twelve I was allowed to play with the grownups if there was a place not being used.

The poker at Pleiku was table stakes. This meant that a person could bet whatever he placed on the table. Generally it was wise to use cash and to also place your checkbook on the table to cover a bet. These stakes were the highest I had ever played but I soon realized that I actually played better when there was more money bet. I almost always won some money or broke even. A typical poker hand would generally net the victor a few hundred dollars at a minimum. The biggest problem was how to dispose of one's winnings without violating the Army's policy on sending money home. The policy basically allowed a soldier to send no more than what he was paid in Vietnam, not counting the money allocated for the family. I was paid each month a total of $250 dollars for purchasing my food, gifts and gambling. Fortunately I often mailed money back to my wife in amounts up to $250 although the mailings occurred more than once a month. I figured that the Army was probably not checking the outgoing mail and even if they were, no one was keeping records as to money transactions. As long as we used American dollars, I had no problem in sending money home but once we were forced to exchange our dollars for script dollars it became more difficult to then convert the script back to dollars.

When not watching a movie or playing poker, the only other and most common activity was drinking. Each night would be some type of celebration and there was always a pilot being transferred back to the States, as his tour would be completed. Champagne was often the drink of choice for these celebrations and everyone would get completely "smashed." Our command never warned the pilots about drinking to access and as long as one could fly his missions, no one was concerned.

The meals at Pleiku were quite flexible in terms of their hours so as to accommodate the pilots varied schedules but not in terms of their cuisine.

Breakfast was served between 6 and 8 am, lunch between 11 and 1 pm and dinner between 5 and 7:30 pm. My favorite meal has always been breakfast in the States but the breakfast served here were powdered eggs that lacked consistency and toast from canned bread that was quite horrible. No milk other than condensed canned milk was available for either coffee or cereal and it would be this item that I missed the most while in Vietnam even though I was never a big milk lover. I was surprised to discover that officers were required to pay for their meals even in Vietnam since they receive a meal allowance. I assumed that the pay allowance would be stopped when you are sent to a combat area. I wondered what the troops in the field did. Would they have to pay for their K-rations? The payment for meals matched the pay allowance and was standard throughout the country although I began to wonder if the meals were worth even the small amount of money that was being charged. I did learn from one of the helicopter pilots that some of them often ate their evening meals at a local restaurant in Pleiku.

On my 8th day at Pleiku a pilot and co-pilot flying an Army Caribou cargo plane did not return to base. The Caribou was the Army's version of the C-123 Air Force cargo plane and had two engines. It boasted an extremely short take off and landing capability. It was significantly better than the C-123. This rivalry between the two services for cargo missions would eventually be settled in the early 1970's with the Army agreeing to scrap the Caribou and all future fixed wing cargo planes and the Air Force agreeing to quit attack helicopter aircraft. While this agreement settled a growing dispute between the two services, it was regrettable since the Caribou was a much better plane than the C-123.

On this day the pilot, Jeff Armstrong and the co-pilot, Dave Regean never radioed any distress but simply did not return from their last mission. Since there was no radar at Pleiku, their approximate location was not even known although it was surmised that they must have gone down to the west or northwest of Pleiku. Unfortunately this area was extremely dense and well developed jungle with the top of the jungle often reaching 100-150 feet above the ground. The Caribou could easily crash and completely disappear from sight by falling below the jungle screen. A massive search was launched for the missing plane but after a five to six hour search by over twenty planes and helicopters, the Caribou and crew were given up for lost.

Later that night the other pilots of the unit to which Armstrong and Regean were assigned were in the club partying as usual. Most of these pilots were like Armstrong and Regean, warrant officers and between 19-21 years old. Although I was not acquainted with either lost pilot, I thought there would be significant morning and despair over their loss.

I found absolutely no mention of either pilot although I did hear one of the unit pilots say, "Well, Armstrong never gave a damn about anyone else who was lost."

The other pilot said, "Yea, but Regean was OK and he had a wife and child."

"You're right, lets have a drink to him," as the two pilots walked to the bar for another round of booze.

Neither pilot was ever mentioned again during my stay in Vietnam and life continued as if they never existed. The pilots and aircraft were never found as to my knowledge. On this night the young warrant officers partied like they did every night with most getting drunk. My reaction to this display was at first shocked but as my tour in Vietnam continued I soon also began to lose track of the men lost and usually would completely wipe their existence from my mind.

On the day prior to my departure from Pleiku for my permanent assignment, I had just returned from a reconnaissance mission. My attention was drawn to the similar OV-1's on the field with "U.S. Air Force" markings. Although our Army planes were painted green, these planes were a dull gray color. What caught my attention to these planes was an accident that I witnessed. An Air Force OV-1 had just taken off to the south from the airfield. Apparently the pilot's plane was not developing full power and the pilot attempted to turn his plane 180 degrees back to the airfield. The one cardinal sin of any pilot especially flying small propeller type aircraft is never attempt to turn when your plane is not developing full power. What made this case even more painful was that the pilot was still attempting to climb higher. Aircraft such as our plane will easily stall once the airspeed drops below flying speed in level flight or a minimum of about 65MPH. As the Air Force pilot began his turn and dropped his left wing the plane stalled and dropped 300 feet on its side to the ground. The pilot was instantly killed.

That night I was explaining the accident to the other 219th pilots and discovered that the Air Force had assigned their own pilots to basically the same mission as our own because they did not believe the Army pilots were capable of calling an air strike for jet aircraft. Consequently a small number of previous jet pilots were reassigned to the OV-1 for this mission. An OV-1 in comparison to a F-105 or other fighter jet is like comparing a bicycle to a Corvette car. The only problem is that the bicycle in this case is capable of killing the driver if he does not have adequate training. From what the other pilots said, the Air Force pilots received only about 50 hours training in the OV-1. They had very little respect for the plane's capabilities in comparison of at least 200 hours for the Army pilots. In this case the lack of knowledge of the aircraft cost the Air Force pilot his life since once he developed engine trouble he should have lowered the nose of the plane maintaining enough airspeed to avoid a stall. If the airspeed is insufficient to maintain altitude, then the pilot must select the best possible location to bring the plane to earth. There is no way to keep a plane in the air once the engine lacks the power to continue to fly. While this problem may seem easy and academic, most pilots refuse to accept this fact when facing similar situations and will crash their planes. In this case the Air Force lost a highly trained jet pilot because the powers to be did not want to allow Army pilots to participate in a common mission. This type of foolishness was consistent with the entire Vietnam fiasco.

One of the more amusing and stupid orders that the 219th received from the high command in Saigon involved elephants. Apparently someone in the ARVN command suggested that the VC were using elephants to transport heavy material such as artillery pieces and ammunition down the Ho Chi Minh trail. Our command gave the pilots the authority to attack and kill any elephants seen in the countryside. It was common knowledge that Vietnam had a few wild elephants that roamed about but none of us had ever seen the Vietcong using them as the ARVN had suggested. Not withstanding the stupidity of the order or the knowledge that the Vietcong was not using the elephants, most pilots jumped at the chance to kill one. On one flight to the west of Pleiku within 25 miles of the Cambodian border I observed an elephant in an open field. I attacked it with two of my HE rockets. Although the rockets struck within ten to twenty feet of the beast, it did not appear seriously hurt and ran for cover in the jungle. The attack gave me a feeling of jubilation. Later as the war progressed I realized the mistake that I had almost made if I had killed the elephant. I felt guilty about my attempt to slaughter an innocent animal and vowed to use more discretion about death even if encouraged and applauded by our high command.

Chapter Nine – Bao Loc

Shortly after my return from An Khe, Captain Leyda called me to his office. "Vince I'm assigning you to a small airfield about 80 clicks south of here. All the pilots under my command will be given assignments to the smaller airfields. Frankly, I consider the assignment better than staying at Pleiku and being under the eye of everyone."

"Sounds great," I said. "When do I leave?"

Leyda continued, "Some of the guys have been ferrying our planes from a Navy carrier off Quin Nhon to Pleiku and your plane should be ready shortly."

"What's the name of the place that I'm going to be assigned?"

"It's a small village called, Boa Loc situated in the Lang Bian Mountains," Leyda said. "It's supposed to be a nice location."

I recall wondering where the hell the Lang Biam Mountains were situated and I wasn't terribly keen on flying in a mountainous terrain but did not say anything about this thought to Leyda. "Have you seen the place?" I asked.

"Sorry I haven't and the locations for the dispersal of the pilots were made for us by higher command. I don't know a damn thing about this place other than it has a MACV detachment for an ARVN regiment stationed there and you will be living at an old college campus of some kind."

I immediately felt better as the prospects of living at a college campus didn't sound bad at all. "Will I be the only pilot from the unit assigned there?" I hoped that Leyda would assign Kellum to the same post.

"Lieutenant Trumball will also be assigned there and will be the senior officer for our detachment based on date of rank. You both will be supporting the MACV unit and indirectly the ARVN although your missions will be basically determined by us."

I recalled 1st Lieutenant Jason Trumball. He was a strange guy who was not really known to me other than an occasional "hello". His home was in Ohio and he didn't have a family other than his parents. He was of medium height and although he looked normal enough, he was quiet and had stayed pretty much to himself at both Fort Hood and our short time in Vietnam. I accepted Leyda's analysis of who was in charge since he was a 1st Lieutenant and I was still a 2nd Lieutenant.

Leyda explained that the mission would also include two mechanics for the two OV-1's. "Your two crew chiefs are Private Jeff Moore and Spec 4 Joseph Wheeler. I met both guys and although I don't really know them, they seem to be OK. Your crew chief will be Moore who will go with you when you depart tomorrow."

"Thanks Captain. I won't let you down," as a broad smile appeared on my face.

"All right get the hell out of here and get to work," as he slapped my behind. "By the way, try to stay out of trouble. I have confidence in your flying ability but have concerns about your diplomacy."

"No problem," I said, as I left Leyda's office.

I immediately went looking for Private Moore and found him in the enlisted man's quarters. We talked for a few minutes and told him to be ready to shove off at 9am on the next day. He didn't impress me with either his attitude or his knowledge of the OV-1. He was in his early 20's with a slight beer belly and hair that was already thinning. He didn't seem to care about the mission and impressed me as having been forced to join the unit against his will. I had no option but to accept the assignment but knew I would have to keep a sharp eye on his work since it could ultimately affect my own well-being. I learned later that Kellum was assigned to Quin Nhon, as Leyda didn't want two close friends assigned to the same location.

Our OV-1s had arrived by ship off Quin Nhon about two days prior to my assignment to Boa Loc and flown off the small carrier deck by Captains John Sinclair and Richard Kowalewski. All the pilots including myself had volunteered for the mission to fly the planes off the carrier. I had to start learning to stop this volunteering thing or it would kill me. Sinclair and Kowalewski flew the planes to Pleiku where they were fitted with four rocket launchers on each wing to be used to mark enemy positions. The rocket launchers would hold smoke, white phosphorous (WP) and high explosives (HE) rockets. The smoke and WP rockets were preferred by our command since they would be more readily visible to fast moving strike aircraft provided by the Air Force and Navy while the HE rockets were intended as a destructive, killing weapon. The HE was much harder to see from the air.

I saw absolutely no sense in the smoke rockets and insisted that my plane be loaded with four WP and four HE rockets. Unfortunately, the OV-1 had no aiming device fitted to the aircraft and the rockets could only be fired at a target with any degree of accuracy when the plane was traveling directly at the target. During the coming weeks I made a number of attacks on targets and used a grease pencil mark on the inside windshield as my aiming device. This simple method was adequate when the plane was perfectly aimed at the target but if wind or any turning movement affected the plane, the rocket could miss its proposed hit by hundreds of feet. The accuracy was also increased the nearer I flew toward the enemy and waited before firing the rocket. Naturally a smoke rocket was the easiest to use since I needed only to advise the attacking jets that the enemy was such and such distance and direction from the smoke. However, if no jets were available and I wanted to personally attack the target then I would have to make a determination based on the enemy's firepower as to when to release the rocket. At least firing rockets added some excitement and feeling of accomplishment.

Leyda saw me off for Boa Loc. "Vince, I haven't seen this airfield but they say it's adequate for your plane. Trumball will be coming in about two days from now, as there is some mechanical problem with his plane. Just take your crew chief with you."

"OK. But how about supplies, food, living quarters, and everything else we need?"

"They'll be provided for you by the Boa Loc unit," Leyda promised.

"Yea, but what kind of unit is this?" I countered.

It was obvious that Leyda had absolutely no idea as to what was available or stationed at Boa Loc. He had only a very rough sketch of the location and personnel although I could not blame him since he really had no way to get all the information. The simplest way to work it out was to just send me there and work my way through it.

Leyda added. "I don't know anything more about the Americans other than the fact they are part of MACV."

"Captain what the hell is a MACV unit?" I inquired.

"It stands for Military Assistance Command Vietnam and the guys assigned to it our intended to train and assist their counterparts in the ARVN units to lead their men." Leyda responded. "But you are not really part of MACV. You're just attached to Bao Loc to provide the MACV support and to fly continuously over the same terrain looking for Charlie. Got it?"

"Right. But do they have authority over me? Can they tell me when and where to fly or are the missions my responsibility?"

"Your command is the 219th but that doesn't mean you can tell them to go to hell. You will have to cooperate with them on their missions but they have no authority to tell you how to accomplish a mission." Leyda said.

I had no idea what his explanation really meant but I assumed that the MACV unit had no authority to order me to do anything and that was how I would explain it to them.

Leyda walked me to my plane helping to carry my duffle bag like a father seeing his child go off into the world for the first time. I believe he was embarrassed by the lack of information he could provide me. I wondered if anyone at Boa Loc knew I was heading their way.

My crew chief, Private Jeff Moore was waiting by the OV-1 with his own duffle bag and a small tool chest. It was obvious the plane would be slightly overweight as it was intended for only a pilot and passenger and minimum of gear. There were the eight rockets attached to the wings. This armament added to the weight for which it was not designed. I knew I would have to be very careful in the takeoff.

The takeoff went much better than I expected. My brief conversation with Moore would continue my skepticism of his ability. He already had a "short timer's attitude" even though he had been in Vietnam for the same period of time as I had been. He seemed complacent and thoroughly uninterested. He mentioned that he had not volunteered to come to Vietnam but had just graduated from crew chief training on the OV-1 and been assigned to the 219th. This conversation did little to remove my fear that my plane would not be taken care of in a professional manner. A pilot's life depends upon the ability and thoroughness of his crew chief.

Our flight was to travel due south for about 80 miles or approximately one hour. My map did not show any prominent geographical features near Bao Loc although it was the first town north of the dividing line between the central highlands and the low areas of Southern Vietnam. The town seemed to be nestled in a band of mountains that isolate the highlands from the lowlands. The flight south confirmed my suspicion that the jungle and only an occasional field or cultivated parcel covered the vast majority of the region. Only one dirt road could be seen from the air and it twisted and turned around every hill and mountain.

I was flying about 2500 feet off the ground and saw little signs of life. There were at this time no large American combat units in 3rd Corp so I was not expecting to see any friendly troops. I also did not see any ARVN troops or camps. The entire area with the exception of Special Forces "A" camps at Ple Me, Cheo Reo and Ban Me Thuot were the only American troops between Pleiku and Boa Loc. 125 mile to the south of Bao Loc was Saigon but there were few American or ARVN troops in that area in-between these locations. Most friendly troops were snuggled comfortably in the protective confines of South Vietnam's capital city.

With no knowledge of the terrain, no radio directional assistance and no distinctive geographical site to compute my location, the search for Boa Loc was strictly guesswork. After an hour of travel I was starting to get a little apprehensive and began to fear that I would look like the biggest fool in the world if I couldn't find this damn place. Suddenly, I saw an opening in the jungle and there sitting on a small rise was what appeared to be a dirt airfield. As I flew closer to the field I could read the words "Bao Loc" printed in white painted rocks near the field. Salvation! I had made it.

I immediately called the Bao Loc station on a frequency provided for me by Leyda. "Bao Loc control this is Headhunter One One approaching for landing."

"Headhunter One One we were expecting you but don't have you in sight."

"This is Headhunter One One, I'm about a mile north of your position at about a thousand feet."

"Sorry Headhunter One One, I can't see you yet."

I assumed that the control had not been use to seeing aircraft approach its station and therefore still had not picked up sight of the plane. Finally I was directly over the airfield and began a circle. I could see no movement on the field. "Bao Loc I'm directly over the field. Do you have me in sight?"

"Sorry we still can't see you."

"Can you hear my engine?"

"No!" came the response.

Was it possible that these guys were that blind or deft or had I made a mistake. Again I looked at the field and the white stones that clearly spelled the words "Bao Loc".

"Listen, I'm directly over the field and can see the name of the field."

"Headhunter One One, we can't see you and the field has no name markers."

Now I was confused. I couldn't be imagining this field. "Is there another air strip near Bao Loc?"

Control responded, "There is a small strip about ten miles to the northwest of Bao Loc but that's Charlie country."

Immediately I gave the OV-1 full power and began as steep a climb as the overweight craft could handle. I expected to be riddled by machine gun fire from Charlie but there was no movement. It was obvious that the Vietcong had placed the rocks near this airfield to perhaps lure unsuspecting pilots to their doom. That place would be my first target when I confirmed there were no friendly troops or civilians located there.

Within ten minutes I could see the town of Bao Loc. It was much bigger than I expected, as there had to be at least three to five thousand inhabitants living there. About three miles to the east of the city I could see the airfield. It was a large dirt strip completely surrounded by a dense jungle canopy.

"Bao Loc control this is Headhunter One One for landing."

"Headhunter One One this is Bao Loc, we have you in sight. The wind is from the east."

I discovered after my landing that the airfield was adjacent to a tea plantation operated by a Frenchman and his family. The strip had been built by the Japanese during WWII and again built north to south. This mistake meant that for the next six months most landings were to test my crosswind techniques to the limit of my ability. My landing went flawlessly.

A Sergeant E-7 John McClintock with whom I would form an immediate friendship and admiration greeted me on the ground. He was a grizzled old timer who had already served in WWII and Korea. He was obviously on the backside of a long Army career and I discovered in short time was the holder of two bronze stars for valor in both the previous wars. He was the type of soldier often played by John Wayne in his war movies. He was a solid, no bullshit type of guy who could always be depended upon to hold his own and carry the younger men. McClintock was a little old for combat assignment in Vietnam at approximately 45 years old and was built like a tree trunk.

As I clamored down from the plane, I greeted McClintock. "Hello Sergeant my name is Vince Capozzella." I always thought that this greeting was the catalyst that formed our friendship since there could not be two more unlikely people to make friends. He was twice my age with many times the experience in both life and war.

"Welcome to the shithole of Vietnam, Lieutenant," McClintock said. "Throw your gear in the jeep and I'll take you to the base."

"Thanks." I said as Moore and I threw the duffle bags in the back and he squeezed next to them. I sat in the front seat next to McClintock. I noticed a small shed on the side of the runway and mentally made a note that it would be a perfect spot for our maintenance setup. The field itself was guarded by a small group of Vietnamese soldiers.

"Are they our they on guard at the field?" I inquired of McClintock.

"The ARVN provide us with a squad of Montagnard troops at both here and the base. The Montagnard are the best local troops available and you will appreciate them more than the ARVN."

This was my first sight of the Montagnard troops. They were to provide for my security at both the airfield and the base where I would live for the next six months. Appearance wise they were even smaller in stature than the typical Vietnamese. Most of the men grew to only about 5'2" and the women to about 4'10". They seemed to have a darker complexion than the Vietnamese and it was apparent these people were from a different stock than the Vietnamese. They appeared more primitive in their facial features than the Vietnamese who had more delicate characteristics. The Montagnards lived almost exclusively in the Central Highlands and were known as fierce fighters. This characteristic alone separated them from the typical Vietnamese. They had no education and lived on average to the ripe old age of about 35 to 40. Traditionally they survived as hunters and cultivated small plots of land on the sides of the mountains. Their main weapon prior to their involvement in the war was a small 18"crossbow. The arrows, which were only straight slits of bamboo with pointed tips and without feathers, were about 8-12" long and had an effective range of only 30-40 feet. Once I saw a Montagnard fire his crossbow at a tree. The bamboo slit imbedded itself for about six inches into the tree trunk. I could only imagine the havoc the bamboo arrow would do to a human body as it slivered itself apart after it struck. These small fighters would leave a lasting impression upon me and impress me as no other Vietnamese fighters would or could.

McClintock drove the jeep at a breath taking speed on the dirt road that passed through the jungle. The road was filed with potholes from the constant rain and little maintenance. The three miles from the airfield to the village was quite eerie since it was obvious that the Vietcong could set up an ambush at any point to take out travelers. It was for this reason that McClintock drove at this high rate. Although I was to travel this road from the base to the airfield and back at least once or twice a day for six months, I could see little advantage for traveling at a greater than safe speed. Obviously McClintock didn't like to drive down this road. I discovered that the road went through the village of Boa Loc before arriving at the college campus. Since this road was the only way to travel to the airfield, I would have to travel through the village for each flight and consequently, if the VC had observers in the village, they would know when we were flying.

Once we arrived at the village, the streets were filled with people. Small shops dotted the streets mingled with shacks made of every imaginable building material. The streets were all dirt covered. I noticed the inhabitants were all of Vietnamese origin and no Montagnards who obviously did not venture into developed areas to dwell. We drove through the village at a brisk pace with the people moving quickly out of our path. Numerous small children ran behind the jeep yelling requests for money.

On the other side of the village we approached our base. McClintock explained, "The base was built as an Agricultural College by the French during the Indochina War back in the 50's. It hasn't been used as a college for many years. The South Vietnamese gave it to us for our use as a base."

"Where are the Vietnamese troops stationed?"

"They're about two clicks away on the north side of the city," McClintock said with a satirical smile on his face.

I realized that he probably didn't have much of a favorable opinion of our allies. "How many troops do they have?"

"There is a regiment of about 600 men but they never send more than one of their companies into the field at any one time."

"Why," I inquired?

"Obviously they're more concerned with their own safety than they are in going after Charlie. In my opinion they go on patrols only because Captain Moyer forces them to go."

Already knowing the answer I said, "Are the ARVN any good?"

McClintock laughed. "You'll find out soon. Oh, by the way, that's your new home, as he pointed down the road.

It was my first glimpse of my new home. The "base" was really a loose term for four white stucco one-story buildings of about 20 by 60 feet. If these building were really a college campus at one time it must have been extremely small. The area was surrounded by a twelve-foot high chain link fence with two strands of barbed wire on the top. Situated at regular intervals were lamp poles with large lights to obviously illuminate the area near the fence at night. Inside the compound area were a series of trenches and bunkers linking all the buildings. There was an open gate at the compound entrance that had no guard although there was a sand bag bunker. We drove through the gate to the center building. This building served as headquarters, bar, movie house and quarters for the higher-ranking personnel. Major Alex Radford commanded Bao Loc MACV. He was a tall, thin, fifties looking man who had a slight stoop when he stood. His Executive Officer was Major Theodore "Ted" White. A tall, thin black man in his late forties. Radford had the demeanor of a concerned father while White didn't show any emotion.

Radford came out of headquarters as we approached. "Glad to have you here at Bao Loc Lieutenant. My name is Major Radford." He put out his hand, which I immediately shook. "We heard that the Army was assigning some recon planes here but had no idea when you would arrive."

"Thank you, sir."

"Major White will show you were you and your crew chief will be housed although I was under the impression that there would be two crews assigned here?"

"Yes sir, the other crew will be arriving within the next two days. All our planes haven't arrived in country yet."

"Get settled and I shall see talk to you after lunch." He turned back to his office.

White proceeded to show me my quarters that were the last room in the most eastern building in the compound. The room held two bunk beds with two hotboxes for clothing. The floors were covered by a beige colored tile and were quite clean. There were twin doors that opened on to a small three-foot high walled patio that ended within ten feet from the perimeter. Sitting around the outside on the patio were four Montagnard troops lying on the dirt with a small fire where they were boiling rice. The group looked very relaxed and obviously not concerned about any attack by Vietcong guerillas during the daylight hours.

I settled into my quarters selecting the bottom bunk and stowed away my clothing in the hotbox. The other hotbox was empty. I assumed it was meant for Trumball and he would be my roommate. I walked to the center building and entered the main door. This led directly into the bar. It was a very small room of about 10 by 12 feet with a small portable bar and two bar chairs. There were two small tables along the wall with two chairs each. The bar was not lavishly filled with alcohol since I observed only one bottle of Schenley whisky on a shelf. There was a small refrigerator behind the bar that I opened and found to be empty although it was at least cold.

I entered a large room off the bar that was the mess area. I sat down and a Vietnamese waiter approached me. He asked if I was interested in lunch. I said it was the reason for my presence. The waiter then told me that I would be required to pay the unit clerk $.75 for the lunch. I agreed to the charge and was brought a meal made obviously from some type of canned GI meal pack that was terrible. After the meal I sought out Major Radford. We sat in his office and discussed my mission at Bao Loc. It was obvious he had no clue to why I was being stationed at his base.

Major Radford asked, "What did they tell you as to your duties? No one has told me a damn thing about your mission."

"Well Sir, I'm to fly daily missions in this province to detect Vietcong movement and any change in the terrain which might indicate their presence. I intend to fly, weather permitting, a mission in the morning and one in the afternoon."

"Are you assigned to MACV?"

"No Sir, I'm still assigned to the 219th Aviation Company, which is a part of the 52nd Aviation Battalion stationed at Pleiku," I responded.

"Does that mean you are under their command on mine?"

Sensing an opportunity for either greater freedom and lacking any definite instructions involving this matter, I quickly said, "Sir, I am under the direct command of the 219th although I would naturally respect any requests for air support that you would make. Any request to directly support MACV operations in the field will in almost all cases be approved since both missions could be completed at the same time."

This response was not entirely false since Leyda told me that our reconnaissance missions took priority before all other assignments and to not let us be used as taxis by local units.

What was to be his usual indecisive response, Radford stated, "OK, we'll give you as much support as we can although we have limited resources. I'll let you work out the details of your missions with my operation officer, Captain Moyer, but if you need anything don't hesitate to come see me."

I replied, "Thank you sir." I left the office and encountered McClintock.

"Oh, Sergeant McClintock, where can I find Captain Moyer?"

Another strange smile came over his face. "You want Captain Moyer?" Before I could answer, he said, "Follow me."

McClintock showed me to another office where I met Captain Moyer. My heart sank a little as Captain Harold Moyer introduced himself. The only way to describe this unassuming man was that he looked like an accountant. His shoulders were narrow and slightly stooped. At about 35 years old he could also easily pass for a 45 year old. He wore glasses and was definitely not the athletic type. At least he was an infantry officer but I doubted that he would be a very effective combat officer. This conclusion was probably my worst that I would make at Boa Loc.

Moyer reached out his hand, "Call me Harry, everybody that I work with in the field calls me that."

"Vince," I said, as we shock hands.

"Basically it's my job to train the ARVN regiment in the principles of combat. My counterpart is a Major Pham Van Tam who's an OK guy as far as Vietnamese go but is weak in leadership skills. So when we go on a mission I normally tell Major Tam what orders to give."

"How many Americans normally go on these missions."

"Usually I'm the ranking American. Sergeant McClintock is one of the team while Lieutenant Sanford, Spec 4 Joseph, and another non-com, Sergeant Simpson, complete the unit. The ARVN will usually commit a company of their troops or about 100 men," Moyer replied.

"Do Majors Radford and White go on some of the missions?" I asked.

Moyer smiled and replied, "Well" as he hesitated, "they have other duties to do around here."

His response left me a little puzzled and I was not to find out until a month had passed that neither Radford nor White ever left the base. They never drove to the airfield and were reluctant to travel the short distance to the ARVN compound or into the city. It became obvious with time that both men were petrified about leaving the safety of the base and lacked even elementary leadership skills. My disgust for the two senior officers would grow with my stay at the base until I completely ignored them both. I had never met two senior officers who I considered such cowards and to find two at the same location was mind-boggling. I had come to Vietnam with the illusion that most American fighting men were positively motivated and certainly would not exhibit any traits that could be considered cowardice. I didn't have the same expectation with our Vietnamese allies but certainly with American GI's, I did. My training as an officer had instilled in me the belief that a leader must always show his subordinates his willingness to place himself in the same life threatening situations as his men. One didn't have to be a hero or be unafraid but shouldn't show his fear. I chalked Radford and White as officers who did not belong in a combat zone and consequently could be either ignored or whose advice would always be suspect. I quickly learned that Moyer and McClintock ran both combat operations and the base.

Moyer then introduced me to Lieutenant Jason Sanford. He was a West Point graduate and had arrived at Bao Loc from the States two weeks prior to my arrival. He looked to be in excellent shape and after meeting him I knew that he was really quite excited about his job. Sanford was awaiting his first mission with Moyer.

I was also introduced to Specialist 4 Joseph, the unit medical specialist. He was a dependable man who had a very slight frame and had a sad look. I would discover within a short time that he had one weakness. He was addicted to morphine and had literally used all the morphine allocated to the base.

The American commitment to the war effort looked extremely weak and I wondered what the ARVN thought of their counterparts. All the men assigned to Bao Loc, with the exception of the 219th personnel were also assigned an ARVN counterpart. I then met Captain Lamont Terole who was an artillery officer and had an ARVN captain from the local artillery unit as his counterpart. Sergeant McClintock's counterpart was the senior ARVN enlisted man who just like the senior officers of both the ARVN and Bao Loc American commanders also never went on missions into the jungle. The meeting with Captain Terole left me a little confused since I couldn't decide whether he was an asset or another dead weight. My meetings with the base personnel didn't leave me with a good feeling since the only men I had a growing confidence was an overage sergeant, a leader who looked like an accountant, a gung-ho Lieutenant with no experience, and a drug addicted medic. Fortunately, Captain Moyer would eventually make up for the glaring lack of leadership exhibited.

The next morning Moyer drove me to the ARVN command post where I was introduced to the ARVN commander, Colonel Tran Binh Teo. The Colonel was thin, in his late 30's and constantly sweating with shifty eyes. He wore a well-tailored uniform that had obviously been starched and ironed.

"What is your mission Lieutenant?" Asked Colonel Tran who was attempting to impress me with an air of casualness?

"Basically, I'm to fly as often as weather permits in the province looking for the Vietcong and any changes in the landscape indicating their presence. The theory is, I will become so familiar with our area that any change in conditions will be known. "

"Does that mean you are available to support my command?"

I immediately suspected an ulterior motive by Tran and explained, "Naturally Colonel, any operation in the field involving both MACV personnel and your command will be supported by me." I emphasized the "in the field" portion of my response since I was not about to become an air taxi for a Vietnamese colonel.

I could tell by his face that my response was not exactly what he had hoped. He responded, "Do you use an observer when you fly?"

I gave the expected answer. "None has been assigned but an observer would probably help. Two pair of eyes is better than one."

"Well, I shall send one of my junior officers to you as an observer. When do you plan to fly?"

"I'll be at the airfield this afternoon and about 8 am tomorrow morning," I replied.

"My man will be there in the morning," replied Tran as he walked away.

I wasn't overly enthusiastic but I couldn't refuse the offer since I would not normally have an observer assigned to me by either the 219th or the MACV unit.

The ARVN compound was primarily a training base but also served as the South Vietnam's government attempt to control the province and keep it out of the hands of the enemy. It was brimming with soldiers many of whom were just sitting around the base smoking cigarettes. I saw no training taking place although the perimeter fence appeared well guarded especially for day light hours.

Moyer and McClintock did their best to make this group of reluctant soldiers into a fighting unit but it did not seem promising at least from my initial impression. I was reluctant to form a final opinion as to the quality of their fighting ability but was prepared mentally for the worst. When I inquired as to other outposts within the unit's area of responsibility, I was advised that they had no units operating outside their perimeter. They did not organize patrols of any kind unless organized by their American counterparts. Therefore if I observed any movement by military type units outside the immediate vicinity of Bao Loc, I could assume they were Vietcong unless Moyer or McClintock advised otherwise. Although I was a pilot, my basic officer training was as an infantry officer. I knew that the failure to operate outposts and nightly patrols was an indication of this unit's inability or unwillingness to meet the enemy in battle. There was also the possibility that there were no Vietcong units operating in the vicinity although that option was slight.

I flew an orientation flight that afternoon to inspect the landscape. To the south of Boa Loc toward the general direction of Saigon were a series of high peaks that reached up to 9,000 feet. There were a series of paths along the sides of these peaks. The paths always wound past small clearings for crops and usually a small grass and dirt dwelling. In the vicinity of Boa Loc, the terrain was fairly flat but with the exception of an occasional clear area was covered by jungle. It grew heavier as one flew west. There didn't seem to be a great deal of farming in the area and no other villages within ten miles of Boa Loc. The main road that originated in Saigon and traveled through a steep mountain pass skirted around Boa Loc and then continued a winding route to the next large city, Dalat. I knew that none of our pilots were assigned to Dalat and since it was over 60 miles away to the northeast, I didn't fly to it. I intended to basically cover an area up to 30-40 miles in every direction from Bao Loc with the exception of the south. This province extended only 15-20 miles in that direction or about 12 miles on the other side of the mountain chain.

The following morning I borrowed a jeep from the base and my crew chief and I drove alone to the airfield. My plane was still parked at the end of the runway and guarded by the Montagnard squad sitting around the shed. I wondered if they sent patrols at night or just continued to sit around the campfire throughout the night.

I was met at the airfield by 2nd Lieutenant (Tee We) Tru Mat Duong. He was a typical small Vietnamese officer with jet-black hair and a contagious smile. He wore a green khaki uniform and I noticed that he was not armed. This lack of weapons seemed curious at first but the mystery was shortly resolved. At least he knew some English. This ability was probably why he had been chosen for this mission. The flight was intended as another orientation flight to help be adjust to the geography of the area as well as the hope that I would spot the VC. I could tell that Tru was not a seasoned soldier and probably had never been in the air with such a small plane.

As I flew around the province I noticed that there were only three highways in the area, Highway 1 running north to Bao Loc and then northeast toward the city of Dalat, a dirt road heading due north toward Pleiku and a smaller road from Bao Loc heading east to the coast. The road-heading north toward Pleiku was obstructed by numerous trenches cut across the road that made it unusable. The other roads were still intact with limited traffic of a few trucks traveling from the south to Bao Loc. About 30 miles northeast of the town I saw an open field with some type of large structure in the center situated on a small hill. On closer inspection the structure was a concrete and stucco fort with a high wall and a series of small buildings inside. The fort looked like one of the French forts that I have seen many times in movies about the French Foreign Legion in Morocco. Obviously the French had built the fort during the French-Indochina War as an outpost against the Vietminh. It was difficult to comprehend how they could possibly believe the concrete walls would protect them against a 20th Century army with modern artillery and explosives. Perhaps their engineers had only one design for a small base. It could also explain how the French were humiliated in their war against all of Indo-China that included Vietnam, Laos and Cambodia.

There were a couple of small hamlets in the area as well as many isolated huts throughout the region. The area to the northwest of Bao Loc was according to my situation maps a Kill Zone. This area was part of the legendary Ho Chi Minh Trail and I had the military option of attempting to kill anyone found in this area.

During the flight, Lieutenant Tru got airsick and threw up in the rear seat. The smell was overpowering and I opened the windows of the plane to clear my lungs of the stench. When we landed, I ordered Tru to clean his mess before the afternoon flight and I told him meet me back at the field at 1 pm. During the morning flight he had said very little although he spoke broken English. Fortunately, I could understand. I told Tru to bring a weapon with him on the afternoon flight. I was in constant fear during my missions in Vietnam was that I would go down in the countryside alone. If I was to go down, I preferred to have someone with me to watch my backside.

After lunch I returned to the field for my second flight of the day and was met by Tru. Again he was not armed, which again upset me. I could not see what use he would be to me if I were to go down in the jungle. The flight was uneventful although the weather was a little unstable. On this flight I flew in the mountain valleys and experienced what would become a constant problem. When flying low in the valleys, the air turbulence was quite severe. Poor Tru got airsick again. Upon arrival at the airfield I gave Tru some rags and water and told him to clean up his mess. He was hesitant but had little choice since I ordered him to do the job. After the cleanup, I noticed that Tru was wearing the traditional Vietnamese style civilian clothing under his uniform. He was wearing black silk pajama clothing. Almost all men wear the black clothing in the countryside and most Vietcong also wear it. I realized that Tru was wearing the civilian clothing for much the same reason I was armed to the teeth – survival. In the event the plane went down, he could easily shed his uniform and slip into the countryside and mingle with the other natives without drawing much attention to himself. A weapon would only hinder his attempt to pretend to be a local villager with no connection to the ARVN. Obviously it was his intent to leave me alone in this situation.

In anger I told Tru, "Tee We, when you come back here in the morning, you will bring a weapon and you will not wear this clothing under your uniform," as I grabbed his pajama top under his shirt.

"But Lieutenant it is nothing and I was told I shouldn't bring a weapon with me," he wined.

"Who the hell told you not to bring a weapon?"

"I'm not sure which of my superiors."

"Now, I'm ordering you to come with a weapon and to wear only your uniform, got it? If I see you without a weapon and with your black clothes under your military uniform, I will report you to Colonel Teo."

This encounter was to be my last sight of Lieutenant Tru and the ARVN never offered to provide an observer to me again. Later that night at the base I told everyone while sitting around at the bar of my dealings with Tru. Major Radford then offered to provide an observer from his own staff. He offered Captain Terole.

Captain Terole was the one man at the base for whom the word worthless would be the primary adjective when describing his character and value. Moyer had advised me that Terole was so bad as an officer that even the ARVN, who were almost all of poor quality, considered him worthless. They had refused to allow Terole to come to their base to instruct and advise his artillery counterpart. This rejection meant that he had no mission in Vietnam and he was so bad that Moyer refused to allow him to participate in missions outside the base for fear that he would jeopardize the lives of those around him. It is doubtful whether he would have consented to participate in one of Moyer's operations anyway. Even his appearance was sickening. He was obviously out of shape, a plump face under a mop of blond hair with a high, squeaky voice. I had noticed him during my first two days at Bao Loc painting the outsides of the four buildings with a whitewash. He was painting the buildings alone without the aid of other Americans or Vietnamese. Major Radford usually gave him menial labor to keep him busy. When Radford made the offer, he was obviously thinking that he could shuffle Terole off on a mission in which he would have no responsibility and needed only to keep his eyes open. Even in this limited responsibility Terole would fail.

That night, Trumball arrived with his crew chief, Spec 4 Wheeler. He quickly settled into the routine at the base. I really had no knowledge of Trumball's flying ability or his personality. At both Fort Hood and Pleiku he was a loner who didn't seem to have any close friends. While we were both stationed at Bao Loc, we would be forced to become a team since our lives would depend upon mutual support. My first inkling of his instability came on the first night. When I returned from my usual stop at the bar for a few hours with Moyer and McClintock, Trumball was laying in his top bunk reading a book. He was reading a book aloud which I could clearly hear.

*"Awake! For Morning in the Bowl of Night
Has fleeing the Stone that puts the Stars to Flight:
And Lo! "The Hunter of the East has caught
The Sultan's Turret in a Noose of Light."*

It sounded like nonsense so I asked, "What's that you're reading?"
"Omar Khayyam's Rubaiyat," he replied.
"Seems like some heavy duty stuff. I've heard of the author and the book but have never read it. Is it good?"
"It relaxes me."
"If it is all like what you were reading, it would put me to sleep in about fifteen minutes. By the way, I don't want to hurt your feelings but could you read it quietly to yourself?" I asked. My request was ignored although he did lower the volume of his reading.

Trumball was already starting to worry me but I would give him the benefit of the doubt as to his flying ability. I already had a couple of good drinking partners at the base so didn't have to concern myself with him. He claimed that he didn't drink alcoholic beverages. It corrupted a person's body and mind. I never saw him take a drink during our time together.

The following morning I went to the field with Trumball, Terole and the two crew chiefs. Terole climbed into the back seat of my plane and I noticed that, at least, he was armed with a pistol. I already had a mild dislike for him since I considered him totally worthless. After about an hour of flying about the countryside, I noticed that Terole had fallen asleep in the back seat. I flew a couple of steep 60-degree turns and he woke up but within minutes was back asleep. The mission was uneventful. In the afternoon I again took Terole as my observer and again he fell asleep within 30 minutes of the start and all my attempts to bring him to consciousness failed. Trumball flew only the morning mission and stayed in our hooch reading his book during the afternoon.

The next morning the five of us again drove to the airfield and again I took Terole along as an observer. This time he was asleep within fifteen minutes of getting airborne. When we returned to the base, I went to see Radford and advised him that I would no longer take Terole with me as an observer. He pleaded with me to give him another chance but I refused to budge on my decision. I was afraid that I would by some unfortunate event have to ditch my plane in the jungle and be stuck with Terole. I still harbored thoughts that I had a responsibility to assist and protect fellow Americans regardless of their value to the war effort.

I returned to the field for the afternoon flight with Trumball and at least got some activity. About 40 miles north of Bao Loc I observed 25 to 30 personnel wearing the standard black pajamas walking across a field in the "kill zone." When they saw or heard my plane, they immediately laid down in the field. However their black clothing and depression of the tall grass in the field was a dead give away as to their location. I wondered why that didn't just attempt to shoot me down and run for the cover of the jungle that was within 100 yards. I recalled a conversation with a Birddog pilot who was stationed with the 52nd before our arrival. He mentioned hearing that the Vietcong were ordered to not fire on our observation aircraft and give away their position unless it was obvious they had been spotted. Fortunately for me these were guerrillas who obviously were obeying orders.

For the first time in Vietnam, I contacted Air Force Control operating out of Saigon on their frequency. I asked for an air strike that they seemed eager to comply. Meanwhile I continued to fly within the area always within sight of the Vietcong in the hope they would have the stupid discipline to remain at their location. A flight of three F-105's arrived and I marked the target with one of my smoke rockets. When I marked the target with my smoke rocket, it was obvious to even the Vietcong that they had been spotted and they began a run to the cover of the jungle. Most of them made it before the jets started their attack.

The jets dropped both high explosive bombs and something that I had never seen before. This new weapon was called a cluster bomb. When the bomb hits the ground, it releases a large number of smaller bombs much like hand grenades that then detonate in a cluster of about 20 by 50 yards. I could see the small explosions impacting the jungle and felt a small degree of pity for the men on the ground. The F-105's did their job and I doubted if any of the enemy could have survived the onslaught of high explosive and cluster bombs.

The lead pilot of the sortie then radioed, "Headhunter One One, what is the body count?"

This was my first exposure to body counts. I responded, "Flight 452 wait one while I take a look." I then flew down to the attack area and attempted to see if I could really see any bodies. I could see five bodies outside the jungle but could not see the casualties which I knew existed within the jungle.

"Flight 452, body count is about 25."

"Headhunter One One this is Flight 452, is this an actual count or a guess?"

I was stung by the tone of the voice and felt as though I had not done my job as it was expected. I replied, "Flight 452, wait while I take another look."

Again I flew down to the area and hoped that none of the Vietcong were in a position or disposition to fire upon my plane which was definitely exposed at this altitude. Again I could only see the five bodies in the open.

"Flight 452, this is Headhunter One One, I have 27 definite casualties, I say again I have a count of 27."

"Well done Headhunter One One. Have a good one." The jets were already streaking south toward Saigon.

I started my return to base feeling quite good about myself. I had learned a number of important lessons today. The first thing was the Vietcong's reaction when an observation plane flies within their vicinity. That was very good news and I would always take care to not give away that they had been observed while I awaited a flight of attack planes. The second was the issue of body count. From the moment I gave Flight 452 a count of 27, I never again gave a round number for kills such as 25, 30, 50, or 75. The numbers would be 23, 31, 54, or 73. Odd numbers implied that I had actually counted the bodies. I could only wonder what the idiots at headquarters must be thinking when they insisted on actual body count numbers. They had obviously never been up in a plane such as mine and looked down into the jungle or fly into a combat area with the enemy shooting at a plane that can only fly at 100 to 110 mph. At least I was a quick learner.

Chapter 10 – A Tiger Hunt

Upon my return I noticed my engine was running rough and we discovered a bad spark plug. Now the replacement of a spark pug is quite elementary which even I could handle. However, we had not been issued any extra spark plugs and it was common knowledge that the unit was short of plugs even in Pleiku.

I approached Trumball, "We need a spark plug if I am to fly tomorrow."

"I don't think we have any plugs here."

"I know that," I said in an agitated voice. "I just wanted to know what you want to do about it?"

"I don't know, what do you think?"

"Well there's no sense in going to Pleiku since they're also short. I think it would make more sense to fly to Saigon and pick up some supplies from the Air Force. It's closer to there than Pleiku anyway." I offered.

"OK, in the morning you go to Saigon and see if you can get some."

"I'm not going to Saigon in my plane if the engine is running rough because of a bad firing cylinder."

"Go ahead and take one of my plugs and I'll wait for your return."

I was not totally upset by Trumball's assignment since I actually had another motive to go to Saigon. It seems that our bar in Bao Loc was out of both beer and whisky with little hope of being resupplied in quite awhile. This flight would give me the opportunity to kill two birds with one stone. Since Trumball didn't drink and actually looked at drinking as a disease, it was unlikely that he would ever transport alcohol or beer to the compound.

In the morning I went to the airfield with Moore and we exchanged the bad plug from my plane to Trumball's plane. He would not be flying today while I went to Saigon. The flight to Tan Sa Nhut airport went without a hitch and I was cleared to land on one of the smaller strips at the airport. I parked my plane near an Air Force unit where some Birddogs were also parked. I entered the nearby Quonset hut and was greeted by an Air Force staff sergeant. I explained my problem and he laughingly gave me a box of twelve spark plugs for our engines and I gave him a Montagnard crossbow. He seemed overjoyed and told me to come back if I needed more parts for the plane.

Next, I located the building that sold beer and whisky. I purchased six cases of beer and four bottles of whisky. The purchases were about all I could carry on two trips to the plane with my booty. I hurried back to my plane and started the engine. I was a little worried that someone would notice me carrying the alcohol and question what I was doing. Carrying alcohol in my plane might be prohibited although I was never advised it was not allowed. I wasn't going to give someone the opportunity to stop me, if possible.

I had not thought about my takeoff from Tan Son Nhut Airport and basically got in line behind all the other aircraft awaiting takeoff. This airport was the busiest in the world during the Vietnam War and here I was in this extremely small airplane standing in line behind ten huge commercial jets. I had gotten into the wrong line and now was committed to taking off down the main runway. The tower control was sympathetic and told me to be patient. Unfortunately it was all I could do to keep the plane from being blown over by the exhaust from the four jet engines directly in front of me. Eventually it was my turn to take off and again I faced difficulty since the preceding jet caused extreme turbulence and I was barely able to keep the plane under control. After getting airborne I returned to Bao Loc with my prize possessions of spark plugs and beer. The bar was lively that evenings as McClintock and I played cribbage and the rest were able to have their first cold beer in over a month. I could tell that the Bao Loc personnel were already beginning to appreciate my presence and they considered my supply efforts to be critical to the base.

The following morning I took care of some unfinished business concerning the fake Bao Loc airfield. I couldn't just call in an air strike on the field since there was no evidence of enemy activity and it was outside the kill zone. Instead I hit the runway with my HE rockets and cratered it sufficiency to discourage anyone from landing on the runway. I never had the opportunity to go to this field on the ground and will always wonder if there was a sinister welcome for me if I had landed there.

As I became more comfortable with my flying situation I began to do more experimentation with my search for the elusive Vietcong. I would climb to about 5-6,000 feet above the terrain and turn off the engine and glide as quiet as possible for miles. The enemy still could see me but at least they wouldn't hear my approach. At first I would restart the engine at 1500 feet but by the time my tour was completed would hold off the restart until about 500 feet above the terrain. My faith in the engine, if properly maintained, was quite high and it never failed to start. I was able to sneak up on three groups of the enemy during my tour and believed the risk was justified. Naturally youth believes it is immortal.

My plane was equipped with a survival pack that was situated under the rear seat. It was bulky, hard to quickly extract from under the seat, weighed at least 90 ponds, and contained items that were totally useless and unnecessary for combat flying. Of the 6 containers of water, I kept three. The food and the fishing gear were discarded. I knew that setting up a survival camp was not an option and didn't believe food was an issue. A water repellent suit was discarded although I kept a small mosquito net that fit over the issue floppy cap. The medical kit was needed as well as the water purification tablets. The final items were a large machete knife and a compass. I then placed the items in a standard military knapsack. It was my belief that survival in the jungle would be determined within the first 48 hours. I had no intention of remaining with my plane in a crash unless there were helicopters in the area and no close enemy units. If I believed I was on my own, I would take only my emergency radio that was always situated in the pocket of my flak vest, the knapsack, my handgun and the M-16. It was my intention to put as much distance between the plane and myself and then begin the task of getting a helicopter rescue.

All the pilots were issued a white colored silk cloth of approximately 12X15 inches. It was stamped with a serial number assigned to a pilot. Printed in the cloth in at least a dozen languages was the following message:

I am an American Soldier. If you assist me in returning to an American base, you will be paid a great deal of money. Thank you for your help.

I never heard of a Vietnamese native assisting a pilot in returning to the safety of an American Base and wondered how much cash they would be paid. I assumed it would be at least $10,000 but then again I may have placed too high a value on our lives.

During Trumball's first week at Bao Loc, I got my first true glimpse of his personality and problems. After dusk Major Radford received a call from the ARVN base. He came into the bar and announced, "I just received a warning from Colonel Teo that a sizeable force of Vietcong have been seen in the area and they are expected to hit either the ARVN base or our own. I want all personnel to go to their assigned defensive position."

Trumball, the two crew chiefs and myself went to our building. Four other personnel also slept there but they were assigned to a defensive position in one of the many slit trenches. The two crew chiefs were assigned to side windows while Trumball and I were to take positions on the patio outside our bedroom. The patio had a small three-foot high block wall that we laid behind for cover. Unfortunately the patio was only ten to twelve feet from the perimeter fence. The light were shining inside the perimeter thereby giving us vision inside the compound while we walked but was poorly designed to give us visibility outside the compound in case of attack. As I peered at the fence and beyond, I realized that the VC could literally walk up to the fence in the night undetected and easily throw a grenade onto the patio. I had expected to see our Montagnard guards near the patio. It is where they normally camped during the night, but they were nowhere to be seen. If things weren't bad enough, there was a lit patio light shining down on us thereby making it easier for the enemy. I jumped up and as quickly as possible unscrewed the light bulb.

As I took cover behind the wall, Trumball said, "God, I hope they come tonight."

"Jason, if the VC hit us tonight, we will probably be killed." This place is defenseless and we're at the far end of the defense," I said.

"I don't care. Let them come. This could be more fun than just flying."

"Are you serious?" I asked.

"Listen, this is the chance I need to prove myself. I hope they come tonight and I'll show all those people back home what I can do."

I looked at Trumball and got very scared. Here I was sitting in an exposed defensive position, waiting for the enemy to attack and I was relying on a complete idiot to assist me. I told Trumball that I thought a nearby trench was a better defensive position and left him mumbling to himself. The VC didn't attack that night. It was a good thing for the base since I'm sure we would have been overrun.

Life at Bao Loc was quite pleasant and often seemed as if the war was far away. The closest city was Dalat and had over 20,000 inhabitants. It was located about 50 miles to the east of Bao Loc. The informal gossip about Dalat was that the Vietcong and ARVN had an informal agreement that neither side would fight for control of the city or in the vicinity. This informal agreement would last with the exception of one minor incident until the Tet offensive in 1968. The city was the most beautiful in South Vietnam and quite different from the other cities in terms of construction. It was situated on a large mountain that looked like an old volcano with its top chopped off. The architecture was very similar to a European city and quite different from all the other Vietnamese cities I saw. The buildings were almost all one or two story stone or stucco buildings. It was said that the French built Dalat and then forbade any Vietnamese from living there unless they were employed in a French household as servants.

About every third or fourth weekend I flew to Dalat and partied with the other pilots that also flew to the airfield. Although Dalat didn't have an American military unit assigned to the city, there were always five to ten Hueys and one or two Birddogs parked on the runway.

I tried to fly, weather permitting, twice a day from Monday to Friday and usually did not fly but once on a weekend if I remained at Bao Loc. Neither the ARVN nor the Bao Loc MACV unit did any combat activity on the weekends and apparently the Vietcong also obliged. The 219th had advised our pilots that they could only fly 60 hours in any one-month period. This restriction was mathematically equivalent to only two hours per day. I thought this quota was ridiculous but I had no choice but to accept the limitation. Consequently I generally flew an average of three hours a day from Monday to Friday and if I was unable to fly due to inclement weather, I would use that time for a weekend flight.

On one Saturday I accompanied Moyer and McClintock on a tiger hunt since this part of Vietnam did have a large supply of the cats. I was invited to join the hunt during one of our weekday binges at the bar.

I did ask Moyer, "What about the VC?"

"I know an area about two or three miles outside of the town to the north that should be relatively safe," he replied. "We'll leave by jeep about 0900 hours and should be finished by noon."

The alcohol I was drinking gave me some false courage and I was too embarrassed to admit my fear to the two men I respected most at Bao Loc and agreed to join the hunt. We were accompanied by five ARVN troops who were hired to act as noisemakers to scare any tigers to our location. The thought entered my mind that the noise would also indicate our location to any Vietcong who were not supposed to be around the area.

Our efforts did lead to a successful hunt when the ARVN supporters alerted the three of us to a tiger heading our way. McClintock was the first to see the tiger and fired three rounds from his M-16 at the tiger. It went down fairly quickly and upon inspection we were all surprised to see that the tiger had only three legs. One of its legs had been either shot off or the beast had lost it during a fight with another predator. McClintock took the tiger back to the compound where he arranged to have it cured and probably shipped back to the states. I imagined McClintock attending a social function and being asked about his activities in this war and telling people about his tiger hunts.

I was able to get a good view of the jungle. It was quite beautiful and I was surprised by the lack of ground vegetation. Apparently the lack of the sun's penetration kept the growth to a minimum. The scene was not what I expected. The only thing that really disturbed me about the jungle was the leaches that inevitably were able to penetrate the clothing and sink into the skin for blood. The leaches usually crawled or dropped onto the clothing through the top of the shirt or where the pants are bloused into the combat boots. I always was able to pick up at least one leech when I would enter the jungle.

It was somewhat funny that my command had absolutely no idea what we were doing in these isolated locations. I certainly didn't inform them about the tiger hunt although they probably wouldn't have cared. Never did I have an officer from the 219th or 52nd fly into Bao Loc and check on our condition or needs with the exception of Leyda on one occasion. Each month either the commanding officer or executive officer would fly to Bao Loc to deliver our pay. Major Lust would land at the Bao Loc field and with the engine still running he would hand us our pay through the open cockpit window and then immediately takeoff for his next site. I always thought they were too nervous about our airfield being situated so close to the jungle for them to drop in on an extended visit. Although there were disadvantages with that situation there was the immeasurable advantage of being allowed to do whatever we felt like.

After three or four days of really poor food at the Bao Loc mess I began to eat my lunch and dinner at a restaurant located in the heart of Bao Loc. As an officer, I was required to pay for each and every meal eaten at a military establishment. At least officers were given a subsistence allowance for our meals. However, this allowance also implied that I had the option of eating wherever I wished and I certainly did not relish paying for food at the Bao Loc compound. The base served only heated C-rations. Major Radford was a little upset when I stopped eating in the compound but there was little he could do to make me change my position. He felt, that the more people that ate at the base, it would increase the purchasing power of the cook and therefore improve the quality of the food. I was more interested in getting a decent meal that had some taste. Trumball ate at the compound. This decision was acceptable to me since I spent as little of my time with him as possible.

There was really only one decent restaurant in Bao Loc. The owner of the restaurant was a small Vietnamese named Tru Mat Kim who spoke very good English. Although I was never particularly fond of oriental food prior to my arrival in Vietnam, I quickly learned to enjoy their style of cooking. Kim would suggest and prepare different dishes and the cost was below what I would have paid at the base. The meat was always a mystery and I assume I ate more than one dog. The Vietnamese have a shortage of beef cattle and had a liking for dog and therefore included this meat in their diets. Obviously they were aware of American dislike of eating dog so they omitted the origin of their meat. Almost all steaks were called "Chateaubriand". This designation implied that it was a quality steak from a steer or cow. When I arrived in Vietnam I weighed about 145 pounds and by the time I returned to the States, I weighed only 123 pounds. The food, the job and the heat were all responsible for this weight loss.

The only two things that I really disliked about Vietnamese cuisine was the milk they put in their coffee and a fish sauce they added over most meals. The milk was more like a thick condensed milk. When poured into the clear glass coffee mug, it would settle to the bottom of the glass in a distinct layer. The fish sauce was called "Nuk Bam" and was made from rotting fish. Once when I was visiting in Quin Nhon, I observed the process of making this nuk bam. Fish are placed in a wood barrel directly in the sunlight along the fish docks. The fish begin to rot and to ferment. After a sufficient period of time the fish are compressed and the juice is bottled. The sauce has three separate labels based on the quality. The first liquid that is pressed from the barrel is a generally a clear fluid and is the cheapest of the three qualities. The second set of liquid is much thicker than the first and more potent in both smell and taste. The final liquid is thick with small chunks of the rotted fish with a very robust smell and taste. The price of these liquids increases with the thickness. I could use the first quality of nuk bam on some dishes but could never get past the smell to use the final two types. However, since the Vietcong usually restricted travel inland, the interior of the country usually had difficulty in getting any of this liquid. If so inclined, nuk bam would have been a great trading vehicle for favors and the procurement of females much like nylons were used during World War II.

Whenever I went to the coast I attempted to secure a couple bottles of nuk bam for Tru. He was quite grateful and would go out of his way to prepare a Vietnamese dish that I had not tried previously. Many of the dishes were made of some type of meat and vegetables rolled into a delicate rice paper which was deep-fried.

The nightlife at Bao Loc was naturally not very interesting. Moyer, McClintock and I often visited the one decent bar in the village. The French built the building housing the bar in the 1930's. It was a three-story building built in a square configuration with a large center court open to the environment. The bar was situated in this large open area with continuous balconies around the two upper floors with single rooms opening onto the balconies. The interesting aspect about this bar was that it also was the main brothel in the village. Frankly I was so scared to death about venereal disease that I never considered hiring a prostitute although the price certainly was cheap. Americans were charged 50 piastas for an hour with a prostitute which was the equivalent of 48 to 49 cents. I often argued with the owner of the establishment, just for the fun of argument, that it was not right that

Vietnamese men were only charged 25 piastas. The prostitutes were pleasant enough to look at but the rooms were terribly dirty. The sheets on the beds were literally black with dirt and discharges from previous clients. The high price for prostitutes did not extend to this remote village and since there were few Americans at the base, the price was low. Only after the huge American buildup later in the year would the price for prostitutes primarily in the large cities skyrocket. The young GI's were literally willing to pay any price for pleasure and a case of venereal disease.

When a new recruit would be assigned to the base, McClintock and I would take him to the bar and I would pay the price for a prostitute. Naturally, at first, I didn't tell them the price and they would be extremely grateful. We also had a running gag that every new man at the base had to attempt to beat the quickest time on record to ejaculate with the prostitute. One young private actually was able to establish a new record in thirty seconds from the time we yelled, "go" through the door of his room. The restaurant usually kept three or four prostitutes busy since they also serviced the ARVN at their nearby base. The bar was usually limited to the Americans stationed at our base or from the Green Berets. It was at this location that we were able to indulge in the Vietnamese beer supply.

The beer produced in Vietnam was not very good but if nothing else was available, it would make do. The price was right at about thirty-five piastas. We had a choice of Bon Ney Bom or Biere LaRue. Both had a bitter taste and about every fifth bottle of Biere LaRue were cloudy with some sediment. I assumed that the alcohol content killed the bacteria in the liquid. At least I never got the "runs" from drinking it.

McClintock introduced me to cribbage. Since I was naturally quite good at cards I learned the game in short time and almost every evening I would play two or three games with him for a beer. No matter how hard I tried or how hard I concentrated, McClintock usually beat me two out of every three games. He was just better than I was and I gained even more respect for him as an intelligent person besides being a courageous fighter.

Chapter 11 – Goodbye Lieutenant Trumball

By late July 1965, things began to heat up throughout the Central Highlands. I was notified by Captain Moyer that he would be leading a company of about 100 ARVN on a sweep of the area to the east of Bao Loc. He asked, "Would you be willing to provide air cover for the operation?"

"Definitely", I responded and added, "I'll let Trumball know what I'm doing."

When I spoke to Trumball, he has some doubts as to both the task and whether he has the authority to assist in this type of mission.

I told Moyer of Trumball's comments and said, "Shit. I don't need his permission to help. When do you push off?"

"Assuming the ARVN and Major Tam are ready, we'll leave at 0600. There isn't any sense in you starting that early since it will take us a good hour to get past the airfield and I don't expect any trouble until we're at least a couple of mile past the field."

I responded, "That will be fine with me. What Americans will be involved?"

"McClintock, Sanford, Joseph, Simpson and myself."

"Just remember that my ability to see 'Charlie' is limited and I could miss him if he is careful."

"Hey, anything you can provide will be a plus from what we are use to."

"Great," I responded. "I'm your man but you'll owe me a couple of beers."

Moyer laughed. "You've got yourself a deal and if you see anything I'll provide the drinks all night."

He then outlined his route of advance. Moyer intended to follow the dirt road past the airfield for an additional twenty miles in vehicles and then on foot to strike due north into the jungle for about ten miles and then to circle back to Bao Loc. The mission would take two days of movement. I agreed to be in the air by 0700. At this time it would place him just past the airfield when I got airborne.

At 0700 I was in the air. The ARVN were late getting organized and the company was just arriving at the airfield when I began to give them cover. The dirt road wound its way through very dense jungle that extended between 50 and 100 feet above the ground. It was impossible for me to see the ground and I could not determine if there were enemy units laying in ambush along the road.

I notified Moyer of my problem. "Roundtree, this is Headhunter One One. It is impossible for me to see the ground near the road. Be advised that I cannot vouch for your security."

"Headhunter One One, read you and will proceed."

"Roundtree, I'll try something a little different." \

I then flew down to within ten feet off the road. The plane was below the top canopy of the jungle. It was like flying in a tunnel although the tunnel roof was open to the sky. There was adequate room between the edges of the jungle that permitted me to fly that close to the road in a jungle area. I still could not see whether any Vietcong were laying in wait but hoped to spook them into firing at the plane if they were setting an ambush. For over 30 minutes I flew back and forth over the column of trucks flying about a mile to their front before turning back for the column.

Finally, Moyer radioed. "Headhunter, you're receiving fire!"

I had nor heard or observed any weapons being fired at me and was seized for a moment with sheer panic as I pushed the throttle to maximum RPM and banked sharply off the road over the jungle. I knew Moyer wouldn't joke about such a serious situation. I reasoned that if I stayed low over the jungle they wouldn't be able to see me and continue the shooting. It worked, as I saw no evidence of rounds being fired and began to climb to a safer altitude.

Just then Moyer advised, "We're receiving fire to our front. Leaving the vehicles and establishing a defensive perimeter to the north."

"Roundtree, I'll be over your position in a minute."

By the time I returned to the vehicles, at least one was burning and a few soldiers were running away from the vehicles to the north where the jungle opened considerably. I could see a few soldiers laying down and firing their weapons at an enemy that I still could not see. What was terribly clear was the fact that the ARVN were fleeing as fast as they could run back toward Bao Loc. The entire company had thrown their weapons to the ground and running to the rear leaving the five American advisors to hold their ground against the ambushers. Finally I could see the Vietcong moving forward in what appeared as a skirmish line. There were about 30 to 40 of them. The five advisors were spread out over about 200 feet and were situated behind the available cover of large standing trees. My heart leaped with excitement. This was my first case of true combat. I could feel the surge of adrenalin and for the moment I ignored the fear of the enemy shooting at my plane. In the excitement I didn't bother to call for Air Force support. They wouldn't have been able to get to our location for at least fifteen minutes. I put the nose of the plane directly at the enemy troops and when within about 1000 feet let go with four HE rockets. The rockets hit near "Charlie." I climbed back to about 1500 feet above the targets and again dove on them and fired my remaining four WP rounds. It was beautiful. The white phosphorous created four large clouds of dense white smoke.

"Son of a bitch, Headhunter," McClintock yelled over the radio, "the bastards are running."

"Is it over?" I asked.

This time Mover's voice came over the radio. "There is still some firing but I can't see them. If you've got any more rounds drop them into that tree line about 200 yards to the east."

"Sorry boss, that's it for me. I'm out of rockets but I can call the big boys. They can be here in about 15 to 30."

"Forget it, Charlie will be far gone by then."

Within a few minutes after the firing stopped and the ambushers had melted back into the jungle some of the ARVN returned to the scene of their flight and picked up their weapons. An hour later most of them had returned and boarded the vehicles and proceeded back to Bao Loc. The ARVN had lost three men with an additional five wounded while the American advisors reported the death of Lieutenant Sanford who fell after the initial retreat of the ARVN.

It was this first engagement that my respect for the ability of Captain Moyer was to flourish. I knew from my relationship with McClintock that he was entirely dependable but I had not warmed to Moyer's ability because of his accountant type look. During this engagement, Moyer was as the leader, cool as a cucumber and solid as a rock against an enemy considerably stronger than the five American contingents. My disgust of the ARVN became quite strong and I wondered how our advisors could accompany them on missions with the knowledge they would probably flee at the first sign of trouble and abandon their advisors. Not even the ARVN officers stood with the Americans.

With the operation halted I gave them cover on the way back but now realized that, at best, I was only providing the ground troops a morale boast and could not provide warning as to an ambush in this environment. Back at the American compound the body of Lieutenant Sanford was laid in an empty room off the bar and MACV headquarters was contacted to pick up the body and to send a replacement. On the next day an Army Huey helicopter arrived and picked up the body. I wondered whether Sanford's wife and parents were told that he had died because of the cowardness of over 100 Vietnamese soldiers.

I returned to my room to ponder the needless death of Sandford. I thought he was a little stiff but I liked him. As I walked into the room Trumball was laying on his bunk with a book. He was reading aloud:

One Moment in Annihilation's Waste,
One Moment, of the Will of Life to taste –
The Stars are setting and the Caravan
Starts for the Dawn of Nothing – Oh,
  Make Haste!

I told Trumball about Sanford's death and he merely replied with a grunt and returned to reading Omar Khayyam. It didn't seem possible that someone could continue to read this poetry week after week without some other relaxation. I suspected that he was close to breaking or insane.

Sanford's replacement arrived within a week and was another 2nd Lieutenant fresh from the States without any combat experience. Lt. Mark Jessman was a graduate from an ROTC program at UCLA. He had graduated in May 1965 and now three months later was assigned to MACV Bao Loc in the middle of the central highlands of Vietnam. He was quite nervous about the assignment and I hoped he would have better luck than his predecessor.

He also had a wife who he had married within a week of his graduation from college. He was a tall lanky Californian and was a little awed by Moyer and McClintock but was more than willing to jump into his duties.

However, my biggest concern was with my flying partner. Trumball was certainly a little eccentric but I was having even greater doubts about him. Two days after the ambush my doubts about Trumball's sanity grew. We were both flying in different areas of the providence when Trumball radioed.

"Vince, I see a large number of VC."

I replied, "Headhunter Two Three, have you called for a strike?"

I knew that no strike had been called and wondered why he would call me rather than the Air Force. Perhaps he wanted me to do the call, as he had never called them before. I also was disturbed that he would use my name over the air as it was common knowledge that the Vietcong monitored our frequencies.

"Vince, I'm receiving fire," he shouted over the air.

"What's your altitude?"

"I'm at 300 feet."

Now that was, as I knew from experience a very poor altitude and responded, "Climb to 1500 feet. Where is your location?"

"I'm thirty miles east of the field."

"I'll be there in about 15 minutes."

Suddenly Trumball yelled, "I'm hit! I'm hit!"

"How bad is it?" I replied.

There was no response. I said, "Headhunter Two Three, how bad are you hit and what is your altitude?" Again there was only silence and I was struck with real fear as I pushed the throttles of my plane to the firewall.

I said, "Headhunter Two Three did you read? I'll be at your location in about ten minutes."

There was no answer. I continued to call Trumball as I flew to a location about 30 miles east of the field. There was no response from Trumball and I began to debate whether to call a higher command to let them now he had been shot down. Something inside my mind hesitated and I wanted to confirm that he was really down and not experiencing radio trouble or some other malfunction. In either case my radio would not have been able to notify anyone unless I climbed to about 8,000 feet since I was in a valley surrounded by mountains. My radios operated by line of sight and I was not high enough to have line of sight with anyone other than the Bao Loc base. I didn't want to climb to 8,000 feet. That height would have been too high to see either a downed plane or the Vietcong unit that was observed by Trumball in the area. I began a frantic search for either the plane or the Vietcong. I could locate neither target and after a 15-minute search decided to return to the airfield to refuel and to notify someone of the situation. I also wanted to confirm in my mind that Trumball had not returned to the field because of a malfunctioning radio.

As I approached the field I could see Trumball's plane sitting in the parking area. I landed and found only my crew chief and a jeep. An inspection of Trumball's plane did not show any evidence of enemy fire or damage.

I asked Moore, "When did Lt. Trumball return?"

"About 30 minutes ago, Sir."

"Did he say anything about seeing any targets?"

"No, Sir," replied Moore with a puzzled look.

I returned to the MACV compound and went directly to my room. Trumball was lying in his bunk reading aloud:

> *They say the Lion and the Lizard keep*
> *The Courts where Jamshyd gloried and*
>   *Drank deep;*
> *An Bahram, that great Hunter – the*
>   *Wild Ass*
> *Stamp o'er his Head, but cannot break his Sleep.*

The blood rushed to my head. "God dam it Jason, what the hell happened?"

In a calm voice he replied, "What do you mean?"

"All the bull shit about the Vietcong and being hit," I yelled.

"I don't know what you're talking about." He then turned to the wall and closed his eyes. I left the room and knew that Trumball was about ready to break but didn't know what to do about it. I wrote a note to Leyda asking him to come to Bao Loc to meet with Trumball. I placed the message on the following supply plane that was heading to Pleiku. My note arrived on the day prior to Trumball's final breakdown.

Trumball was flying a reconnaissance mission and was returning to the field. I had already landed and I was checking my engine as he approached for a landing. Although I was never impressed with his flying ability, his approach for this landing looked terrible. He came in much to fast and with a steep bank. I immediately knew Trumball was in trouble. He hit the ground hard and bounced on the Birddog's spring designed landing gear that could absorb most minor misuse. When the plane stopped bouncing, he applied full breaks and ground looped the plane causing the right wing to hit the ground and then collapse on its side. Wheeler and I ran to the plane. Trumball emerged from the cockpit without a word.

"Jason are you OK?"

Trumball had a strange look on his face and his eyes looked straight through me. Again I asked, "Are you OK?"

He walked past us without any response and got into the jeep parked on the side of the field and drove away. He had not spoken one word. Trumball gunned the accelerator on the jeep and it leaped forward at a high rate of speed. It didn't travel but a few hundred yards before he struck a tree on the side of the road destroying the front of the vehicle. During the vehicular accident, Trumball struck his head on the steering wheel causing blood to flow down his face. He was badly shaken and still didn't seem to know where he was or what he was doing. Wheeler and I drove him back to the base and called the medic, Specialist 4 Joseph to look at him. Meanwhile I radioed Pleiku with the bad news. I only gave them the news about the two accidents and hinted that Trumball was injured with minor injuries that did not require hospitalization. I suggested Captain Leyda might want to talk with him.

Apparently this communication along with my previous note was enough to warrant an inquiry by Leyda. The following day he arrived in his Birddog. We talked about the situation and I explained the sequence of events to him. Leyda was obviously concerned about Trumball's sanity and became convinced that Trumball was off the deep end. Leyda went to the compound and talked with Trumball for about an hour.

Leyda came out of our hooch and walked up to me. "Vince, I'm taking Trumball back to Pleiku with me. He's in bad shape."

I laughed. "You don't have to tell me."

"I'll send someone from Pleiku down here to take his place. You know Lieutenant Burrows?" He asked.

My mind brought up a picture of Burrows as I responded, "He's a good man. I could do far worst."

"OK, then it's settled. You keep everything here under control and I'll send Burrows down in a couple of days."

"You've got it."

"By the way," Leyda said as he walked away. "Let's keep Trumball's condition between us."

"You mean the guys here or the 219th?" I inquired.

"I mean the Bao Loc personnel. There's no reason to have them aware that we have a problem. Right?"

"Right!"

My final sight of Trumball was as he boarded Leyda's plane with his copy of Omar Khayyam's poetry in his hand. I never saw him again. I heard that he was transferred back to the States and probably given a medical discharge. Leyda never discussed him even when I made inquiries.

Chapter 12 – Promotion and The Ace of Spades

Trumball's replacement was 1st Lieutenant Robert Burrows. Burrows was a slightly overweight officer who was a pleasant guy. He was placed in command of our two-plane unit based on his rank of 1st Lieutenant while I was still a 2nd Lieutenant. Unfortunately Burrows' rank and appointment to command would result in his eventual replacement. Burrows arrived in a new Birddog and advised me that I was to report to our commander of the 219th, Major Lust, the following morning.

I took off from Bao Loc at 0700 and arrived at Pleiku in the early morning. I reported to Major Lust and wondered if I was going to be blamed for Trumball's collapse. Instead, Lust advised me that I was scheduled to be promoted to 1st Lieutenant the previous week. I knew that my promotion was due and was awaiting word to put on my 1st Lieutenant insignias. This promotion was almost automatic for all 2nd Lieutenants unless they were dead.

Lust said, "Cappy, the Pentagon has informed us that you are being passed over for promotion."

I immediately knew that Major Lamont, my battalion commander from Fort Leonard Wood, had kept his promise to get me. Somehow that last efficiency report and probably a personal letter to the Pentagon had been enough to deny me my promotion. I said, "Sir, I know exactly why I'm not being promoted."

"Well, go tell it to the 52rd Aviation Battalion commander. He wants to see you. I made a pitch that he contact the Pentagon to arrange for your promotion based on your record while assigned to me and your work in Vietnam. Good luck."

As I walked to the office of Colonel Theodore Winslow, I wondered what new kind of trouble I was facing. Would I be labeled as some kind or retard or loser and given some really stupid assignment? I was announced to his office by the First Sergeant.

I walked into the office, saluted and said, "Lieutenant Capozzella reporting as ordered, Sir."

Although I had never seen the colonel before, he stuck me as a very pleasant and kind man. He said, "You probably don't know Lieutenant but I have never in my entire career heard of a 2nd Lieutenant being passed over for promotion to 1st Lieutenant. Have a seat and tell me why you're not being promoted."

I then proceeded to explain the situation at Fort Leonard Wood and with Major Lamont. Colonel Winslow told me to come back and see him in two hours. I visited with the other 219th pilots and picked up a couple cases of beer and a few bottles of booze that I stowed in my plane. I then went back to Colonel Winslow's office.

"Well Lieutenant, I have reviewed your personnel file and your accomplishments since arriving in Vietnam. The MACV unit in Bao Loc thinks you're exactly what they need and are singing praises of your work. I have also relayed this information to General Westmoreland's Headquarters in Saigon. The commanding general is granting you a battlefield promotion as of this date." My heart leaped with joy. At least I wouldn't be embarrassed in front of the other guys in the 219th.

"Thank you, Sir. Thank you very much"

"Naturally Lieutenant, you will miss a couple of weeks of seniority but at least you got your promotion. Major Lust went to bat for you and I guess you owe him some thanks also."

"Sir, thank you for your efforts and concern and I will also thank Major Lust."

"Listen I don't mind looking into situations like this one and I don't mind putting my neck on the line when someone is getting the job done out here. Keep up the good work."

That night I gave one of the usual champagne parties for the officers of the 219th. At the party I thanked Major Lust and bought him a bottle of champagne. The promotion revitalized me and I felt better about my commanding officer.

While at Pleiku, I also advised the head crew chief that I wanted an insignia painted on my plane. Since our arrival, I noticed that many of the pilots were painting various insignia on the front fuselage of their planes. About four of the Pleiku planes had a shark's mouth and teeth painted much like the WWII Flying Tigers. I wanted something that would not only identify the plane but also discourage other pilots from flying my plane when I was not using it. The unit was short of planes for all the 219th pilots. The pilots at Pleiku used any plane that was available at the field for missions. When I arrived for my conference with Colonel Winslow, one of the 219th pilots took my plane for a local mission. His action meant I had to stay the night at Plieku instead of immediately returning to Bao Loc. At least he didn't say anything about the booze in the back seat.

Pilots in combat tend to be very superstitious. Although I did not consider myself to be superstitious, I confronted this situation once. I noticed that prior to every mission I donned my uniform and flight gear in the same manner. I had a routine as to which piece of gear to put on although there was no need that it had to be done in the same order. I decided to change the order of dress before the next mission. As I prepared to dress, I convinced myself that it was unnecessary to change the order of dress since I was not superstitious. My order of dress was good luck and had kept me out of serious harm. I guess in retrospect I had only proven that much like the majority of other pilots, I too was superstitious.

I decided to paint an insignia that I did not feel would cause me harm but might discourage other pilots from flying the plane. I decided upon a picture of an ace of spades. Historically, at least for card players the ace of spades is considered the death card. As a frequent card player, I had always looked at the ace as a card of power and not death. I asked the ground crew to do me a favor and put the ace of spades on the fuselage of my plane. The ace was painted on both sides of the fuselage by morning when I took off for Bao Loc. The insignia did discourage other pilots from flying the plane but would also have unforeseen consequences for my new partner, Lieutenant Burrows.

While I was still at Pleiku, the Operations Officer advised me that I could have my plane fitted with an armored seat. The normal seat is made of canvas and obviously would not have impeded the penetration of enemy bullets or shrapnel. The armored seat was quite large extending to the top of my helmet when I was seated. Unfortunately the seat weighed in excess of 250 pounds. The weight meant that, when I flew, the seat would be the equivalent of a second passenger and if I took a passenger in the rear seat, the plane would be overloaded. Although the plane could still fly with this extra weight, the margin of error for flying at low level in the mountains with their constant downdrafts would be a serious issue. I told the operation's officer that I would pass on the seat. Instead I placed an extra armored vest on the seat to protect my rear and vitals. I figured that the most common weapon fired at me would be AK-47's whose bullets would have the same penetration power as our own M-16's. The armored flak vest on my seat and around my chest gave me all the security I believed I would need. If the Vietcong were using 50 or 60 caliber weapons, then the armored seat wouldn't be much more protection and I would be in serious trouble anyway.

Back at Bao Loc, Burrows and I hit it off perfectly. He was a good pilot who was not afraid to do his job and never tried to pull rank on me. We were a good complement to each other. I tended to be slightly mischievous with the plane while he was steady but conservative.

Our contingent of observation planes was increased by two in late July. The Air Force assigned two of its converted jet pilots to the Bao Loc airfield Apparently I had been giving them enough missions that they felt justified in assigning these two pilots since as a mere Army pilot I was not trusted to handle the job. The two pilots were Captains Wayne Laird and Taylor Briggs. Both were graduates of the Air Force Academy and had volunteered for this assignment. The pilots were both in their late 20's and in fairly good shape. As pilots we tended to hang together but in our conversations together Laird showed a disposition that was not to my liking. I noticed that he didn't associate with Moyer or McClintock and seemed to look down his nose on the Army combatants. It was no surprise that he got along with Major Radford and Major White. Laird made his opinion of the Vietnamese very clear. He believed that the only way to win the war was to kill as many of the people as possible. He often commented that most of the natives were against the United States and therefore did not deserve to live. His philosophy was not too alarming since many of the American military felt the same way and I tended to write it off as mere bluster. I kept my distance from Laird and he in turn didn't want to come to our bar in Bao Loc. This location is where Burrows and I spent most of our off duty time.

After a week at Bao Loc, I heard Laird call for a strike on a target. I continued to complete my observation sweep of my sector and finished for the day. At the evening get-together Laird bragged about the strike in which he claimed credit for destroying an enemy tank. He explained that the tank was within a mile of the old French fort. I was quite skeptical since the use of tanks by the Vietcong was unheard of and unlikely especially in this area of heavy jungle. The next morning I was flying before the other pilots were airborne. I flew to the old French fort and sure enough I observed a large vehicle in a field about a mile away from the fort. Burnt grass and large craters surrounded the vehicle. I flew at tree top level over the vehicle. I could clearly see the vehicle was an oversized bulldozer. From the layers of rust on its body, the vehicle had been abandoned many years earlier. The bulldozer was a tracked vehicle and at a very high altitude could pass for a tank but certainly not at the altitude needed for observation work. I gave Captain Laird credit for spotting the tractor. I had overlooked it but I was also critical at least in my mind that he had not recognized the vehicle for what it truly was. I continued on my mission and in an hour I heard Captain Laird again call for an air strike on suspected Vietcong tanks. Using a second flight of three F-105'd, Laird attacked the rusty bulldozer and claimed yet another VC tank. That night at our usual drinking get-together, Laird brought up the subject of the tanks.

He said, "If those VC tanks are still there tomorrow, I'm going to call another strike to finish off the job."

I responded, "You know those tanks you are destroying are one rusted, old French bulldozer."

"Bullshit, those were tanks on both days. They even fired at me."

"You are talking about the vehicle a mile south of the old fort, right?"

Ignoring my comment, Laird said, "I know a tank when I see one."

"I'm willing to bet all the money I can raise that these tanks you are claiming are one old bulldozer," I countered.

"I'm not going to make any silly bet with you," he sneered. "Tomorrow I'll finish the job."

My heart was pumping at full speed. "If you call in another flight of jets, I will notify your command that you have used nine jets and countless bombs to destroy a rusted out piece of junk. You won't be able to get a job piecing together garbage for the Air Force when I'm done with you."

Laird stalked from the bar and I knew I had handled his reprimand poorly. I had acquired an enemy who would not forget this humiliation that occurred in front of the entire Bao Loc American garrison.

The next morning I half expected the idiot to call another flight of jets for his imaginary target. He was quiet the entire day. In the afternoon, I showed Burrows and Moyer who was acting as my observer, the bulldozer. The area around the vehicle for at least 100 yards was devoid of any vegetation and yet the vehicle looked almost untouched by the bombs. At least Laird was correct when he said that they needed to finish the job since the bulldozer was probably in the same condition as it was prior to the attack by six jets. My victory over Laird would have ramifications within a month as secretly he vowed to get Burrows and I.

Three days after the bulldozer incident the Air Force was at it again. Captain Brigg was flying about 35 miles northwest of Bao Loc when his engine seized up on him. He made a forced landing in a field. The uneven field ripped his landing gear off the plane. Considering the circumstances, it was a good attempt. Fortunately he was not seriously injured and was able to call for help with his emergency radio. Both Laird and I were in the air at the time and arrived over Brigg's location at the same time. I immediately called for helicopters to pick him up. Meanwhile Laird was starting to get nervous over the wait for the chopper and radioed me.

"Headhunter One One this is Winston Three One, I'm going to land on the road and pick up Brigg."

I looked down at the location and could only see a broken road that had enough clearance for only about 200 yards. Although this area was only a few yards from where Brigg was standing, the road was too chopped up for a safe landing and I responded, "Winston Three One, if you attempt a landing here, you will destroy your plane."

"Well we have to do something or the VC will get him."

"There isn't any movement around him, lets give the choppers more time."

"No, I'm going down."

Since I didn't think there was any sense in continuing the discussion, I replied. "OK, but you will have to make a really good landing."

In my mind I could see the reasoning behind Laird's attempt. A successful landing and extraction of his wing man in the face of an imaginary onslaught of Vietcong might win him the Distinguished Flying Cross or higher with enough bullshit.

Laird began his approach and as I expected he hit hard and ground lopped his plane causing damage to the wing, bent propeller and a destroyed engine. Laird was able to walk away from the plane and within minutes had joined his partner on the ground. Laird radioed me; "Headhunter One One I think you can make it if you land a few yards further down the road."

"Winston Three One, I'm not going to attempt a landing which could end with three planes down within one hundred yards of each other."

"Are you refusing to try?"

"You're damn right! Anyways you know the plane only holds two people."

"We can squeeze into the back."

"Forget it," I replied.

Within five minutes I received a call from a flight of three Army Hueys that I directed to the crash site. They arrived and picked up both Brigg and Laird without incident. The Huey pilot radioed, "What the hell happened, did they collide?"

I said, "No, one of the planes had engine trouble and went down and his partner attempted a landing to rescue him."

"The second pilot must be a real hotdog."

"Yep!"

The choppers picked up both Brigg and Laird without incident and without any enemy fire. They were back at the Bao Loc base within 20 minutes. Later that evening they both boasted of their exploits as if they had confronted a large enemy force. I expected they would recommend each other for some type of medal.

Lieut. Capozzella waiting to board C-130 for flight to Vietnam

Lieuts. Capozzella and Kellum at bunker at Pleiku Airfield

Pilots of the 219th (Lt. Capozzella front row right)

Hooch maids cleaning boots for pilots

OV-1 "Birddog" in flight over Central Highlands of Vietnam

Pleiku Airfield Base

Enlisted personnel assigned to the 219th

219th pilot and Vietnamese workers at Pleiku

Chapter 13 – Tea & Ms. Raye

From the end of July thru the end of October 1965, my life became somewhat routine. Each day I flew looking for "Charlie" and occasionally I was lucky enough to find small units. Although I generally called for air support to mop up the VC, once in a while I would use my own rockets to make an attack. Since the air support was much more effective in killing power, it was more logical to use either Air Force or Marine air power. Only when no air support was available or the target so small did I engage the enemy with my own firepower. However, I often would attack areas of the jungle in the kill zone with my grease gun where I knew the Ho Chi Minh trail had a branch. I wondered whether I ever hit any of the enemy after spraying an area with over 300 rounds from that weapon but it certainly passed the time of day and broke the monotony of the missions. Occasionally I was awakened from the daily routine by something different.

Captain Moyer met me at the airport one afternoon and asked, "Would you be interested in meeting the local French tea plantation owner?"

"Sure," I responded.

The tea plantation was only about two miles away from the airfield and I had often flown over the area although there was never any evidence of VC activity in that location. I assumed the plantation owner had made some type of deal or payoff to the VC to continue to operate. I wanted to see how tea was grown since I didn't know if tea was harvested from a small plant or just flowers. Moyer's invitation was an opportunity I could not ignore.

"The owner is Marcel Duvail and as far as I know he was here prior to the French war with the Viet Minh and also when the Japanese occupied Vietnam. He has a lot of stories about the old days and is quite pleasant," explained Moyer.

"It sounds interesting. Let's go."

We drove the jeep to the plantation. The main house was a one story building but quite large and could have been used in a tropics movie starring Clark Gable. All the windows had shutters and the roof was made of tied palm branches. The plantation was well kept and there were numerous workers moving around the compound. I saw no evidence of defensive positions in case of attack and none of the workers or Duvail carried a weapon.

Duvail was expecting us. Here was a distinguished looking man of about six feet and with a thin but hard looking body. His hair was salt and pepper. It gave him a mature look of someone with an important message.

He walked to the jeep with his arm extended and in very good English said, "Good to meet you, Lieutenant. I've seen you fly over my home a number of times and now we finally meet."

"I'm happy to meet you Mr. Duvail," as we shook hands. I immediately liked this man and marveled at his achievements in such a hostile climate and political environment.

Turning to Captain Moyer, Duvail offered his hand and said, "Nice to see you again, Captain. Would you gentlemen join me on the veranda for some tea? I promise you the tea will be fresh."

We sat on large bamboo chairs while a servant brought two large teapots and cups. "I want you to try the typical dark tea that is shipped to Europe and also some local flowered tea that is very special, quite expensive and in short supply."

After a cup of the dark tea I was poured a cup of the flowered tea that was quite light looking but had a strong flowery aroma. I tasted the tea. I immediately disliked it but tried not to show my feelings. "It's not bad but very different than what I'm use to drinking."

"I'm very proud of this tea and it is my favorite," Duvail said.

Changing the subject, I said, "How long have you been in Vietnam?"

"I came here as a young man in 1932 and was able to purchase this land from another Frenchman who really didn't grow any crops. Through some hard work and good fortune I was able to develop a tea plantation and make a little money. Although the climate here tends to wear down Europeans, it's excellent for tea and other crops if the land can be cleared. Are either of you farmers back in the states," he asked?

"No. I'm from a city in upstate New York," I responded while Moyer said he was born and raised near Chicago.

"Too bad. Living in the country is much better than city life. That's one of the reasons I came to Vietnam."

"Mr. Duvail, back in the states I'm a history buff and have always been fascinated by the Japanese invasion of this area and the French Indochina War. Could you tell me a little about it from your own prospective?"

"I was both unfortunate and also lucky when the Japanese came to Vietnam. My Vietnamese wife was an active supporter of those people fighting the Japanese and they killed her in reprisals for some sabotage. On the other hand, the Japanese felt the production of tea was important to their war effort and allowed me to harvest our tea although the tea went directly to the Japanese military at a very low charge. Eventually I developed a commercial relationship and found that, if I did not openly oppose them, they left me alone. As for the conflict between the French and the Viet Minh, most of the fighting was to the north. Fortunately it spared my plantation."

"The VC also seem to leave you alone," I said in more of a statement of fact than a question.

"My philosophy with the Vietcong has also been, if they leave me alone, I will leave them alone. Over the years I have developed a relationship with the local leaders and the people. They have allowed me to operate without much difficulty. It's in everyone's interest that some commercial enterprises remain in tact for whoever wins."

"Obviously the VC doesn't have an urgent need for tea so at least you're safe from them taking your finished product but do you have to pay them to remain without harassment?" I asked.

"Lieutenant, unofficially, I pay the Vietcong and the local government and military to leave me alone. I favor neither side and just wish that I can live in peace without their interference. Up to this point I've been successful."

We continued our discussions and I learned after the Japanese had killed his wife during their occupation, he didn't remarry and had no children. He seemed quite content to run his business and remain at the plantation for the rest of his life. I wondered as he spoke whether the war would allow him to continue with his idyllic life. In my opinion, eventually someone or some group would decide that he would either have to join their movement or be eliminated. Duvail was a fascinating man but I felt somewhat sorry for him since he lived in a dream world that would someday come crashing down around him due to no act of his own choosing. We said our goodbyes after a short tour of the plantation. Duvail gave both Moyer and I standing invitations to return to the plantation and if there had not been a war, I would have taken him up on his offer. As it was, this was the first and last time I would see the man.

On the way back to the Bao Loc compound, I said to Moyer, "The guy has a great place but I doubt the war will continue to bypass him."

"Yea, but he will continue for as long as he can. He told me last week that your missions were making it more difficult for him to remain neutral."

"How so?" I asked.

"The VC feel your missions have stepped up the war in this province or at least that is what Duvail was told."

"Well obviously he has made some type of commitment since giving you information like this sort of makes him an informant for us."

"That, Lieutenant, is why I often have a cup of tea with the man," as Moyer laughed.

Just then our jeep drove pass a beautiful girl of about twenty years old who looked like any French or American girl one would see in those countries. She was squatting along the road with her dress pulled up as she was peeing. I had seen Vietnamese woman doing the same thing on a number of occasions but never a white woman.

"Look at the girl by the road," I said.

"What about her?"

"She looks like an American or French girl. What is she doing here?"

"She's half French and half Vietnamese although raised as a Vietnamese. Supposedly her father was a French soldier stationed here during the war against the Viet Minh," responded Moyer.

"It just seemed strange seeing her by the road taking a pee."

I wondered whether some soldier in some future war would see a similar scene involving a half American and half Vietnamese girl.

A few days later I was at the compound when a radio call came to Bao Loc MACV that an important VIP was arriving at the airfield in an hour. The message did not include the identity of the individual but only requested to have someone meet the plane at the airfield by 2 pm. Since there were not many individuals willing to leave the safety of the compound for a ride through the jungle to the airfield, Sergeant McClintock and I decided to meet the plane.

At 2 pm a twin engine Army plane landed at the field. McClintock and I drove the jeep up to the plane expecting to meet a high-ranking member of our military. Instead we saw a woman leave the plane dressed in a green khaki army uniform with the insignia of a full "bird" colonel. However this woman was no military person since I recognized her as Martha Raye. Ms. Raye was a comedian who achieved fame and recognition as a member of the Sid Caesar television show. Her trademark was her overly large mouth. Naturally both McClintock and I were shocked by this arrival. After greeting her with a warm handshake, I walked to the plane and grabbed her bag that was handed to me by a crewmember of the plane.

As Ms. Raye walked to the jeep where McClintock was standing he yelled to me, "You mean we drove through the jungle to pick up this god damn broad?"

I was so startled and embarrassed I really couldn't think of anything to say. I wasn't sure if he was just having a joke at her expense but I should have known better.

He turned to Ms. Raye and commanded with no cheerfulness, "Get in the back of the jeep." He then turned and climbed into the driver's seat as I helped Ms. Raye into the jeep. The plane departed after the pilot told me that they would be back at noon on the next day to pick up Ms. Raye.

She was obviously completely intimidated by this encounter and never uttered a word on the entire trip back to the base. However, McClintock continued his attack upon her presence and the inconvenience of driving to the airfield.

He muttered, "God damn broads shouldn't be allowed in a combat zone. Damn woman prancing around Vietnam in a colonel's uniform who don't know a fucking thing about this war."

I never said a word as I was too embarrassed to think of an answer and wondered what she was thinking and how she had gotten into this mess. Unfortunately this encounter with Sergeant McClintock was only the beginning of an adventure that would undoubtedly be remembered by Ms. Raye as one of the worst experiences of her life.

When we entered the compound, Ms. Raye was met by both Major Redford and Major White. Although they had many shortcomings as leaders, both were quite gracious in their welcome. Ms. Raye's spirits were obviously raised as she smiled for the first time and advise everyone that she would be putting on a one-woman show after dinner. She was shown to her room adjacent to the base's small bar.

One day prior to Ms. Raye's arrival, the Bao Loc MACV received another replacement. His name was Staff Sergeant Clarence Merritt. The sergeant had just arrived in Vietnam two days before his arrival in Bao Loc and from the looks of his demeanor he was petrified of this assignment. The timing of his arrival and Ms. Raye's visit would be the catalyst for the next humorous and tragic incident in Vietnam.

Ms. Raye was scheduled to put on a small show later that evening. Almost the entire complement of personnel stationed at the base were in the bar drinking beer waiting for the show. It was just after 8 pm and it was quite dark outside when Ms. Raye walked into the bar. She was still wearing her colonel's uniform and began to talk with the men. I was in the bar as usual with Captain Moyer and Lieutenant Burrows and we had been drinking heavily for about two hours. Ms. Raye had been in the bar for only a few minutes when suddenly we could hear a noise like a hard rain hitting the metal roof. Unfortunately the rain was the clatter of small arms, machine gun fire and explosions. Although the firing sounded close it was actually about a mile away in the direction of the ARVN base. The sky was lit as the tracer rounds could be observed through the front door and windows. The tracers were quite a spectacle since most of the shots were fired at an angle of at least 60 degrees above the horizon and would have had difficulty hitting anyone over 10 feet from the shooter. I guessed the people shooting were firing from behind protective cover and had their weapons above the cover and shooting without really aiming their weapons. From the spectacle it was also obvious that both attacker and defender were employing the same ineffective firing positions.

The first person to respond to the firing was Sergeant Merritt. Before anyone could say anything or even move, Merritt jumped out of his seat holding his M-16 and swung the butt at the light hanging from the ceiling of the bar. The light bulb shattered with a large noise, pitching the bar in darkness. Merritt then ran to the closest front window and instead of opening the window smashed the glass pane much like one would see in an old western and gangster movie. The rest of us were in shock watching Merritt make these idiotic decisions. As a group no one other than Merritt and Ms. Raye moved. She jumped to her feet and in a shriek that had to be heard for at least a mile, screamed holding her head and dashed into her room. She ran to a corner of the room where she crouched into a fetus position and began to whimper.

After the shock of this comic opera passed, the remaining participants in this play grabbed our weapons and leisurely left the bar to go to our defensive positions. Sergeant Merritt was left in the bar peering out through the broken window while Ms. Raye continued to whimper in her room.

McClintock couldn't resist a parting shot saying, "I told you that these damn broads don't belong out here."

We spent the next three hours looking into the darkness beyond our fence perimeter awaiting the attack by the Vietcong. The attack never materialized although the firefight at the ARVN camp continued for another two hours. I doubted that the ARVN or VC had inflicted many casualties since most of their tracer rounds continued to be fired into the air.

We returned to the bar after the emergency had apparently subsided. Ms. Ray was probably still huddled in a corner. None of us had the courage to go into her room and check on her. After a ten-minute wait, Major White came to the bar. He spoke to Lieutenant Burrows and me, "There are two women at the ARVN compound who were injured during the attack. Could we possibly med evac them out in your airplanes tonight."

Burrows quickly responded, "Major, I'm too loaded to fly a plane tonight. It would be a big mistake to attempt a mission after drinking."

"Colonel Teo would take it as a big favor if the more serious of the two woman were airlifted out," as White looked at me. I felt a pang of guilt since someone really needed medical assistance and I was too drunk to offer assistance. Finally I knew I had to make an attempt to help.

Although I was also quite drunk but knew I could fly or at least the alcohol thought I could still fly. "Alright I'll take her," I responded. "Where does Colonel Teo suggest I take her?"

"Colonel Teo said that he could make arrangements to have Vietnamese medical personnel meet a plane if you could fly her to Saigon."

"Well at least Saigon is large enough and bright enough for me to see even without navigational signals," I countered. "Have the ARVN meet us at our airfield."

Truly I was not in any condition to fly the Birddog and thought it was a hopeless mission with an idiot for a pilot. Burrows, McClintock, Moyer and I drove a jeep to the airfield. Surprisingly, Major White followed in another jeep with two other personnel. Unfortunately the Bao Loc airfield was not equipped with any night takeoff or landing lights. In addition, the plane could hold two sitting occupants counting the pilot but was not equipped to carry a person in a stretcher. The planes were not fitted with any directional equipment for flying directly to another location and consequently had to use dead reckoning or follow a landmark such as a road. In the darkness obviously following a landmark was out of the question and no vehicles traveled on the roads at night during the war. To make matters even worst, it had begun to rain. This condition meant that even if my dead reckoning was accurate we might miss Saigon because of the weather. If we missed Saigon, the plane would certainly run out of gas and I would be forced to make a crash landing in the dark and rain. This situation gave me two unhealthy and dangerous choices and when my inebriated condition is factored into the equation, a long shot for success.

Burrows looked again at me and asked, "Vince, what do you think?"

"This is crap Bob, the odds aren't good although I would certainly bow to your request to take this mission." He gave me a look that I read 'forget it.'

Major White interceded, "You know this woman will probably die if one of you doesn't fly her out."

Before I could respond, Burrows answered, "Major, frankly I already said that I'm too drunk to fly a plane and if I did and crashed, I would be court-martialed." Burrows had effectively removed himself from the situation. His position left me holding the bag.

"I'll give it a try but I have serious doubts." Although my response was true, I still believed that I was invincible and not destined to die in this hellhole.

By this time the ARVN had brought the two wounded woman to the airfield. Major White notified them that only one of our planes was available and therefore only one woman would be flown to Saigon. With the help of Captain Moyer, I removed the rear seat in the plane. We were able to place the woman with her stretcher into the fuselage of the plane with her head positioned toward the front of the plane. The medics had already hooked her up to an IV. We hung the IV on the ceiling near my head. The victim was not awake and I wondered whether she had been drugged or simply in a coma. I worried whether she would awake during the flight and begin to scream or attempt to free herself from the restraints.

I walked to the front of the plane and addressed McClintock. "We will need to light the runway. My landing lights are not sufficient for me to make a safe takeoff."

McClintock said, "We could put some lights on the sides of the runway. What do you think?"

I through out the question, "Is it possible to rig some smudge pots of lighted gas?" I remembered seeing the same technique used in a movie about World War II pilots.

"I'll take care of it," said McClintoch.

"That would help but I also want someone to take the jeep to the end of the runway and face my takeoff with the lights on so that I will know where the end is located."

"I'll do it," Burrows offered.

I got into the plane with everyone clustered around. "Here goes nothing," I offered with my bravest face.

Someone gave me a cup of coffee. I gulped it down with the hope that my head would clear up even more. I was starting to regain most of my wits since I had agreed to fly the mission.

Burrows said, "Vince don't leave the area if you're not certain the weather will allow you to land at Saigon."

"Bob, you can bet I'm not going south unless there is a good chance of success." I had my doubts about the success of this mission since the rain was coming down in the proverbial 'buckets'. My respect for the changing Vietnam weather was still as high as it could get.

Our medic, Spec 4 Joseph had arrived at the field and warned me that the plasma would only last about an hour and a half and must be removed when it emptied. I thought to myself that if the bottle emptied when I was still in the air, I would be in serious trouble as the flight to Saigon was a little over an hour away.

This distribution of weight caused by the stretcher laid down the fuselage would cause a tail-heavy attitude and I mentally made a note to compensate for this condition. The smudge pots were lit and I started the engine. Burrows had driven to the far end of the airfield and parked his jeep with the lights on pointing down the runway at my plane. I felt confident about the takeoff but still worried about the rain. I knew from flying in this condition that once airborne I would be unable to see out the front window.

The plane started without a flaw and I taxied to the takeoff position. I took off without incident and climbed to five hundred feet. The clouds were far too low to negotiate above the mountains between Bao Loc and Saigon. Any higher would place me in the clouds and force me to fly on instruments. This plane was not designed to handle IFR flights. I began to circle the town of Bao Loc that I could see out my side window. I was not going to climb into the clouds and head toward Saigon with only the hope that the weather would clear sufficiently enough to allow me to see the city and the airfield. For over an hour I circled the town hoping the rain would stop. The plasma got lower and lower and finally I called the Bao Loc radio to tell the guys to relight the smudge puts for my landing. They returned to the airfield and relit the pots. I felt terrible that I had failed to fly this woman to safety but I was not going to risk both her life and my own on the hope that the weather was clear over Saigon. Surprisingly I made a safe landing and the woman was returned to the medical facility at the ARVN compound. I was relieved the next day to learn that she was recovering but that the other woman had died during the night due to her wounds.

The following morning I didn't see Ms. Raye and went to the airfield for my usual morning recognizance flight. Moyer and McClintock went to the ARVN camp to help bring some semblance of stability to our allies. When I returned to the field at about noon, Ms. Raye had already boarded her plane and was well on her way to a more desirable spot. No one ever admitted taking her to the field. Ironically our paths would cross before I returned to the States. I never again saw any VIP entertainers visit Bao Loc during my six-month stay at the camp.

Chapter 14 – Strange Customs

While driving to dinner at Tru Mat Kim's restaurant, I noticed two Vietnamese people that caught my eye. The first was a woman who was probably in her late 40's but look more like 60. She was sitting along the side of the road begging for money. I threw a fifty piastas coin in her hat lying on the ground in front of her. She said something in Vietnamese and gave me a wide smile. Her smile showed two rows of completely black teeth that had a shinny pearl like quality to them. I asked McClintock about her teeth and he said, "They get black when they chew chi-chi nuts."

"Why do they chew the nuts? Are they some form of narcotic or drug," I asked?

"They may have some narcotic in them but mainly natives, who are very poor and live in the hills, chew the nut to kill their teeth. Since they don't have any dentists in the hills and can't afford to come to the cities for treatment, they kill their teeth when they start to rot."

I turned and looked back at the woman and was swept by compassion and pity. "Imagine kissing someone with a mouth like that. Ugh!"

Later that evening as we were walking out of the restaurant I saw an old man sitting in front of one of the many shacks that lined the street. His left arm and hand were supported by a piece of wood attached to a chair. The reason for the support was because his left index finger had a nail that was easily two feet long. The nail did not extend for two feet but as it grew, it wound into a spiral that I estimated was at least two feet long with at least three complete 360-degree spirals. The nail was brown with age and quite ugly although one had to wonder how it could be grown without breaking.

I said to McClintock, "Do you see that man's nail?"

"Yea, I've seen him sitting here before."

"What do you make of the nail?"

"He's making a statement to anybody that sees him."

"What do you mean Mac?"

"Lieutenant I think you realize, that when he moves, he must support the nail with his other hand or the nail will break. If he does anything that requires use of his left arm or hand, the nail will break. He's telling the world that he doesn't do anything with this arm and in fact doesn't work. It's his way of bragging that he does not need to work."

"That's a lot of effort and worry to make a statement like that one. I would just have someone bring me drinks while I sat on a swing in front of my house all day."

"Well, that just what he's doing but with a nail instead of a swing and he probably can't afford to drink alcohol. Remember these people are not Americans and have different ways to express their feelings."

As we left the area I realized that McClintock was right. I could not continue to judge and analyze the Vietnamese as I would Americans. Their culture did not necessarily support similar ideas and ways of expressing their needs. I thought of the American effort to bring democracy to South Vietnam. These people had no knowledge or desire for our democracy. They were merely content to be allowed to live in peace and scratch out an existence. The lack of involvement gave them a chance for survival. Our government would be far more successful and welcomed in the country if we offered education and medical assistance. I imagined the impact America could have achieved if we pumped even a portion of the money already spent on the war to the effort to improve the way of life of these poor people. All we seemed to be doing was to prop up an unpopular government and to kill those that opposed our offer of democracy. This lesson would remain with me for the rest of my life.

Shortly after Ms. Raye departed Major Redford notified me that Colonel Teo was hosting a dinner and party at his headquarters for the officers of the MACV unit and the pilots. We went as a group to Colonel Teo's command and were ushered into a large dining room in a very plush home at his base. There was a long table with a tablecloth that reached the floor in the dining room with plates and silverware already set. In the middle of the table was a silver cover that was obviously covering some type of food. When everyone was seated, Colonel Teo gave a short speech of welcome followed by toasts to the successful outcome of the war and to our two countries. Colonel Teo then announced that he had ordered a special treat for dinner. The special cuisine was under the silver cover. When the servants who were Vietnamese soldiers lifted the cover, I saw the top of a goat's head. It was clamped to the table so that the animal was immobilized under the table. The skull had been cut and I saw the warm, raw, bloody brains of the goat. The animal was obviously now dead. Colonel Teo dished into the brains with a spoon and suggested everyone help himself to this delicacy. I have eaten many things but this was my limit and I declined and wondered how anybody could eat uncooked, warm goat brains.

After dinner to my surprise a number of the ARVN officers who attended the meal sang Vietnamese songs. Colonel Teo explained that it was a Vietnamese custom, at least at the base, to sing for their entertainment. Even Colonel Teo sang and was quite good. Perhaps he had missed his calling since I didn't consider him a very competent military officer. He then asked the Americans to sing. A number of us sang a song and when it came time for me to perform, Burrows and I sang as a team. We sang, "Home on the Range". It was probably one of the few songs that I knew the words and was easy to sing. I was more than happy to return to the compound where I would not have to display my lack of singing talent.

Chapter 15 – Special Forces

At the end of September, Bao Loc was changed by the arrival of a Special Forces "A" team. The team was commanded by Captain Barry Larson and included Lieutenant Nat Winters as his executive officer. Interestingly, Winters was a classmate of mine from Officer Candidate School at Fort Benning, Georgia. I liked Winters but never considered him a close friend. My friendship with Larson would grow, as we seemed to be similar in our attitude about life and the war. Larson was outgoing and gave me the impression of a man who enjoyed command and was good at leading men. He even looked the part of a leader standing about 5'10" and in great physical condition.

On the first day after their arrival at Bao Loc, Captain Larson ordered Lieutenant Winter to lead the squad outside the village and set up a camp for one night as practice for future operations. Larson flew with me as we gave cover to the squad and he watched with interest the execution of his order. Winters led the squad to the edge of a clearing just outside Bao Loc and set up a temporary camp about an hour before dusk.

Larson radio Winters, "What are you doing Seaside Two?"

Winters responded, "Seaside One, this is Seaside Two, we are setting up camp and have already established a perimeter."

"Seaside Two, we never establish a camp during daylight hours when Charlie can see and pinpoint our location."

"Sorry Seaside One."

"Now breakup that goddamn camp, get back into the boonies and re-establish the camp after dark. Do you read me?"

Winters responded meekly, "Will do, Seaside One."

I felt bad for Winters but had to agree with Larson. He was attempting to ascertain Winters' knowledge and combat experience. He was obviously lacking. In Winters defense he had been assigned to Larson for only two weeks that was his length of time in Vietnam. He had much to learn about warfare but was lucky since he would be learning from someone who obviously knew his business.

The Special Forces team stayed within the Bao Loc compound for the first three days of their arrival after the exercise. It seemed natural for me to hang around with the Special Forces officers although Winters was often given tasks to prepare the men for their mission.

On the second day, Larson asked, "Vince, would you mind if I was your observer tomorrow during your morning flight"?

"Always glad to have another American as an observer on these flights," I responded. "Be ready at 0800 hours for the ride to the airfield."

That night as usual, Captain Larson and I settled down in the club and drank until we were barely able to walk. He explained that he needed a recognizance flight to the north of the base to scout a nameless village about 20 miles away. The following morning I recall the weather was perfect. My crew chief drove Larson and me to the airfield and after takeoff we flew leisurely over the village, about which Larson was interested. There were about twenty huts lining a small dirt road with a number of cultivated fields outside the village. I did not observe any indication that the village was fortified or under the control of the Vietcong although it was usually impossible to see evidence of this type.

After circling the village twice, Larson said, "Vince, can you land on that dirt road so that I can take a walk into the village?"

I was dumbfounded, "Why would I want to do that?"

"Listen, my team intends to set up a camp at that area and I want to know what we are facing".

"Jesus, Barry, that village could be under the control of the Vietcong," I responded.

"It looks pretty quiet to me."

"Hell, the ARVN haven't been able to even get up here since I arrived at Bao Loc and looks can be pretty deceiving".

"Well, fly right over the village and see if there is any reaction."

"OK, but I'm not agreeing to a landing. If I was to wreck the plane on this kind of stunt, they would take my wings."

"Just take a close look."

I flew about 20 feet over the village on two passes and with the exception of an occasional look at the plane; the three or four villagers that were visible did not seem concern. It reminded me of the joke among the pilots. If after flying over a Vietnamese and he runs, he's a Vietcong, if he doesn't run and seems unconcerned, he's a disciplined Vietcong. I wondered whether these villagers were the disciplined Vietcong.

Larson said, "It looks pretty safe to me, OK?"

"I don't know. This is a foolish risk for a sightseeing trip."

"Vince this is really important. If there are no VC, then I can move my team up here immediately and stabilize this area with a minimum of bloodshed."

"All right, but if there is one shot, we're leaving."

Already I was regretting becoming friends with Larson. Sitting in his shoes I probably would have made the same request and hoped that the pilot was a little short on smarts.

"You've got it" Larson relied with a growing confidence.

Looking at him I realized that he had no fear of facing the enemy on the ground even with me as a backup. I took the plane on a straight in approach as if I intended to give the village a third once over. The road was narrow but surprisingly quite level and the landing went flawlessly as I landed away from the village thereby giving me as much room as possible from anyone with a weapon. I then turned the plane 180 degrees and taxied toward the village ready to again turn the plane for an immediate exit. When no shots were fired I again turned the plane and figured to take off in the opposite direction of the village in case of trouble. Larson climbed out with his M-16 at the ready and began the 100-yard walk into the village. I set the breaks with the motor idling and exited the plane also with my M-16. We approached the village with Larson about 20 yards in the lead. All I could think was that this mission was insane. I had to take my hat off to Larson; he didn't seem concerned or show any sign of fear although his approach to the village was slow and deliberate. At the edge of the village I stopped and took a defensive position while Larson walked to the opposite end and back. I looked back at my plane and I calculated the time it would take me to run the distance and get the plane moving. I was as scared as I had ever been while in Vietnam. What we were doing was insane but I couldn't say no to Larson without admitting my fear and also felt a need to give him a chance to accomplish his mission.

Larson walked down the middle of the road into the village. His gun was at the ready but he would have been an easy target for a Vietcong in one of the huts. I couldn't help but admire his courage but also thought he was crazy to take this risk. I began to evaluate the situation. If Larson was shot at and hit, what should I do? The smart move would be to immediately run like hell back to the plane and get airborne. That idea made me feel guilty as I would be deserting my comrade and yet I also knew there was little choice. I also wondered how I would report losing Larson who was my passenger in my plane. Naturally I was guilty of violating my unit's directives and showing poor common sense. Finally Larson turned and walked back toward me as I retreated toward the plane.

Larson said, "OK, I've seen enough unless you want to see more."

"No, I'm satisfied." I felt relieved that we were heading back to my plane and safety.

"Let's head on back to the field."

"Barry, you owe me big time tonight at the bar."

"You've got it."

I never reported our activity to my command, as they would have gone ballistic. Being curious is one thing but to be foolhardy is another? However, the flight did earn Larson my respect and admiration and hoped that I had earned his respect. From that moment Larson often took my advice as to a course of action recommended from my viewpoint in the air as opposed to his on the ground.

That night we began drinking after dinner and by 10 pm we were both drunk. He and I got into a friendly argument as to whose job was the more difficult and dangerous. Finally, Larson made a $100 bet that he could fly my plane without any prior experience and instruction. I took the bet to humor him knowing that we would never find out the truth. When I excused myself to visit the men's room, I returned to find that Larson had left the bar.

I asked McClintock, "Where's Captain Larson?"

"He took a jeep to drive out to the airfield to fly your plane. He seemed awfully eager and said that you had given him permission."

"Are you kidding?"

"No Sir, I normally don't kid."

"But that's crazy, you shouldn't have let him go."

"Lieutenant Capozzella, he's a captain and what he does is his own business. I'm not sure he could even find his way to the airfield in his present condition."

"God damn it! That idiot will try to fly the plane."

"Yes sir. That's what he said he would do."

I immediately jumped into another jeep and drove to the airfield where I found Larson sitting in the cockpit of the Birddog attempting to get the plane to power up. Fortunately after every mission I always disconnected the battery by a switch under a plate on the floor of the cockpit. Larson was not aware this switch existed.

I said, "Barry you can't even figure out how to turn the engine on much less fly it. Admit you know nothing about an airplane."

In his drunken stupor, Larson responded, "You turn it on and I'll show you."

"No way," as I turned to leave with the relief of knowing that he would never be able to start the engine in his drunken state.

We returned to the compound and in the ensuing weeks, Larson often asked what he did wrong. I always responded that the plane was extremely complicated and a person needed a great deal of experience to even start the engine. Naturally he knew this answer was total nonsense but I never turned the battery switch on with him present.

A few days later I was sitting in the bar at Bao Loc with the Special Forces team. It was late and I was looking out the window and watching a Vietnamese civilian gather the insects that had been killed by the bright compound flood lights just outside the camp. I asked Larson, "What do you think they are going to do with those bugs?"

"They're going to fry them with their rice. These people are so poor that they lack protein in their diet and inspects are often the only source of protein. I've tried it and it's not too bad in a pinch."

"I suppose I could eat bugs but I prefer not to," I responded.

One of Larson's sergeants then added, "Hell, I like bugs. I even like them raw."

I then saw in the window a huge bug that had the characteristics of a winged hippopotamus. It was over an inch in length and width and had smaller bugs flying around it and landing on its surface. I turned to the sergeant, "Eat that bug and I'll buy you a beer."

"I would eat that bug just for the taste but I'll take the beer."

He picked up the bug and placed it in his mouth and clinched his teeth. The bug was still alive and made a squealing sound. He then crunched down on the bug and swallowed it. The sergeant then reached into his mouth and pulled out the bug's wings and said, "I really don't like the wings."

We all burst into laughter and I bought him two beers for breaking up the boredom of the night.

Chapter 16 – Ia Drang Valley

My routine of flying, drinking and comradely with the Bao Loc base was broken in November. Up to this time period in the war, the use of regular North Vietnamese Army (NVA) units was virtually unheard of against American units. There were of course rumors that the North was sending units into the South but it really was not official information. Apparently, the buildup of US personnel was prompting the North to match our move.

A regimental size unit of the NVA attacked the Special Forces camp in the Ia Drang Valley. This was the same camp that had been so accommodating to me when I first arrived in Vietnam. The 33rd NVA Regiment was pushed away from the camp by an ARVN relief column that was badly mauled before the intervention of massed American artillery paved its way to the base. The artillery unit was supplied by the First Calvary Division. This soon to be famous unit was given the order by General William Westmoreland to destroy the 33rd before it found sanctuary in Cambodia. The 1st Brigade under the command of Colonel Elvy B. Roberts was assigned this task and employed the techniques that would become quite routine over the next eight years. His troops were airlifted by squadrons of Hueys and Chinooks to landing zones on the enemy's flank and rear to begin the mission of destroying the NVA. Meanwhile the 66th NVA Regiment reinforced the 33rd NVA Regiment. Colonel Roberts' unit unfortunately had been airlifted into a hornet's nest and the enemy outnumbered them. However, the 1st Cav had no choice but to attempt to defeat the enemy or give the entire Ia Drang Valley to the NVA and VC.

The First Cavalry Division as well as all other American units operating in the jungle removed from large bases was unable to communicate with the higher commands. Units operating in close proximity to each other could usually talk to themselves but to no one else unless in direct line of sight. In the valleys and dense terrain, this was impossible. The answer was a flying communication device capable of relaying messages between these units and headquarters. That relay device would be the pilots and planes of the 219th.

On the 14th of November, I was temporarily recalled from my duties at Bao Loc and along with Lieutenant Tracy Winthers, Headhunter 22, assigned to assist the 1st Cav. At first I assumed our mission was to provide radio relay, artillery and search and destroy missions against the enemy. On my first mission in the battle zone I was communicating with a small unit that was in a firefight with the NVA. I attempted with some success to adjust artillery against the enemy. However as I flew at an altitude of about 1500 feet above the terrain, I noticed an enemy weapon emplacement with was manned by the NVA with what looked likes a quad-thirty caliber anti-aircraft gun. I cannot understand how they were able to miss destroying my plane. However, my plane was hit with three rounds of the fire. The rounds struck the fuselage and tail section but fortunately did not affect my controls. The gun so unnerved me that I flew behind a hill and began an immediate climb for safety. The opportunity for artillery support missions that I employed out of Bao Loc was readily available here. Unfortunately this enemy was not the small Vietcong units that operated near Bao Loc but full size NVA units with supporting heavy weapon units. I attempted one more time to direct artillery but was unable to accomplish the mission due again to intensive antiaircraft fire. Artillery fire control from the air was normally completed between 1500 and 2500 feet above the terrain but the intensive anti-aircraft fire meant almost certain destruction without being able to complete the mission and I was consequently driven away from the battlefield at that low level. Attempts to control the artillery from a safe altitude was senseless since I would be unable to observe the enemy. The enemy was smart enough to realize that at a high altitude, I could not be hit by their antiaircraft fire and also was unable to observe them unless they gave away their positions.

After the mission in which I encountered the anti-aircraft fire, I returned to Pleiku and reported the situation to Captain Tom Scott who was the Operations Officer. Scott was visibly upset about the damage to the aircraft and probably about the danger to my life, "What the hell happened to your plane?"

"I was flying at about 2000 feet directing artillery fire when they hit me," I lied.

"Why were you flying so low?"

"Well I had to see where the rounds were hitting and it was above the 1500 foot limit."

"You knew they had large caliber weapons that could reach that altitude," Scott insisted. "You're lucky to be alive and your plane will take a couple of days to repair."

I began to wonder if he was more concerned about my plane or me. "Well, you can't have it both ways. If you want us to fly in close support of the 1st Cavalry, then we will be at risk from these weapons."

He answered, "I'll have to speak to the CO and get back to you."

Within an hour my command ordered our planes to provide only radio support for the 1st Cav. that we could accomplish at an altitude of 8,000 feet or higher. Winthers and I decided to divide the missions into four three-hour relays by alternating missions every three hours. This meant that our planes would be flying with little or no reserve fuel since a Birddog could only fly four hours at normal RPM's. With three hours over the target and a half hour flight going and returning from the area would put us at the extreme limit of flying time. In order to accomplish the mission using these parameters, I would have to reduce the RPM's to the lowest possible setting to conserve fuel. This rationing would prolong my normal flying limit by an additional thirty to forty-five minutes.

I was provided with a loaner plane from my company so that I could continue to fly. I hated these missions, as they required me to fly circles high above the fighting while relaying messages from the ground troops in exposed conditions to rear echelon commanders. The troops on the ground must have felt that they were on their own since they had no ability to communicate directly with their command network. They were usually excited and in many cases almost incomprehensible. I would have to ask them to repeat their messages. This action made them even more agitated and excited. Their requests for reinforcements and support were often ignored or they received replies such as "can't do" or "will take your request under advisement". These messages usually meant nothing could be done. In defense of the rear command, there really was little they could do to reinforce these units since they were usually in the middle of thick jungle and the 1st Cavalry was short of troops. I felt helpless in this position, as my voice was the only reassurance the troops on the ground were receiving and I usually had to relay short messages of psychological encouragement but no actual messages of assistance heading their way. In addition the troops on the ground were usually uncertain of their exact position or just plain lost. Attempts to drop smoke so that I could locate their position were usually inadequate at my assigned altitude and consequently I was forced to ignore my unit's orders. I would dive toward their position and then climb as fast as possible to a safe altitude. It was my opinion that if I couldn't see the enemy they would have trouble seeing me and the jungle canopy made it difficult to shoot up at planes. Over open ground was a completely different situation. For once I was thankful to be flying over areas of thick jungle. Usually I was able to locate a unit and provide them with their position. Unfortunately some of the small unit commanders did not always accept my determination of their location. It was also obvious that the NVA was capable of listening to my radio communications with our ground units and benefit as to my information. I attempted to disguise the information but in reality it would not take a genius to determine what I was telling the ground troops. I no longer used compass heading but rather would advise the unit as to their location by where they were in relation to a prominent terrain or smoke.

    The U.S. Army at this point in time did not have sophisticated communications equipment in Vietnam for our use that would deny the enemy the ability to eavesdrop. Also there was no system of using codes to disguise our communications. I was never advised as to the use of passwords and frankly never heard them used by the ground troops.

    The North Vietnamese also began to play havoc with our radio signals. They could disrupt the signal completely or they would broadcast over our frequency with constant clatter. I knew it wasn't the ARVN inadvertently using our signal since it would be the same voice talking endlessly in Vietnamese. His voice like most Vietnamese voices has a high pitch. The constant chatter, high pitch and strain of constant flying began to irritate me. I had by this time developed a limited but useful command of certain vulgar Vietnamese words and would respond to this person in vulgar adjectives of his personality and parentage. The operator would normally respond in equally vulgar English responses. Unfortunately, these outbursts did not keep him off the air. I could usually override his signal when I was communicating to the ground personal because of my altitude but the North Vietnamese usually interrupted the ground unit's signal at some point.

Although I was terribly frustrated and exhausted with these missions, I did believe we were accomplishing some good results. On one incident, the 1st Cav. asked me to help locate a squad of men who had not retuned from a scouting mission. After about an hour of search I heard a faint reply on the radio frequency they were operating.

I called, "Zebra Three this is Headhunter One One."

"Headhunter One One, this is Zebra Three, have you been looking for us?"

"Command was wondering about your situation. Is everything OK?"

"Headhunter, relay to command that we had to take a detour because of Charlie and are trying to make our way back."

"Do you need assistance?'

"Well I could use some help in pinpointing our exact location."

I knew immediately that they were lost but they wouldn't admit it to their command or me. "When you see or hear me fly over you give a short 'now' message."

Disregarding my previous orders about altitude I drove down to tree top level and after about 5 minutes of flying heard a short "now" from Zebra Three. I had to determine a way to tell them their location without a code and without the enemy discovering their location.

Finally I radioed. "Zebra Three, could you see me when I flew over your position?"

"Roger that."

"OK, I'm going to make a another fly-over your position, heading the direction you should take to return. Understand?"

"You've got it Headhunter One One."

I lined up on a heading of about 75 degrees. This direction would take them back to their unit area and I flew over their position.

"We see you Headhunter and have the azimuth. Thanks."

I immediately altered course in the event the enemy was nearby and were able to determine the direction the unit would be traveling. I answered their last message, "No problem guys but take care getting back." The squad made it back to their unit without any losses and I felt I had accomplished something good for the day.

After three days of three hours on station as radio relay and three hours rest before the final three-hour duty, it was apparent that Winthers and I alone could not keep up this intensity. Another pilot, Lieutenant Stanley Silver, Headhunter 20, joined our team. With a three-man relay I flew 3 hours and then took a break of 6 hours before my final flight. On special occasions we also flew short radio relay flights at night. Radio reception often improved at night for the ground troops. On the fifth day in support of the 1st Cavalry Division, I celebrated my 25th birthday by flying two more long missions. The radio messages took their toll on us because the men on the ground were often frantic in their requests for help and direction. At times I could not understand their messages due to the constant crack of small arms and asked for repeat of a message. The poor radio operators on the ground were expectantly short of patience.

On the day of my birthday, Captain Leyda greeted me as I returned from my last mission of the day. He said, "I've checked the records and you have already exceeded the maximum flight time of sixty hours for a month by five hours."

"Listen I feel good and I really don't see why we can't ignore that rule for this mission?"

"Vince, it's the Flight Surgeon at Pleiku that came up with the sixty hour a month flying time, not me. Tomorrow morning you will report to the doctors to be examined. If they give the OK, I don't have a problem with you continuing to fly."

Reluctantly I said, "Fine, I'll see him tomorrow before my next mission."

At 0800 hours I was standing in the office of Major Bacon who basically asked how I felt and authorized me to fly an additional 20 hours without performing any physical tests. On the 18th I was reexamined by the flight surgeon and cleared to fly to 100 hours. By the 22nd, I was again examined by the same flight surgeon and cleared to 120 hours.

My attitude about my flying ability had greatly increased with my flying experience. I believed in an emergency that I could literally reduce the speed of my plane to a mere 45 mph and land on a large tree in the jungle and walk away with only minor scratches. Fortunately, I never had to prove this belief. My ego as to my flying ability in any kind of adversity was growing. However, after hitting 100 hours of flight time in 22 days I noticed my coordination was beginning to lag. Doubts as to my ability began to creep into my mind and my landings became more ragged. This situation was the first time I began to seriously question my ability to perform even simple flying tasks. On the 25th, Captain Leyda observed my landing at Pleiku and greeted my plane. The landing was unusually hard and I barely managed to keep the plane on the runway. I was brought to the flight surgeon who attempted to test my reflexes by having me cross my legs and taping my knees. He got very limited response and ordered me grounded for two days of rest.

The last six days of flying prior to my ordered rest, I was asked to land at the Duc Co Special Forces camp and to pick up some wounded men of the First Cav. The Birddogs were not really suited for this mission since there was only the one seat behind the pilot. The seat could be removed as I had done in Bao Loc previously. This action meant I could transport one wounded GI. I was reluctant to transport the wounded in this manner without a medic. I met a medical officer on the ground at the Special Forces camp and he asked if I could transport the wounded. As I looked into the medical tent I was overcome by the number of GI's awaiting flights to a more secure and better-equipped medical facility. It was also obvious that a flight in my cramped plane for soldiers with severe wounds was not in their best interests. A medical officer said, "Do you have any problem with taking these men to Pleiku"?

"Doctor, I really don't think it would be wise to have me transport them. Wouldn't it be wiser to have them evacuated by helicopter?"

He responded, "Your right but I would like to get as many of them to safety as possible in the shortest of time."

"I can understand that but I can't attend to the man if an emergency develops in the air."

"No problem", he responded, I'll have an orderly go with you."

I realized that he had no conception of the capabilities of my plane. "Doctor, my plane can safely hold myself and only one passenger. An attendant would make the plane way over weight and I can't do it."

The doctor looked puzzled, "I thought you could take two passengers. Listen, would you have any objection to removing some bodies that need to be brought to Pleiku for shipment to the States before they deteriorate even further?"

My stomach took a jump and I was repulsed as I realized what he was saying. On the other hand the doctor had the look of someone making an extraordinary plea and I couldn't refuse the request.

"Sure Doc, I will help in any way possible."

Meanwhile my mind was going through every possible reason to refuse the request but I was unable to utter any other words. I began the removal of corpses. I made five trips from Duc Co with either one body or one body and bags filled with body parts that day. The floor of my plane was drenched with the blood of these poor men and I loathed the missions. It seemed illogical to remove the bodies one at a time but it was obvious in the heat the sooner a body was taken to a location that could handle the situation was better than nothing. The bodies were already decomposing and the smell compelled me to fly with all the windows open for ventilation.

The thought of the handling of dead GI's had never entered my mind. I always maneuvered myself away from the disposition of dead soldiers prior to this event. I thought about my own situation. I dreaded the thought that if I were killed, my body would be placed into a body bag and then thrown into the rear of an airplane for removal to a unit designated for handling bodies. Another part of my mind easily rejected these thoughts since I still believed God didn't intend for me to be killed in some forsaken jungle. I often wondered if the other pilots and the guys on the ground felt the same way but it was impossible to know since the talk of dying was never discussed throughout my tour in Vietnam. Discussions as to God were not discussed accept by chaplains during mass. These were subjects best left in the inner recesses of the mind and if brought to the open could suggest that I was frightened or feared death. Obviously both of these conclusions were true at different times of my activities but I never admitted them to anyone. My only visible sign of fear was the constant biting of my mouth and lips when I was in serious situation or danger. My mouth was constantly tender since I normally bit myself on almost every mission.

During one of my breaks at Duc Co I observed a different manner of handling the dead. There were literally hundreds of VC and NVA dead in the area. The U.S. military out of concern of disease and disgust at watching bodies deteriorate had the job of disposing of them. Consequently, I observed the burial of the NVA casualties in mass graves prepared by bulldozers. A hundred bodies would be pushed into excavated holes by the bulldozers and then covered with only a foot or two of dirt. This preparation of the burial sites was similar to the methods that the Germans used to hide their killings of "undesirables" during World War II. Obviously the U.S. had no choice in our removal of these bodies and I doubt if a more honored burial technique crossed anyone's mind, including myself. However, these mass burial sites would become in the second half of my tour a reminder of the insensitivity of our troops after prolonged combat.

The battle at the Ia Drang Valley was winding down and finally my unit replaced me in support of the 1st Cav. I took only the one day of rest ordered by the Flight Surgeon and returned to Bao Loc. For the remainder of the month, I flew only one prolonged mission or two short missions each day to get my flying legs back.

I read in the Stars and Stripes newspaper that there had been massive anti-war protests in forty American cities on October 14th and 15th. At first I was angry and then disillusioned that the people back home were not supporting the war. However, I also realized that even my view of the war was changing. While I still agreed with President Johnson and his advisors that winning the war were vital to American security and freedom, I also was beginning to doubt that the war could be won using the South Vietnamese Army as the main force. It was also apparent especially after the Ia Drang Valley campaign that something was motivating the North Vietnamese Army far more than their counterparts in the South to win the war. Most of the people seemed to think of the American forces as intruders and as unwanted guests in this fight even though we had been invited by their leadership to assist them. Perhaps the leadership needed the American military to prop up their unpopular government and to provide financial assistance. The money usually went into the pockets of the Vietnamese leaders but the common people seemed to want to be left alone to continue their lives. There didn't seem to be this universal demand by the South Vietnamese people for the right to vote and democracy that was being presented to the American people by our leadership. If all these issues were taken together, then perhaps the war was not something that was in the best interests of the American people.

From letters by relatives and friends I learned that the President and his advisors were labeling the dissenters as being unpatriotic and undermining the war. I began to wonder whether I was being unpatriotic by having doubts in our efforts. I knew that I was giving the war everything I had. I wondered if killing people, who disagree with you, was necessarily patriotic. I could not be a dissenter but I also thought I was fighting for the right of these dissenters to voice their opinions. In a few months I had evolved from a right wing supporter of the war to a supporter who had doubts as to our legitimacy in the war and of our ability to win the war.

I hoped that the war would somehow begin to show signs of our victory or success. This movement toward our final victory would need to come from the American forces and the spirit of our fighting men. My own situation with the men, who were assigned to assist me to accomplish my mission, was an indication of what the future would become.

Upon the conclusion of one afternoon flight, I told my crew chief, Private Jeff Moore that an oil change was due and to have it completed in time for my morning flight. He basically had enough time to do the oil change either that late afternoon or early morning. When I returned to the airfield for the morning flight, I began my pre-flight inspection. This procedure was conducted before every flight. When I raised the cowling to the engine, I immediately saw that the oil cap had been left off the engine. The oil cap on an airplane is a critical component and not only must be secured but must also have a medal wire safety mechanism. The wire prohibits the removal of the cap unless it is being conducted by a mechanic. If the oil cap is inadvertently left off the engine, almost certainly the engine will spit out the oil through this opening and will freeze-up causing the plane to go down.

Although I was aware that Moore had a poor attitude about being in Vietnam and the Army, in general, I expected him to do his duty as a crew chief to the best of his ability. I was furious with him and gave him a verbal dressing-down. He seemed to take my reprimand very nonchalantly. No further action was taken against him but I decided that from that point on, I would conduct my inspections with the utmost diligence.

On the following day as I conducted my inspection, I again was checking under the cowling and found lying on the engine a large wrench. I do not know if the wrench would have caused serious problems with the engine in flight but it was serious enough to cause me to wonder about Moore. I'm certain the wrench had been left on the engine in retaliation for the dressing-down Moore had received the previous day.

Moore was sitting near the maintenance shed by the runway. I called him over to the plane. He approached without any sign of distress or urgency.

"Moore, look under the cowling and tell me what you see."

He took a quick look and responded in a sarcastic voice, "An engine?"

"Listen you asshole, this may seem funny to you but I'm dead serious. Look again but this time look at the top of the engine."

"Oh yea, I was wondering where I had left that wrench," as he reached into the engine and took the tool in his hand.

"Moore, I think you left the wrench there on purpose," I countered. "I could have you court-martialed for what you did yesterday and now today."

"Lieutenant, you can do whatever your heart wants. Anyway, I wouldn't intentionally do a thing like that."

I could see that this discussion was a losing proposition. I turned to the maintenance shed where Spec 4 Joseph Wheeler was sitting and called him over to my plane.

"Joe, do you think you can do the maintenance on two planes," I asked?

"Sure Lieutenant, no problem."

Again I turned to Moore, "If you go near this aircraft again, I will have you court-martialed. Do you understand?"

"Yea," he responded again in a sarcastic voice.

"Yes, sir!" I barked with my face only a few inches from Moore.

"OK, yes sir."

"You listen to me loud and clear, private. If there is the slightest thing wrong with my plane from this moment on, I shall see that you spend the rest of your life in Leavenworth. Now is that clear?"

"OK, Lieutenant you've made your point but what are my duties?"

"Basically I don't give a fuck what you do but you will remain at the Bao Loc compound doing every shit detail I can come up with. You are not allowed at this airfield again and if I see you near this plane, I will either shoot you or have you arrested."

"This isn't right, Lieutenant."

"Alright I'll give you the option of having me report your incompetence and sabotage of my plane to our command or accepting these duties. Take your pick."

Moore lowered his head and said, "I'll take the compound duty. I can use the rest."

I knew that he would do everything possible to avoid duty but I was just happy to get him away from my plane. In the future I would keep an eye on him and if there were ever an attack on the compound, would keep him always in front of me. I had absolutely no trust in him and guessed that he would have no qualms about retaliation. He didn't realize that I had no qualms about him either.

Chapter 17 – The Gonorrhea Fiasco

The Special Forces made an impact upon the Bao Loc base in more ways than just militarily. About two weeks after they first arrived, the men stationed with the MACV command began to come down with gonorrhea. The Special Forces troops had taken full advantage of the cheap price of the prostitutes in Bao Loc but had also introduced them to venereal disease. Surprisingly this problem was not an issue before their arrival. By the fourth week, eight of the men in the base had the disease that included at least one officer, Lt. Jessman. To acquire a venereal disease by either an officer or high-ranking NCO was the kiss of death for one's military career at this point in the war. Fortunately this disease was easily cured by treatment with penicillin. However, the penicillin for the treatment of the eight men was not available in Bao Loc.

The medic, Specialist 4 Joseph, approached me. "Lt. Capozzella, we need penicillin for our guys and I don't have enough for their treatments."

"Yea, I heard about the problem. Why not just requisition some?"

"Saigon would never give us penicillin without demanding the reason for its use and demanding the names of the guys with VD."

"Well, I doubt the 219th has any or would be willing to send it to me without some explanation."

"Is there any way you could get some for us unofficially in Saigon?" he asked.

"Shit. Are you sure there isn't some other way to get some?"

"No. Couldn't you fly to Saigon and trade for some. You're always able to acquire other things that aren't exactly supply items."

"OK, Joseph, I'll speak to Lt. Burrows about taking a run down there but you will be responsible for getting me some trade items."

"Thanks Lieutenant."

I found Burrows in our room and explained the situation to him. Neither he nor I had a problem with the disease but we felt an obligation to help the guys out since it would affect their careers.

"I've got no problem with you going to Saigon. You will have to make the flight on the QT," Burrows said.

"I'll leave after the morning flight and if there is a call for me from headquarters, cover it."

"Will you be coming back or stay there the night?"

"I might as well stay the night and get some R& R." I responded.

"No problem but don't get into any trouble or we'll both take the fall," he warned.

"Hey, I'll be like a mouse hiding from the cat."

After lunch I took off for Saigon with a bag full of trading material. The trading material included three cross bows made by our Montagnard friends. I was fairly certain that I had enough material to make a trade. I landed at Tan Son Nhut Airport without incident and looked for a suitable place to park my plane. The airport controller had not given me any parking instructions since almost all aircraft landing at the airport are either permanently housed at the field and know their parking instructions or commercial aircraft that park near the airport terminal located on the opposite side of the field from military operations. I taxied the L-19 to where a group of F-105's were parked and protected by eight-foot walls of sandbags. I left the plane behind one of these sandbag revetments without any worry as to safety or discovery. The plane was not visible from the command buildings and I didn't think anyone would be concerned about this small aircraft even if noticed.

After a short inquiry as to the location of the nearest medical detachment, I found a medical aid station located in a Quonset hut near the airfield. It was an Air Force unit. When I walked into the station a Specialist 5 Thompson greeted me. I explained in as vague a description of my dilemma as possible and was pleasantly surprised when Thompson offered enough penicillin for our post. After getting the drugs I gave Thompson the trading material. He refused the offer but I insisted that he accept. My mission was now complete and it was approximately 4pm. Now all I needed to do was to find suitable quarters. I walked to the tent city that had housed me and the rest of the 219th upon our arrival in Vietnam. The sergeant in charge of the entrance to the compound asked me for my orders assigning me to the compound. When I explained that I had no orders, I was declined entrance but was told that officers are often housed in a large BAQ (Bachelor's Officer Quarters) and also the Palace Hotel in downtown Saigon.

I took a taxi into Saigon and went directly to the officer's billets but was informed that they were full for the night and it was doubtful whether there would be any billets available for me. I entertained thoughts of sleeping in my plane but decided it would be far too uncomfortable. I walked to the Palace Hotel and again discovered that it was also full. The military clerk at the reception desk told me that the hotel was filled with high-ranking officers of the U.S. military. I wondered why all these officers were here and not in the field with their troops. It was only then that the term "Saigon warrior" was beginning to become an integral part of the military slang. The concept of "Saigon warrior" infers that a great many officers and enlisted personnel were assigned to duties in the vicinity of Saigon because this assignment was a safe haven for their tour in Vietnam. Although I realized that it takes more personnel to support combat troops than the combat troops, it was apparent that there were thousands of troops in this city and very few troops in the field fighting the VC. It would be this disapportionate number of personnel in the relative safety of Saigon and other large cities as opposed to troops on the ground seeking out and destroying the enemy that was in my opinion the reason for our failure to defeat the VC before the huge influx of NVA troops.

With no room, I contemplated returning to Bao Loc but decided against it since it would be dark by time I returned to the airport and got airborne. Instead I went up to the bar in the Palace Hotel. It was located on the top floor. As I sat down at the bar for a beer, I noticed sitting a few chairs down from me a woman dressed in Army green fatigues. Yes, it was Martha Raye. She was leaning over the bar from her bar stool and obviously quite drunk.

I walked up to her and said, "Hello, Miss Raye."

She looked up but didn't return my greeting.

"I'm Lieutenant Capozzella. I met you when you toured my base at Bao Loc."

Again she looked up but I could tell that she had no idea as to who I was or the name Bao Loc. "Oh, hi," she responded in an obvious drink induced slur.

"Well nice meeting you again," as I turned to leave.

"Would you like my autograph?"

"No thanks, I already have one," I lied.

I walked back to my seat and finished my drink. I decided to get a taxi and to locate a civilian hotel where I could put up for the night. Before I could leave the hotel I ran into a former pilot training classmate, Lieutenant Jeff Avery. We had a few drinks discussing the good old days and he kept me amused with some stories about my friend, Lieutenant Barry Taylor.

Taylor was assigned to the southwest of Saigon in a village in the Mekong delta with the 220th Aviation Company doing basically the same assignment as I was doing. Taylor had the exact same Birddog as I was flying and also had two bomb pods that would hold four individual rockets. While all the pilots wanted more firepower and destructive ability, the plane had severe limitations since it was not intended to be an attack aircraft. Pilots attempted to fix bombs on the wings or like me would drop grenades out the cockpit and fire rifles or small machine guns out the cockpit windows. Taylor decided to mount a rocket pod on each wing of his plane. The pods held seven rockets each and were designed for the Huey helicopters. They were quite heavy. Somehow Taylor was able to get a mechanic to mount the pods on his bomb shackles on each wing. With this load he took of on a search and destroy mission. He located some VC in the delta and commenced an attack on the enemy. Unfortunately, the mechanic had wired the rockets to all fire at the same time when the firing button was pressed instead of one rocket at a time. All fourteen rockets were ignited and shot at the same moment. The firing probably completely stopped the flight of Taylor's plane but the force of the ignition literally tore the rocket pods away from the wing carrying a significant portion of the wing's skin with them. Although the plane received substantial damage, Taylor was able to limp back to the airfield. Lieutenant Avery said that Taylor was able to escape any punishment since it was an honest attempt to strike at the enemy. The common sense was lacking since the pods truly created an unsafe flying condition. The pods would have eventually caused Taylor greater difficulties from the stress it created on the wings.

Avery also told the story about Taylor's run-in with the Cambodian Air Force. Apparently, Taylor had gotten slightly lost on a flight. This situation wasn't unusual considering the lack of directional equipment aboard our planes and his lack of superior navigational techniques. However, Taylor was so lost that he flew over twenty miles into Cambodian air space and the Cambodian Air Force scrambled two jets to intercept Taylor. The Cambodian pilots attempted to force Taylor to fly to a nearly airfield in Cambodia where he would probably have been interned and used as propaganda against the United States. Fortunately the Cambodians had contacted Taylor on a frequency monitored by the American Air Force. Our command sent three of our own jets to assist Taylor. The Cambodians backed down and flew back to their base with their tails between their legs while Taylor was escorted by the three jets back to Vietnamese air space and safety. Again Taylor escaped this incident without any reprimand. The stories lightened my spirits and I decided I had better secure someplace to spend the night.

I left the hotel and flagged a nearby taxi, preferring to travel quickly in a regular car rather than one of the many rickshaws that filled the streets. I told the driver to take me to the nearest hotel that would probably have rooms available. He understood the situation and drove for about ten minutes into the heart of Saigon. As I looked out the window at the narrow streets and cluttered apartment buildings with all manner of clothing drying on makeshift clothes lines, it reminded me of a scene from the movie, "The World of Suzy Wong". The driver stopped in front of a fairly large four-story hotel that from the patrons standing around catered to an almost exclusive Vietnamese clientele. I was slightly concerned as I had never visited this part of Saigon before and I didn't see the large groups of Americans near the bars or attempting to procure a prostitute on the street.

I entered the hotel and noticed the clerk's station situated between two open staircases that serviced the second floor. The lobby was clean and the floors were marble while the ceiling was easily over twelve feet high. A number of sofas and cushioned chairs were situated in the lobby and reminded me of old hotels in the states.

A room was available although the clerk knew only a smattering of English. His lack of English put me on guard since I knew that the hotel did not normally cater to Americans. Yet I wasn't overly concerned as a bellhop showed me to my room on the third floor. It was a spacious room with its own sink, toilet and bidet all situated in the open space of the room. This was the first time I had ever seen a bidet but I was at least familiar with its function. The bed was situated somewhat in the middle of the room although the headboard was against a wall.

As yet the U.S. military high command was not concerned with terrorism targeting our personnel and consequently had issued an order that no American personnel were allowed to carry any weapons in Saigon from the nearby military bases. I had disregarded this order as I felt it to be insane and foolish. Frankly I had no place to leave my weapon other than in my airplane although I had stowed my M-16 behind the passenger seat in the fuselage. In my overnight bag I carried my .45 caliber Browning semi-automatic pistol. I took it from my bag and laid it under my pillow for reassurance. I double-locked the door to my room and since I was dead tired, I fell immediately into a deep sleep.

At approximately 2 am I emerged from my deep sleep into a half sleep and half awake state. I hallucinated that there was a large rat under my bed but that it was so large that it was literally moving the bed. Since I greatly feared being attacked by rats as I sleep as a result of my initial experience in Pleiku's tent compound, I realized in my state that it must be a stupid dream. As I drifted toward consciousness, I realized that, in fact, my bed was moving and this was not a dream. As I lay on the bed it appeared to be moving up and down. My mind raced with a plausible reason for the bed to be moving. Quickly I rejected the concept of an earthquake since the rest of the room was not moving. It had to be a person or something under the bed causing the movement but I knew when I had entered the room that there was nothing under it. I silently reached under my pillow and retrieved my pistol. I immediately cocked the weapon for firing. Slowly I crawled toward the side of the bed. The bed was still moving up and down. As I peaked over the side of the bed and under its frame, I had my pistol extended in front of my face. I was beyond fear since I had to know what was under my bed that could be making this motion. Suddenly, I could see under the bed and saw a man's eyes looking into my own eyes. Only the top of his head was visible. Under my bed was some type of large trap door. Apparently the foot of the bed was sitting on the front corner of the trap door and as the person attempting entrance lifted the door, he also lifted the bed. Startled I reacted by shoving my pistol into the opening of the trap door at the person's head. He immediately backed down and slammed the door on the barrel of the pistol. I was tempted to fire my gun at the man but the thought of killing a person with a weapon that was not authorized, flashed through my mind. Yet, I knew I had to investigate the location under my room as it also could contain explosives or a group of VC who would now storm the room itself.

I pulled the pistol out of the door opening and jumped from the bed. Only one thought was in my mind, to seize the would-be intruder. Wearing boxer shorts and with the gun in my hand, I raced out of the room. I knew the man was on the second floor and I ran bounding three or four steps at a time down the stairway to the second floor. When I reached the second floor, I attempted to find the location under my room. I expected to find another hotel room. My search was unable to locate the room and it seemed as though the hotel was divided into two separate parts.

I ran down the next flight of stairs to the main lobby and must have looked like a mad man dressed only in my shorts and waiving my pistol. Surprisingly the clerk did not appear to be overly concerned or fearful and attempted to get me to return to my room. He didn't seem to understand the situation or at least was playing dumb. I refused to return to my room and decided to conduct my search to that portion of the hotel serviced by the stairway on the other side of the clerk's desk. I bounced up the stairway with my gun still in my hand. At the top landing of the stairway I could see another set of stairs continuing toward the third floor. Upon inspection I could see that this stairway ended at the ceiling but had a trap door. I climbed the stairs and pushed on the door. It gave way with only a great deal of effort. I peered into the opening and realized it was the trap door situated under my bed. My questioning of the clerk failed to obtain any reasonable explanation as his knowledge of English had deteriorated considerably.

I walked back through the lobby up to my room where I remained in an uneasy sleep for the remainder of the night. I again placed the edge of the bed on the trap door knowing that an entry attempt would again awake me. Early the next morning I left the hotel in a taxi for the air base. I will never know if I was an intended target for thieves or assassination. Obviously I had been placed in that particular room by design and it was by sheer luck the bedpost was sitting on the corner of the trap door. I felt extremely fortunate to be alive and learned another lesson in Vietnam. Nothing is, as it seems.

Unfortunately my trip to obtain penicillin had more dire consequences than just my adventure in the hotel. My flight back to Bao Loc was uneventful and the troops with the venereal disease were grateful that their problem could now be treated without any consequences. All of the guys with the problem had gonorrhea that was quickly and easily cured with the drugs.

Prior to my trip to Saigon, Major Radford had asked me to take over the supervision of securing movies for the compound and arranging for the evening movie. It was logical to select me as I was the only person who occasionally left Bao Loc and would have the opportunity to trade a movie. Most movies were seen four or five times and I would arrange to exchange it to another base for their movie that they had seen four or five times. The most logical and easy trades were with the Special Forces camps that I liked to visit and make contact with on my flights. Although there was only one Special Forces unit operating in my district, I would often fly to camps outside my area of responsibility. They were always glad to see me. The responsibility for the movie did create a problem.

The artillery officer at Bao Loc, Captain Terole, always had free time at the compound since he was not assigned any duties at the camp or with the ARVN because of his worthlessness. He would often tinker with the movie projector to keep himself busy. Consequently the projector seldom worked and when it did operate was always out of focus. After being given the assignment by Major Radford, I took the projector to Saigon on one of my legitimate stops and was able to trade the broken projector for a functioning projector through the Air Force supply. When I returned with the projector, I told Specialist Wheeler, who ran the projector in the evening, to not allow anyone to touch the projector except him. I had given Wheeler this order in the bar and loud enough so that everyone including Terole could clearly hear the order and understand my true meaning. Basically, I was telling Wheeler to not allow Terole to touch the projector. I emphasized the instructions with the phrase, "This is a lawful order that I expect you to obey." Naturally the order was somewhat ludicrous since it had nothing to do with our mission and it would be difficult for an enlisted man to refuse to allow a captain to do something. I hoped that just my conversation with Wheeler would be enough to discourage Terole. I was wrong.

After securing a movie from an Air Force flight that stopped at the airfield to unload some supplies, I was looking forward to the film that evening. I gave the film to Wheeler and told him to run it at 7 pm. When I arrived for my evening drink and movie at the bar, I noticed Captain Terole tinkering with the projector. He had broken this projector also. Wheeler was sitting in the bar along with Major Radford, Major White, Sergeant McClintock and Specialist Moore.

"Wheeler get over here," I barked. "I gave you a direct order that no one was to touch that projector without my approval. Who gave Captain Terole permission to touch the projector?"

Immediately I could see amusement on the face of McClintock and amassment on the faces of Radford and White. Terole merely looked up from the pieces of projector spread out on the table in front of him.

"Sir, Captain Terole just took the projector from the table and started taking it apart," Wheeler answered.

"God dam it. I don't give a fuck who took it. You were given an order not to allow anyone to touch it."

Terole had now stood up from the table and walked to where I was talking to Wheeler. "Lieutenant, no enlisted man can give me an order especially one from a Lieutenant. The projector wasn't working properly."

In a rage I turned to Terole, "Captain, I'm in charge of the projector and the movies and I'm telling you to keep you're funking hands off that projector, is that clear. It was working perfectly when I brought it here yesterday."

Terole was visibly shaken by my attack. "You can't talk to me that way."

"I'll talk to you anyway I want. Keep your funking hands off the projector."

"I'll have you court-martialed for this."

"Shit, you couldn't court-martial a turd," I said as I walked away from him before my anger made me td something more.

As I walked out of the bar with a beer in my hand, I could hear Terole complaining to Major Radford.

The following morning, as I was leaving for the airfield, Major White walked up to my jeep and told me that Major Radford wanted to speak to me. I walked to his office and sat down in front of his desk.

"Lieutenant Capozzella, Captain Terole made a complaint to me about your conduct. He says that you were disrespectful to him last night."

I almost smiled since Radford didn't seem to want to admit that he was a witness to the confrontation. "Sir, you put me in charge of the movies and projector and that idiot broke the new projector after breaking the old one also."

"I know that and I will deal with it."

"Sir, I realize that Captain Terole has no function at the base and frankly doesn't do anything here but he is a pain in the ass."

I knew that Radford would be concerned about this statement since he allowed Terole to sit around all day although I don't know what else he could do with him.

"Lieutenant, you just can't talk to him that way in front of enlisted men."

"Sir, if you promise to keep him away from me and the projector, I will not yell at him again in front of enlisted men."

Radford stood up and offered his hand as if we had struck an agreement. "Alright I shall order Captain Terole to stay away from you and the projector. Will that satisfy you?"

"Yes, sir. Also keep him away from the airfield as I don't want him near my plane either."

"OK Lieutenant, it's a deal."

That confrontation was my last contact with Terole. He not only avoided me but also kept his hands off the projector. The war was ridiculous. I had been publicly discourteous to an officer that outranked me and was able to get his commanding officer to order him to stay out of my way as if he was the offending party. In reality the war placed a premium on someone who had value and discarded those who were a liability. Terole was fortunate that he was not assigned to a combat unit in the field. He was definitely a candidate for a fragging. I doubt he would have survived the war if he had not been assigned to Bao Loc.

Later that night I was sitting on the veranda outside my room attempting to communicate with the Montagnard squad guarding the compound. They were squatting around a fire cooking their supper. One of the soldiers had his small son of about six or seven years old with him. The boy was very cute and I offered him some candy that he accepted. The soldier then asked through a Vietnamese interpreter, "Are you interested in the boy?"

"No," I responded. At first I was uncertain as to his meaning. I hoped he wasn't asking if I was interested in the boy for sexual reasons.

Instead he asked again, "Are you interested in taking my son to the United States and wish to buy him?"

"No, I just wanted to give him some candy."

"I will sell him to you for one thousand piastas."

"No, I'm really not interested."

Apparently he thought I had opened up negotiations for he then responded, "Five hundred piastas!"

"No."

"One hundred piastas!"

"Sorry I can't."

Finally he said, "I will give him to you for free if you take him to the United States."

I was touched by the soldier's desire to give up his son so that he could secure a better life than the one that awaited him in Vietnam. I explained to him that it was impossible for me to merely take the child aboard an aircraft and return to the United States. He was obviously disappointed and I felt very sorry. I gave the soldier five hundred piastas. It was less than $5.00 to purchase something for the boy. Whenever I saw the soldier after that night, he always went out of his way to flash a smile and a wave at me.

There was one other Birddog pilot assigned to Bao Loc. This pilot was a Lieutenant in the ARVN Air Force. His name was Khu Tru Huong although we called him "Crash" both behind and to his face. His nickname was obviously earned as a pilot who had already crashed three Birddogs, all on poor landings. Obviously he was a disaster as a pilot. This situation was compounded by the fact that he truly believed he was a great aviator. He dressed the part of a World War I pilot with an old fashion pilot jacket and always wore a white silk scarf wrapped around his neck. I usually ignored Crash since he was also a coward. He was afraid to fly his plane more than a mile away from Bao Loc and spent all of his flying time flying circles around the village at a very high altitude. I could never understand why the Vietnamese and American authorities continued to give him planes to wreck.

Crash often would argue with me that he could fly better than the rest of us and especially in an air-to-air dogfight. The Birddog was obviously too slow as an air-to-air combat plane but he envisioned himself the second coming of Baron von Richthofen. I finally accepted one of his challenges for a dogfight. The match was to take place directly over Bao Loc. I knew the MACV advisors would be watching and assumed that the ARVN compound would also be a spectator to the event. Crash had probably bragged to his friends that he would beat an American pilot and wanted them to see the event. I knew that I could easily beat Crash in a fight since I was both a better pilot but also because there were areas I would fly, which he would not. It was agreed that Crash would have the first option of getting on my tail and see if I could shake him off. As promised I allowed him to get behind me over the village and then I placed the plane in a hard downward drive heading away from the village. I leveled out at tree top level and headed north over the jungle. As predicted, Crash was unwilling to fly that low or over the jungle and quickly broke off the flight and headed back to Bao Loc. I continued north for a few minutes and began to climb and circled back. When I reached five thousand feet, I returned to the village where Crash was flying his normal circles. It was easy to get behind his plane and announced my arrival on his plane's frequency.

"OK, Crash it's my turn. You couldn't stay on my tail and now try to shake me off yours." I was already only 100 yards behind him and slightly higher. The elevation gave me an advantage.

Crash responded, "I thought the game was over."

"Well it was agreed that we would both have a chance to stay on the other person's tail. This is my chance or do you admit defeat?"

"Let's see what you've got Headhunter," as Crash began to twist and turn in the air. Actually Crash had the faster of the two planes since his plane did not have the rocket pods that caused my plane to fly slightly slower because of the drag on the wings. He could easily have left me in his dust but he was unwilling to fly in any configuration other than a circle in which I could maintain my position. Finally after a few minutes my plane was position directly behind Crash on a heading toward a zone that no friendly forces or people were allowed to live or travel. This was the "kill zone". I armed one of my rockets and released it in a direction that would take its flight path within fifty yards of Crash's plane and would hit after its flight in the kill zone. Crash obviously saw the rocket streak past his plane and he became completely unglued. He almost lost control and immediately began screaming over the air, "You're trying to kill me. That rocket almost hit my plane."

"Not quite Crash."

"You can't shoot a rocket at me," he yelled.

"Who was shooting a rocket at you?" I radioed.

"I just saw the rocket fly past my window."

"No Crash, I was firing at what I believe was a VC build-up."

"Bull shit!" With this statement he flew directly to the airfield and landed.

I expected him to be waiting for me when my flight was over a few hours later but he had left the area. Within a week I heard that he had asked and received a transfer to Saigon. Naturally no one felt his departure was a great loss although I heard that he made a claim through his intelligence service for recognition that he and I had jointly attacked a VC unit and killed ten VC with my rocket attack.

Two days after my return from Saigon for the penicillin, Lieutenant Burrows and I received a call over the radio that Captain Leyda was making an unannounced and unscheduled landing at the airfield and wanted us to meet with him.

Leyda landed his Birddog and walked up to where we waited off to the side of the field. He was not smiling and did not greet us with his usual friendly chatter.

Burrows broke the ice and said, "Nice to have you visit us, Captain Leyda."

"Maybe not so nice."

"Is there a problem?" Burrows asked.

"Let's forget the formalities." Leyda turned to me. "Were you in Saigon a couple of days ago?"

"Saigon? Let me think a second."

My mind raced as to what I should say. Obviously he knew something about my trip but how much was the question. I decided to play as stupid as possible without making him overly excited with anger.

"Cut the bullshit, Vince, your plane was seen there."

"How do you know it was my plane?" I continued to stall.

"Because it was seen and that stupid 'Ace of Spades' was on the fuselage."

I tried to figure an answer that would satisfy him and yet continue the coverage for those guys with the disease. "Oh you mean a couple of days ago. Sure I was in Saigon getting some supplies."

"What supplies?" Leyda asked.

He had us but I didn't know what to say. I really didn't want to take him into our confidence about the situation. "Just some stuff needed here."

"And who authorized this supply mission?"

Before I could give an answer, Burrows stepped forward. "I did."

"You gave Capozzella permission to fly to Saigon to get supplies for this compound?"

"Yes."

Leyda countered, "Who gave you the authority to change the mission of the 219th here?"

"I assumed I had the authority. Isn't that why you put me in charge?." I was really amazed as to how much guts Burrows was showing. I didn't really expect him to cover for me. Obviously Burrows had known about the mission and could have stopped me but I really never truly considered asking permission.

"Well you assumed wrong."

"What now?" Burrows asked.

"You're relieved of command here. Tomorrow I want you packed and back at Pleiku. I have another job for you."

"Sir, I was the one who flew to Saigon," I interrupted.

"Right, but Burrows let you go. He is the ranking man here from the 219th."

"I'm really the guilty party."

"Yea I believe you're probably the most guilty but that's the way it is going to be."

"How about me?" I asked.

"Vince, you're in charge."

I could hardly believe my ears. They were relieving Burrows for something I had done and then rewarding me by putting me in charge.

"Captain, this isn't right."

"Tough." Leyda walked away from us toward his plane.

I followed him and said, "Who are they sending to replace Lieutenant Burrows?"

"No one. Pleiku needs more pilots and they feel that you can handle the mission alone."

"Fine."

Leyda stopped and said, "Look Vince, you're a good pilot. Just knock off the crap and do the job assigned. Since you're our only pilot here, the buck begins and ends with you. Any slipup and you take the fall. Clear?"

"Yes. How about the extra crew chief?" I asked.

"Send one of them back with Burrows."

"Right."

Leyda stopped as he was climbing into his plane. "Be careful of the Air Force pilots here. It was one of them that contacted Major Lust and told him about the flight to Saigon."

"That bastard."

"That may well be but obviously they don't like you. See you later and be safe," he responded. Leyda climbed into his plane and returned to Pleiku.

The following day Burrows left with Private Moore. I was finally able to get rid of Moore and to keep Spec 4 Wheeler as my official crew chief. As they were boarding the plane I could not help but take a least shot at Private Moore.

"Private, I advised our command concerning you laxity with aircraft and they promised me that they would give you special supervision."

Moore turned to me, his face flush with rage. I could tell that he wanted to say something to anger me but he perhaps thought better of his position.

"Thanks Lieutenant, I'm sure we will meet again."

"I doubt it, but if we do, you will probably end up in a stockade."

That meeting was the last I ever saw of Moore. I heard later that after only a month back at Pleiku the command grew tired of his attitude and shipped him off to another assignment in Korea.

Although I hated to see Burrows leave especially under these circumstances, I was delighted to have total freedom in terms of flying. I was free to fly whenever and wherever I wanted without any interference from anyone. The Bao Loc command had no authority over me and Pleiku was a long way from here. Actually I flew more missions with the Bao Loc MACV advisors and the Special Forces unit then I did before. The situation was made even sweeter when the Air Force pilots were ordered to return to Saigon for further assignment. It seems as though their talents were needed where they would do the most good, in a jet fighter. Their departure did not mean any lost to the mission as I was certain as to my ability to maintain coverage in the province and attacks against any VC movement. My only concern was the loss of companionship in the area that did offer a degree of security. It was difficult to contact someone if the plane was low or I had to make an emergency landing.

After Burrows departure things returned to a somewhat normal pace. I continued my two a day flights but noticed a decrease in VC activity. One incident prior to the departure of the Air Force pilots had unusual implications. When looking back, it always made me feel good about my time in Bao Loc. I was flying my daily morning mission when I observed a group of approximately thirty Vietnamese dressed in black and carrying what appeared, from an altitude of 1500 feet above the terrain, to be rifles. What made the situation even more suspicious was the fact the group was in the automatic kill zone established by the Vietnamese High Command.

I immediately flew to an altitude of 3000 feet above the terrain to enable my radio transmission in the call for an air strike. I was able to contact a flight of three American jets to the south of the province who promised to be at my location in 15 minutes. In the meantime, Captain Taylor Brigg, the Air Force Birddog pilot also flew to my location. I was becoming concerned about the target as they didn't seem to be acting like typical VC. They neither took cover nor attempted to lie down to avoid being seen. They were now situated on a road near a large truck with a great deal of jungle cover nearby. I couldn't understand why they didn't melt into the jungle. By now with two planes circling overhead, it was obvious they had been seen.

The three jets arrived and the flight leader contacted me. "Headhunter One One, this is Copra Six. Please identify target and mark their location."

I was now beginning to be worried that I had made a serious mistake and finally responded, "Copra Six, wait one while I take a closer look."

I put the nose of the Birddog down into a steep dive and flew away from the target over the jungle canopy. Upon reaching a few feet above the trees I turned the plane to intercept the target. Within a couple of minutes I flew over the target. A group of men and women were climbing into the truck and instead of rifles; they were carrying farming tools such as rakes and hoes. They looked up but didn't seem to be concerned and continued with the loading. I began a steady climb.

"Copra Six, this is Headhunter One One, mission is terminated, I say again, mission is terminated. Target is friendly."

"Headhunter One One, this is Copra Six, are you sure you want the mission scrubbed?"

"Affirmative, Copra Six."

"Roger, have a good one and call us again when you get another target."

The jets departed and I returned to my mission. Later that day at our routine get together at the bar in the compound, I met with Captain Brigg and Captain Laird. Captain Brigg brought up the situation with my friendly target.

"You looked like a total fool today, Lieutenant. You don't call for an air strike and then call it off when they arrive."

"Well, from my altitude they looked like VC and they were in the kill zone," I responded.

"If they were in the kill zone, why didn't you attack them?"

"Because they weren't VC."

"What difference does that make?" countered Brigg.

"To me, a big difference. What's the point of killing innocent Vietnamese simply because they're in the wrong place?"

Brigg continued, "I would have killed them all. You certainly were justified and now you look like an idiot. We'd be better off if all the Vietnamese were dead."

"You mean, free the Vietnamese from the communist by killing everyone? Now that is one intelligent position."

"Why not?"

"I'm not going to discuss it any more if you can't see the point."

With that statement I walked away and went outside the bar with my drink. This idiot couldn't understand the humanity of sparing the innocent. I also had another motive for not attacking people who are not VC. For every innocent killed by the United States, we create two or three family members who become VC. Unfortunately in the war there were thousands of men like Brigg and it was this moment that the seeds of my questioning the American involvement were sowed. I didn't see any difference between a Vietnamese family and an American family. If someone was to kill one of my children and they were innocent of the situation, I would certainly become an avowed enemy of the killers. I don't think many Americans ever understood this problem. Too often we looked at the Vietnamese as having different morals and motivation than our own but in reality all humanity acts very similar to each other. I witnessed Vietnamese families acting with the same motivation as our American families and displaying the same grief and rage as we would have displayed.

Fortunately, the Air Force command ordered Captain Brigg and Captain Laird to another assignment flying jets. They left two days after the incident involving the civilian targets. Their departure had nothing to do with the incident and was due to the fact that the Air Force was finally realizing that the Army pilots could perform the mission of locating and marking targets. It was a foolish waste of training to take jet trained pilots and put them in Birddogs where they were frankly out of their element.

Chapter 18 – The Roadblock & the CIA

One of the issues that continued to fester upon me was the unwillingness of the ARVN command to pursue the VC. Since my arrival in Bao Loc in July, I had observed what appeared to be a VC concentration approximately 20 miles south of the town on the main highway to Saigon. To reach this spot I had to cross a fairly high chain of mountains. They seemed to be enclosed in clouds most of the time. The highway ran through these mountains in a steep valley with the road situated about a third of the way up the mountains. Often I had to fly through the valley to get to the target because of the low ceiling. I detested flying through the valley because the VC were often situated above my plane that made their shooting more effective. Fortunately they never mounted any large caliber weapons in the valley on such occasions.

When I first observed the VC problem, it appeared as though a large group of delivery trucks were parked on the highway. I flew low over a line of vehicles and could see about twenty trucks were on the road with a large group of people near the first truck. Every ten to twenty minutes a truck would continue the trip north on the road thru the pass. This group of people milling around the lead truck were always dressed in the typical Vietcong black pajama uniform and were carrying rifles. The first time I flew low over the convoy and the suspected Vietcong, they began firing at my plane with their rifles. I was very lucky to escape harm since the area was open and not a jungle setting. It was apparently a checkpoint to inspect vehicles for weapons and a VC extortion problem. I discovered later, that depending on the size of the vehicle, drivers were required to pay a fee to pass the roadblock.

At the next meeting of the MACV and ARVN commands, I reported the roadblock. Immediately the ARVN command denied such a roadblock existed although I was just as forceful in stressing the point that it did in fact exist. Each week I would fly over the roadblock at about 2,000 feet. I couldn't attack the roadblock because of the numerous innocent truck drivers and their vehicles. Instead I would drop a smoke bomb out the window near the checkpoint. The VC would always grab their weapons and shoot at the plane that was too high to be hit by these weapons. This comedy continued for three months with my harassing tactics against the VC, the continued reporting of the roadblock at the monthly intelligence meeting with the ARVN and the ARVN command's continued denial of its existence. Finally I submitted a written report through the MACV intelligence channel. Within a month I received a response.

The response to my report was the arrival of an intelligence officer from Saigon. The officer arrived on the monthly supply plane at the end of October 1965. Kermit Zanmiller was a young man in his early 20's and wore green fatigues without any indication of rank. I was told by McClintock that Zanmiller was an employee of the CIA. The agency provided intelligence assessments for the Army. They did hold Army rank but did not tell people their rank. This secrecy meant they could hold any rank from private to senior officer. I suspected that Zanmiller's rank was closer to private. McClintock's attitude toward Zanmiller showed his contempt for his position.

Upon meeting Zanmiller, I attempted to be cordial since his mission was to confirm my report concerning the VC roadblock and I had never had contact with the CIA previously. On the day following his arrival, I briefed him on the situation and agreed to fly him over the area. When we arrived over the checkpoint, there were over thirty trucks lining the road. I dropped my usual smoke bomb on the position and about ten VC began to fire their rifles at the plane. Zanmiller became quite restless and insisted I stop this maneuver and return to the base.

That evening the MACV and ARVN intelligence briefing was held at the MACV base. As usual I gave my assessment of the VC roadblock and called on Zanmiller to verify my report.

Zanmiller stood up and said, "I'm not sure what I saw."

I immediately jumped to my feet and said, "Did you see the line of trucks stopped on the road?"

"Yes, but they may have had a mechanical problem with the lead vehicle."

"So one vehicle has a problem and thirty have to stop?"

In a deadpan voice he responded, "I guess so."

I continued my challenge of his report. "Did you see the VC shooting at the plane?"

"No, all I saw was a group of people milling around."

"I guess that milling around scared you so much that you asked me to leave the area."

"What do you mean by that," Zanmiller shouted as he rose and took a step toward me?

Quickly Major Redford, rose and situated himself between Zanmiller and me and said, "Well, we have two different reports. What now?"

"If the thirty trucks were lined together because of a breakdown then tomorrow certainly there should be only at most one or two trucks at this location. I will take Zanmiller and return for another look in the morning," I said.

Zanmiller immediately countered my suggestion, "Sorry I have to return to Saigon and wouldn't have the time for another flight with you."

"Bullshit!" I then sat down with the realization that I was wasting my time.

The ARVN commander, Colonel Teo interjected, "We still have only the report of Lieutenant Capozzella. It is contrary to our own reports and now the report of the representative of the American Army's intelligence from Saigon. We will continue to monitor the situation since I don't know what else to do."

I countered, "Colonel we can mount a force of your troops to go to the checkpoint and conduct an operation."

"I see no point in that conclusion, Lieutenant. This meeting is adjourned."

"Sir, if your command is unwilling to act upon my observations regarding the enemy, then I can see no logical reason to fly missions to assist your troops. It's obvious, I cannot be believed."

This statement was merely a veiled threat to withhold air support for the ARVN command. I suspected this maneuver might motivate them to action. However, Colonel Teo made no response and the meeting was over.

After the departure of our Vietnamese allies, I went to town to have dinner at my restaurant. I realized that Zanmiller had lied to provide a face saving alternative to the ARVN. I couldn't understand why the CIA would even bother to send someone to Bao Loc if they had decided to cover the situation. It was this type of farce within both the American and ARVN commands that worked against our best efforts to be successful. We were more concerned about the ARVN's feelings than winning the war while they were interested in doing as little as possible that could jeopardize their job or their lives. Upon my return to the MACV compound I went to the bar for a few drinks. Zanmiller was at the bar and walked up to me. He made no mention of the flight, the roadblock or our disagreement.

He asked, "When can you give me a ride back to Saigon?"

Sensing an opportunity for revenge, I said, "Sorry, my plane's not a taxi."

"It was my understanding that you would support my mission here."

"Right. And I did support your mission by flying you to a road jam. No one ever mentioned that I had the responsibility to chauffer you around Vietnam after finishing the mission," I said.

"Look I could order you to fly me."

The Bao Loc group was listening with some amusement to our discussion. I responded, "Zanmiller, unless you can show me a rank on your collar higher than this" as I pointed to my Lieutenant bars, "your order doesn't mean shit to me."

"Listen we aren't allowed to show our rank. I could be a captain and outrank you," responded Zanmiller.

"Yea, and you could be a private trying to show your importance." I turned and walked away from him.

"Does this mean you won't give me the ride?"

"Now you're really getting smart."

Turning to Captain Moyer, Zanmiller asked, "When is the next plane due in here?"

Smiling, Captain Moyer responded, "In about five or six days."

Zanmiller turned to me and said, "What the hell am I suppose to do for a week here?"

"Well, if you're in a hurry, I'm sure the ARVN Colonel will loan you a jeep and a driver and you can drive to Saigon. Perhaps on the way you can stop and give that truck driver with the mechanical problem a lift." I said to the roar of laughter from those listening to the conversation.

At this point Zanmiller stumped from the bar and returned to his temporary quarters. He remained in Bao Loc for the next six days when he boarded a flight with our supply plane. His intrigues while awaiting a flight, however, did not stop with the roadblock situation. While eating dinner about two days after his departure, Tru Mat Kim, the owner of the restaurant approached me with an intriguing story. Zanmiller was aware I ate my meals at the restaurant and approached Kim with a proposition. Kim was asked to keep an eye on me and to discuss politics since Zanmiller questioned my loyalty to the United States. In return for his services, Kim would be paid $200 per month and was given an address and telephone number to contact with the information. Both Kim and I laughed about the absurd offer that was made even more absurd by the fact that Zanmiller made no mention of information regarding the VC. It was difficult for me to comprehend that the CIA was more interested in an American flyer that was upset with the CIA for falsifying military information than they were interested in the enemy. That situation only highlighted in my mind the opinion the United States would not be successful in Vietnam.

Chapter 19 – Dalat & Mistakes

In early November 1965, I decided to take an unofficial break in Dalat. Although Dalat had no American troops assigned to the city, a small number of ARVN were stationed there. However, I never heard of them taking part in the war. The city's fairly large airfield was situated on the top of what looked like an old volcano. Actually the rim of the old volcano surrounded the airfield and was about 50 feet higher than the field. The city was beautiful and the area quite calm. It was a going joke that both the VC and the Americans refrained from military operations near Dalat and used it as an R & R location. When I arrived early Saturday morning, the field was already crowded with two Birddogs and six Hueys. Obviously there were other pilots and crews with the same intensions as my own. I spent the day walking through the city and looking for any bargains. Finally I settled in a nice bar were I met two other pilots that I knew from Pleiku. Naturally we became quite drunk before the night was over.

Throughout my stay in Vietnam I was proud of the fact that I didn't cheat on my wife. This situation was motivated by both my desire to remain faithful and my fear of contracting the many venereal diseases. It was on this trip that I came the closest to breaking my personal vow. We were approached by a number of available Vietnamese girls at the bar. As usual I would offer the prostitute a price that was ridiculously low and inevitably the girl would grow frustrated with the price and stalk away calling me "Cheap Charlie". However on this occasion, a prostitute who called herself "Alice" accepted my ridiculous offer. I was caught in a dilemma. I didn't want to now refuse and show the other pilots that I wasn't interested in a beautiful Vietnamese woman and yet I had no desire to break my vow. The prostitute literally dragged me from the bar and led me to an upstairs room that she obviously used for this type of liaison. My mind was scrambling for a logical way to get out of the situation and I decided to merely go to the room, pay her the agreed upon fee and stay a reasonable time before returning to the bar. When we walked into the room, I sat on the end of the bed. Alice encouraged me to take my clothes off and probably concluded that I was shy when I hesitated. The room held only a bed, a hotbox clothes hamper and a dresser. The prostitute took off her black dress and walked to the hamper to hang the dress. When she opened the door that had a full-length mirror on its front, it suddenly fell off its hinges and landed squarely on Alice's toes. She screamed in pain and crumbled to the bed. I was fairly certain her toes were broken. Somehow I felt that this accident was an omen from God to remain faithful. I threw some money on the bed and made a hasty retreat to the bar. I told the other pilots of the incident. They thought the story was humorous.

I stayed the night in Dalat in a local hotel. At approximately 4 am I heard a series of at least four explosions. I awoke and looked out the window but didn't see anything unusual and did not hear any gunfire. I was armed with both my pistol and M-16 and was not worried about any attack. I went back to bed and upon waking at 8 am went to the airfield. When I arrived at the field, I was shocked at the scene. Four Hueys and one Birddog were completely destroyed by explosives set by the VC. Fortunately my plane was spared. I knew that the Army would soon be investigating the attack and the field would be swarming with people. I jumped into my plane and flew directly to Bao Loc and never heard anything about my involvement in the attack at Dalat. There were reports that a number of pilots were in serious trouble for being at Dalat without orders or a mission. I wondered how they would explain why they took an aircraft without orders to a location not occupied by American military personnel and partied. I was very fortunate to escape this incident and promised myself to avoid a similar situation.

To my dismay, Captain Moyer's tour of duty in Vietnam was over by the first week of November. His replacement, Captain Seth Jamison, was a West Pointer and seemed to walk around with a large chip on his shoulder. I assumed, as a black man, that he had ample reason to be aggressive with white people but also thought he should, at least, give them the opportunity to be decent. Jamison did not become a close friend or drinking partner. He also arrived at Bao Loc with Master Sergeant John Davis who assumed duties as ranking enlisted man. I knew that Sgt. McClintock was due to be transferred out of Bao Loc to the States at the end of November and wondered how these two men could possibly replace our best combat personnel. Captain Jamison took an instant dislike for McClintock whom he referred to on at least two occasions as "the old dinosaur". McClintock merely accepted the criticism with a grunt and avoided both of the new men. I explained to Jamison about McClintock's military achievements in WWII and Korea as well as his steady performance against the Vietcong. Jamison merely stated that McClintock was past his prime and should be put out to pasture. I always thought Jamison was intimidated by McClintock and wanted to keep him as far away as possible so that no comparisons could be made.

Captain Jamison decided to lead a small unit of American personnel and a company of ARVN into the countryside as an orientation exercise. I suspected that he really wanted to see if he was up to the physical demands and the quality of our allies. I promised to give him logistical support. As soon as he was traveling into the interior of the jungle off the road, I would provide a daily contact to report his situation. Jamison had decided not to take McClintock on the mission. I knew this decision was foolish since McClintock was the most experienced man in these operations.

The group was trucked about ten miles to the east of Bao Loc and then marched straight into the deepest jungle. On the second day I contacted Jamison and discovered everything was going as anticipated with no sign of contact with the VC. On the fourth day of the mission on my daily contact, Jamison advised that Master Sergeant Davis had experienced a heart attack and would be moved by stretcher to the nearest location available for helicopter pick-up.

Jamison said, "Headhunter One One, where is the nearest open ground suitable for a helicopter to pick-up the Master Sergeant."

Jamison's location was unfortunately in heavy jungle growth and I could not see his personnel from the air even when directly over their location at tree top level. There was a decent opening about a days march to the north. This direction was away from the road and Bao Loc.

I answered his question, "Drumbeat Five, there is a location about five miles north on a heading of about 330 degrees. You should be able to march there by tomorrow morning"

"Do you know our location, Headhunter One One?" Jamison's voice sounded quite agitated.

"Drumbeat Five, I'm fairly positive I have your exact location but I shall make another pass and you give me a 'now' when I pass overhead."

I turned the plane and drove to the location I was sure where Jamison was located. At the exact spot he yelled, "Now."

"Drumbeat Five, I have your location pin-pointed. Take heading of 330 degrees for about five miles."

I realized that this information was not what Jamison wanted to hear as he instinctively wanted to head back home to safety and I was sending him in the opposite direction. However, if the issue was to obtain the earliest medical evacuation possible, then my choice was correct.

"Headhunter One One, do you know how to read a map?"

I attempted to ignore the attack but responded, "This is Headhunter One One. I've been flying for two years with maps and haven't gotten lost yet."

"I think the shortest way to a landing zone is straight south."

"Drumbeat Five, there is nothing to the south but jungle and it will take you three days to hit something." I did not want to give any VC listening on the frequency an opportunity to pin point Jamison's location.

"Headhunter One One, I'm heading south and request you give us a flyby in the morning with direction to the nearest landing spot in that direction."

"Roger Drumbeat Five, I will contact you tomorrow morning." I flew off to another part of the province since circling vainly over Jamison would only give the VC an opportunity to discover his location. In my opinion his stupidity might cost the Master Sergeant his life but he was in command in the jungle.

In the morning I returned to Jamison's vicinity and discovered with conversations with him that he had only proceeded about traveling two or three miles from his previous day's location. I asked, "How is the Sergeant doing, Drumbeat Five?"

"He's doing OK, Headhunter One One. Can you give us a direction to the closest landing zone?"

"I hate to tell you this Drumbeat Five but your closest location is still to your north."

"God dam it, that's not possible," yelled Jamison.

"Look Drumbeat, I can only give you what I know to be correct and you are traveling in the wrong direction."

Recovering himself, Jamison radioed, "Headhunter One One, we will proceed to the south and expect you to make contact tomorrow morning."

"Roger that Drumbeat."

I thought to myself that the Captain was one dumb son-of-a-bitch whose animosity against anyone who disagreed with him would probably cost a man his life. There was little I could do to help since I didn't outrank him. What made matters worst was Jamison's refusal to take McClintock on the mission since he didn't think he would be able to handle the rigors of the march. We all knew this logic to be stupid since McClintock had been on numerous such missions over the last year. In reality, Jamison didn't want people to think there was someone on the mission who knew more than him. I couldn't imagine a more illogical reasoning. If I were on the ground in the jungle in the vicinity of the VC, the first person I would want with me would be McClintock.

I returned to Jamison's location the next morning and determined that he had traveled only three miles since the previous contact. He was still 8 to 10 miles from the road leading back to Bao Loc and at the pace he was moving would take at least two more days.

"Headhunter One One, can you give me a fix to a suitable location for a pick-up now?"

I hated to even answer as I was now truly worried about the Master Sergeant. "Drumbeat Five, your nearest location is the highway and I anticipate at your present speed will take another two or three full days of travel."

"That can't be possible. I know there must be a location nearby."

"Sorry Drumbeat, I truly can't see any suitable location and I assume you must now realize that since I can easily find you that I can also find you on a map."

"Alright Headhunter, do you have any suggestion."

I knew that response took a lot for Jamison to say. "Drumbeat Five, if the patient is in need of emergency medical treatment, I suggest you clear a spot in the jungle for a line to be dropped to pick up the passenger without landing the helicopter."

"Alright Headhunter One One, I will begin clearing a spot. Come back in about six hours to see if it is clear enough for a pick-up and if OK to contact Med Evac."

"Roger, Drumbeat see you in six."

I returned to Bao Loc and immediately arranged for the Med Evac to accompany me to Jamison's location at the agreed upon time. Time was critical and I didn't want to risk waiting another day or even an extra hour now that Jamison was taking the appropriate action. Upon our return to the unit's location, the American and ARVN troops had cleared an area of about ten by ten feet. This was ample room to lower a line to pick up Master Sergeant Davis and the pick-up came off without any problem. He was quickly transported to a hospital in Saigon where he recovered although I never saw him again. As for Drumbeat Five, it took the unit another two days to reach the road where I had trucks waiting to transport them back to Bao Loc. Needless to say the command was literally physically broken when they returned. Jamison did not speak of the situation again and I wondered if he would take my advice next time on an operation.

Within a week of Jamison's fiasco on his first mission with the ARVN, I was advised that both he and Colonel Teo had decided to send a detachment of troops south to the VC roadblock. At a mission-planning meeting I was shocked when it was decided to send a company of troops via truck to the location. I argued that the trucks would have to pass through the steep valley on a narrow road built on the side of the mountain. Stressing the point that no ARVN or American troops had been on this road for over two years and the VC controlled the mountains, an ambush was highly likely. Jamison argued that an ambush was unlikely if I provided cover with my plane. I argued that my coverage could not guarantee a safe journey as the VC were skilled in camouflage and my plane had only limited ability to spot them.

I suggested, "Sir, only a small unit such as a platoon is needed for the operation. They should also be airlifted to selected strike locations by helicopter before dawn to surprise the VC."

Jamison countered, "Lieutenant this is not a priority mission and obtaining helicopters will be impossible."

I asked, "Captain Jamison, have you made an attempt to secure helicopters?"

"Lieutenant, I don't need to make such a request since both Colonel Teo and I have decided that a company sized force is needed and we cannot obtain enough choppers to move that many men. Moving them by truck is the only logical and acceptable method of travel."

"Captain, I've flown through that valley many times. The area is controlled by the VC and they would need only a handful of men to stop the convoy since the road is narrow and movement would be limited."

Colonel Teo interjected, "Lieutenant, my lookouts in the valley have assured me that there are no VC either in the valley or on the road south of the valley."

This statement surprised me since I have never heard of such lookouts previously and doubted the accuracy of the statement. "Colonel, if such lookouts really exist then the should be able to observe what I see every time I fly in the valley. The risk of sending a convoy through there is extremely high and in my opinion very foolhardy."

"Colonel Teo and I believe the risk is acceptable, Lieutenant. You will provide coverage for the movement beginning at 0800 hours tomorrow," replied Jamison.

"Will you be leading the convoy, Sir?" I asked Colonel Teo.

He flushed but immediately regained his composure and said, "This is a company size operation. I shall remain with my regiment while Captain Jamison and our company commander lead the expedition."

Captain Jamison ended the conversation and said to me, "0800 hours."

I shrugged my shoulders and said with resignation, "I'll be there, sir."

I watched from the ground as the ten trucks, two jeeps and one armored troop carrier were loaded. A jeep with a 50-caliber machine gun lead the way with the armored troop carrier also with a 50-caliber machine gun followed the jeep. Captain Jamison sat in the first jeep and I had to admire his courage although I questioned his sanity. Naturally, neither Colonel Teo nor his American counterpart, Major Radford were participating in the mission. On this movement Captain Jamison had agreed to allow Sergeant McClintock to accompany the mission although he was placed in the jeep that was the last vehicle in the convoy. McClintock had expressed doubts as to the probability of success and I'm sure he didn't object on this situation to being in the rear of the convoy.

I gave the convoy a thirty-minute head start because I didn't want to begin flying in the valley too soon and possibly alert the VC. The weather was as usual terrible this early in the morning over the mountains and I couldn't see the tops of the mountain peaks. They were immersed in a thick layer of fog. I flew down the valley with the sides of the mountains looming above the plane and silently wondered if the VC would shoot down at me. The valley was also covered with a haze. It made even this attempt limited. My crew chief, Wheeler, was my observer and he had opened the cockpit windows for better sight and had also stuck his M-16 rifle out to provide fire support, if needed.

I made two passes each way through the valley when the convoy began its climb up the road. The road passage was about a mile long. I could not see any sign of VC activity although this negative observation did not reassure be that the VC did not exist. I had a deep premonition that the convoy would be hit and felt guilty since it was my continued reports regarding the roadblock that had set this terrible chain of events in motion. The convoy had gotten only a quarter of a mile through the valley when the VC sprung their attack. Jamison was hit with the first opening of fire by an automatic weapon. I had already flown past the ambush location and was not over the convoy when the firing began. I was unable to fly a 180-degree turn until I was completely out of the valley. Upon my return I could see the convoy was in trouble and the troops had jumped out of the vehicles and were either fighting back along a ditch or running down the road toward Bao Loc. Three trucks had driven off the road and lay smashed to pieces on the valley floor.

"Switchblade, this is Headhunter One One, what is your situation?"

Only McClintock responded, "Headhunter, this is Mac, we have a funking mess down here. That asshole Jamison is down and the ARVN are looking to diddy out of here."

"I'll do what I can for you Switchback. Take care."

Unfortunately I now had to fly again to the north side of the pass to turn the plane around to again assist the troops. On this run through the valley I unleashed four of my rockets and hoped they would not inadvertently hit our troops. The rockets did have some affect, I'm sure, on the VC as Wheeler began an uninterrupted attack with his weapon toward the VC. There was no sense in calling for air support from the Air Force as the jets would be unable to see the target due to the cloud coverage and the mountains. Again I flew down the valley did a 180 degree turn and back again for my second attack. I fired my final four rockets as I noticed that five of the trucks were backing down the road with the ARVN troops running ahead of them. I made one more pass to the south and a return trip firing with my "grease gun" and Wheeler's weapon. The fighting appeared to be over as I made this final pass. I could see our troops were tending to the wounded and killed and were carrying them down the road. The fact that the ARVN bothered to see to the wounded and dead was a little surprising but I assume they were unable to flee to the rear and forced to seek cover in the vicinity of the ambush. Therefore, when the VC pulled back, the ARVN were still reluctantly at the scene.

I continued to fly over the retreating column as they walked down the mountain road to the lowlands where the convoy vehicles that survived were waiting to transport them back to Bao Loc. After landing at the airfield I went back to our compound and was there when McClintock returned with the wounded, Captain Jamison. I felt sad over his wound but I was unable to pretend that I was deeply touched since he had by his own actions lead to this fiasco. My lack of feelings toward Jamison was motivated by his attitude and also by his uselessness in a combat situation. I would certainly have felt terrible if Moyer or McClintock had been killed or wounded since they had value in a combat zone. Stupidity and arrogance had little value.

I firmly believe that if Jamison had used a little common sense and military judgment instead of trying to placate the ARVN, the ambush would have been avoided. Jamison needed only to arrange for the airlifting of a platoon of troops in the early dawn hours to the vicinity of the roadblock. The VC troops were not strong enough to withstand an attack by 30 to 60 men. However, I also knew that even if the attack on the road block was successful the VC would simply have waited for the troops to be pulled out and reestablish the block or move it into their mountain sanctuary.

At the joint meeting with the ARVN commanders on the following day, I was a little shocked by the announcement of Colonel Teo. He said, "As recommended by intelligence sources of both out allies and our own troops, forces of the Republic of Vietnam have successfully attacked and eliminated a road block established by the Vietcong on Highway 14. I want to congratulate all those personnel who took part in the action. Major Tam estimates that our forces killed over 100 Vietcong with only minimum casualties to our own troops. Unfortunately Captain Jamison was wounded but performed bravely as he assisted Major Tam's attack on the VC roadblock. I recommend the American forces recommend Captain Jamison for a medal for his bravery. Well done gentlemen."

Major White stood up and announced, "I concur with the assessment of Colonel Teo and will notify MACV command of the success of all our troops in this splendid achievement. Major Radford advised me that he intends to recommend Captain Jamison for the Silver Star." He then looked at me and asked, "Does anyone else have anything to add to our report?"

I stood and said, "I have nothing more to add to the reporting of the success although I wonder how the roadblock was eliminated without getting to within five mile of the location?" As I sat I wondered if anyone had picked up on my sarcasm.

It was difficult to restrain myself but I realized that other than provoking both the ARVN and the MACV leadership, my true report would have accomplished very little. Actually everyone with the exception of McClintock and I were satisfied with the operation. The ARVN and MACV could report to their respective command structure their success on destroying a large number of enemy troops and a roadblock. They would magnify their success with each command supporting the other and thereby earn for themselves some measure of complements and reports in their personnel files to perhaps assist them for their next promotion. The alternative was to admit both a military defeat and their own incompetence.

In reality the operation was a dismal failure. Our forces lost over fifty personnel killed, wounded or missing including Captain Jamison plus numerous weapons and vehicles destroyed and abandoned. The VC still controlled the mountain pass and continued with the roadblock. Prudently I never mentioned the roadblock at a joint intelligence meeting again. I continued to report its existence in my own reports to my own command although I had no idea what they did with this information. Life continued at Bao Loc as it had before the defeat and eventually Captain Benjamin Russell, who would distinguish himself as a competent leader with limited military energy, replaced Captain Jamison. I never had the opportunity to become very friendly with Russell and neither the MACV nor ARVN mounted another operation or patrol again while I was stationed at Bao Loc.

The other casualty of the ambush was an American that wasn't even on the mission. After Jamison was wounded, McClintock and the survivors attempted to provide first aid. They discovered the first aid kits did not have the required three morpheme syringes. None of the kits that had been issued that morning by medic Specialist 4 Joseph had the syringes. When the survivors returned to Bao Loc, an inspection of the unit's medical kits determined that the entire morpheme supply was missing. During interview, Joseph admitted that he had taken the morpheme for "a medical condition." He was immediately transferred to Saigon for some disciplinary measures and perhaps some type of cure although he was probably just dishonorably discharged.

My crew chief and I returned to the VC roadblock a few days after the ambush and the VC were at it again. I flew over their checkpoint at 2000 feet above the ground, too high for their rifles. When I saw they were shooting. I dropped a couple of smoke grenades and saw that they didn't bother to run as they had in the past. Today, however, I had a surprise for them. I flew down to 1500 feet above the terrain and Wheeler dropped two class jars out of the rear window while I dropped one jar out my window. The jars were big enough to hold a grenade fairly securely and the pins were pulled before the jars thrown out the windows. They landed about 75 yards from the VC and I could see some of them running toward the jars to perhaps inspect them. The jars had broken upon impact and released their armed grenades. They exploded within a few seconds. I felt some measure of satisfaction as I could see at least three of the VC lying on the ground as casualties. I flew over the checkpoint again and rocked my wings in a victory salute although I doubt they understood.

Mt enthusiasm for my duties began to diminish the longer I stayed at Bao Loc. With the exception of my assists to the Special Forces group operating in the district, there was little presence of our forces to stop the VC. Captain Larson had established a temporary base at the Vietnamese village we had visited a few months earlier. A wall of brush and barbed wire now surrounded the village although the VC did not make an attempt to penetrate its defenses. Larson even had the road leading into the village made more accommodating for small aircraft like the Birddog and I would visit the compound once or twice every week. On these visits I often brought Larson a couple of cases of beer for which they were grateful.

My crew chief, Specialist Wheeler was my next incident in Vietnam. We got along very well and he often flew as my observer on my daily missions. I taught him how to fly the plane from the rear seat. The knowledge gave him something to do to break up the monotony of the days. In return I was able to relax in the plane. I found that the loud engine noise and constant vibration had the effect of making me become terribly sleepy after about thirty minutes of flying time. To compensate for this sleepiness I would light a cigarette every fifteen minutes while flying. There were no restrictions about smoking in the Birddog either from safety or military considerations and I found that the anticipation and the smoking helped keep me awake. Unfiltered Lucky Strikes were the cigarette of choice although I would also smoke Pall Malls or in a pinch, Camels. When there wasn't much to see or do while I was flying with Wheeler, he would take the controls and I would light up and just relax in the front seat.

Wheeler began to complain of being tired and experienced alternating periods of feeling cold then hot. The new medic at Bao Loc was satisfactory in the performance of handing out minor drugs but was woefully inadequate as a medical practitioner. At first he diagnosed the problem as the flu but since Wheeler seldom showed any temperature above normal, this diagnosis was discounted. We were all at a loss to explain his condition until I finally announced after two days of symptoms that I was fairly certain that Wheeler was suffering from malaria. Without contacting my command I flew Wheeler to the costal Army base at Phan Thiet where I brought him to a local Army medical facility. The facility agreed to take Wheeler in as a patient and that they would contact me in a couple of days.

I decided to take a short tour of the base and naturally went directly to the Officer's Club. When I walked into the bar at about 2 pm it was already crowded with officers having a drink. As I walked past the men standing at the bar some one yelled, "Hey Vince."

I turned and saw to my amazement my long time college roommate, Brian Eddy standing at the bar. I had not seen Eddy in over two years since he attended my marriage ceremony as an usher. Here he was now in the uniform of an Army lieutenant assigned to the Signal Corps.

Eddy and I had met during our first year at Clarkson College of Technology in Potsdam, New York in 1958. As roommates we shared everything including our failure to obtain high grades at college although he eventually was able to complete his education. We eventually joined the same fraternity, Theta Chi, where we again continued as roommates. Eddy and I had both joined the Army ROTC at college. I had to admit that he took the ROTC studies much more serious than I and upon completing college had been required to join the Army. It was Eddy who arranged for my reunion with my future wife when I returned to visit the college after I had enlisted in the Army in 1962.

Consequently, seeing him at an obscure Army base in Vietnam was quite a pleasant surprise. We spent a few hours drinking at the bar and reminiscing about the good old days at Clarkson before I finally announced that I had to return to the airfield to return to my base at Bao Loc. I never saw Eddy again and assumed he made it through the war without any problems although I did take the time to look up his name at the Vietnam memorial in Washington, D.C. to see if he was included as a casualty. He wasn't on the list.

I returned to Bao Loc without Wheeler and conducted the minor aircraft checks on the plane that even I could manage. I figured that I could proceed without my mechanic for about four or five days without any difficulty and assumed I would be contacted in a day or two by either the medical facility or Wheeler. Finally on the fifth day, not receiving any word from either source, I flew back to Phan Thiet. I was shocked when I returned to the medical facility to discover that Wheeler had been evacuated to a hospital ship and would not be returning to Vietnam. Apparently my diagnosis of malaria was far off base. The doctor advised me that Wheeler had two different types of venereal diseases. I had heard through the grapevine that there was one hospital ship designated as taking only patients with venereal diseases and that some of the diseases were literally immune to penicillin. I wondered what would happen to someone who contacted such a strain of venereal disease. Apparently if the rumor was true, the U.S. military had no intention of releasing these people on an unsuspecting American population and starting an epidemic for which there was no cure. I never saw or heard from Wheeler again and do not know his fate. My fate was quite different as I had to break the news to my command at Pleiku that Wheeler was no longer in Vietnam and had been evacuated some three or four days earlier and that I was flying my plane without the benefit of a crew chief.

Captain Leyda again flew down to Bao Loc where he and I held an afternoon meeting. He complained about my failure to notify my command of administrative details although he also said the command was pleased with my flying performance. Major Lust felt that I was not showing total respect for the officers of the unit by my failure to keep them abreast of the situation in Bao Loc regarding my crew chief. I had to disagree somewhat with this argument since I only had contact with Captain Leyda and occasionally with

Major Lust. It was difficult to have respect for a commander who when visiting my base would land, taxi to the takeoff position, and with the engine still running would toss my pay out the window and immediately take off. I let this complaint slip by and hung my head dutifully until Leyda was finished.

"Look, Vince, try not to get into anymore trouble while you're here."

"Captain, I'll do my best but there are a lot of people who are either stupid or just plain cowards."

"Unofficially I agree but you still have to deal with them in a respectful manner. Will you give it a try?"

I answered, "No problem."

"Vince, you will probably be rotated to Pleiku after the first of the year anyway. The CO thinks that it would be better for morale and efficiency to change all the pilots who are at the remote assignments with the guys from Pleiku and visa versa."

"Well, it makes no difference as to where I fly. There might be more action in the north anyway."

Captain Leyda got up from his seat and said, "Fine."

As he was leaving I asked, "Captain any word about my R & R?"

On my last trip to Pleiku I had turned in a request for R & R or Relaxation and Rest leave, which was a one-week trip to either Hong Kong or Bangkok, Thailand. Later the options for the Vietnam veterans would be expanded to include trips to Australia and Hawaii. I had requested the leave for the end of December.

"Oh yes, I understand that you got Bangkok leaving Saigon on December 24th and returning on January 1st. I'll let you fly down to Saigon on December 22nd to give you a few extra days."

"Great! And thank you for your support, Sir."

"Now let me get out of here before I find something else to ball you out."

Captain Leyda had also brought another crew chief for me to Bao Loc. Private Tyrone Johnson was new to me and told me that he had arrived in Vietnam in October and been assigned to the 219th. He was a black man from Nashville, Tennessee and had enlisted in the Army the previous year. I got along well with him although we would really only be together for one month before my R & R and transfer to Pleiku.

I took Johnson on a few orientation flights and decided to fly over the VC checkpoint to the south of Bao Loc. I flew over the high mountains separating our valley from the fairly level plain that stretched to Saigon. As usual the checkpoint was still operating although I didn't try to harass them. On the return flight I climbed to about 9,000 feet. This altitude was about 2,000 above the mountains. There were two layers of scattered clouds, one above us and one below us. As I flew I noticed the layers were becoming denser and seemed to be converging as I approached the mountains. I continued to fly under visual rules since the plane did not have enough instruments to fly under instrumentation rules. In a short time I lost visibility of the ground and the top layer had also become solid. It was not possible to weave in and around the clouds and I was going in and out of them.

Finally I ran out of any sight with the earth or clear sky. I was completely in the clouds although I continued to look for the ground or the sky. After a few minutes I realized that I had better check what instruments I did have. Pilots realize, that if one was to fly without sight and the plane was to slowly either dive or climb, the pilot's inner ear that notifies us of change would be fooled into thinking you are still flying straight and level. On this occasion my ears had been completely fooled. The instruments indicated my speed was approaching the red line for excessive speed, the climb and dive indicator was pegged on the down side and the turn and ball indicator was pegged on the left wing. This meant that in the few minutes I had not looked at the instruments and had flown into the clouds, the plane was in a steep dive to the left. The normal procedure to correct such a condition is to cut the power to the engine to reduce speed, level the wings and raise the nose to level flight until the airspeed drops. Unfortunately I was obviously now below the level of the mountain peeks that I could not see. To simply raise the nose of the plane to climb would put the plane into a downward skid. This case was much like a driver who finds that he car is skidding on ice and needs to turn. He must wait for the car's tires to obtain traction and also for the speed to reduce before entering the turn. I didn't have the luxury of time and for a brief moment my mind said, "Hell with it, I've had it." Then my desire for life and adrenalin kicked in my actions. Instead of reducing power, I ordered the engine to give me every last drop of power, leveled the wings and then instead of putting the plane in level flight, I raised the nose into a climb.

The plane shuttered and went into the expected skid downward. The RPM's were pegged to the extreme red line condition and then slowly I could feel the power overcome the skid and the plane began a slow and agonizing climb. After a few minutes I did see the ground. It was a mere twenty feet below the left wing of the plane and was definitely the side of a mountain. After two more minutes I finally relaxed and brought the plane back to normal flight.

I turned to Johnson and asked, "Did you realize the plane was in a dive back there?"

"Yes sir, I thought it was your intention to do that but you sure as hell scared the shit out of me coming that close to the mountain."

"Next time, Private Johnson, you have permission to ask me what I'm doing and to remind me not to fly into clouds."

This incident was my closest brush with death and again was the result of pilot error. I was also intrigued by my first reaction of accepting the inevitable and wondered if most soldiers have that same resignation when they see the inevitable hand of death come their way.

A few days later I received word from the MACV command that some VIP's and a high-ranking Army commander, rumored to be General William Westmoreland, would visit Bao Loc. The day prior to the visit a Chinook helicopter landed bringing additional American security and a team of men with devices to inspect the airfield for bombs. Within an hour the team located a bomb buried in the middle of the airfield and which by its condition and the hardness of the dirt had been buried for quite some time. Apparently I had been flying and landing on the bomb for over five months. Because of the bomb, the security team determined that Bao Loc was too unsafe for the visit of the VIP's and Westmoreland. The mission was cancelled.

Frankly, I didn't think very highly of General Westmoreland and felt that the position of Commanding General in Vietnam had become too complex and demanding for his abilities. He has a tall West Pointer with service in World War II and Korea and by the time he took command in Vietnam in 1964, looked every inch like the kind of man to lead our army. His demeanor and good looks helped to promote him to this position but did little to help our forces win the war. I never did get to meet the general and really I wasn't sorry.

The VC in my area were becoming more disciplined and experienced in ways to avoid being seen by me on my daily missions. I suspected that they were moving at night to avoid me and in the day stayed under the jungle canopy. My requests for air support diminished as my sightings diminished. Some of the pilots in the other areas were experiencing the same situation although they continued the requests for support by bombing suspected build-up area in the jungle and supply routes. However, this type of bombing was a hit or miss with the emphasis on miss. The pilots continued to report VC casualties on these missions even if they had no idea if anything or anybody was hit. At least the VC casualties continued to rise daily and the high command was probably satisfied. I had trouble wasting bombs and effort by the Air Force on such missions and would not call for support without some idea that I would be doing damage to the VC.

I continued with some horseplay while at Bao Loc and at least once almost cost me my life. A number of the Bao Loc personnel were at the airfield including McClintock and Captain Russell. I decided to show them some fancy flying by diving at the runway and buzzing the field. The plane was headed perpendicular to the runway and as I passed over the runway, I was so low that my landing gear struck the runway while I was flying at the maximum speed. I didn't really think hitting the gear was much of a problem but to my amazement the strike caused the gear and then the entire plane to vibrate quite violently. As I raised the nose of the plane to fly over a large hill to the east the plane began to sink into the valley surrounding the field. Apparently the vibration caused the lift under the wings to be compromised and without lift the plane could not fly even though the engine was turning at maximum RPM's. The valley was solid jungle and I knew that I would finally have to prove my theory about landing on the jungle canopy without serious bodily injury. Fortunately the vibration began to diminish as I approached the top of the jungle and the plane began to develop lift sufficiently to begin a climb over the hill. The plane was no more that ten to fifteen feet above the jungle when I was saved. I chalked that episode up to another foolish activity that could have resulted in my death in an attempt to be a showoff.

Chapter 20 – R & R

As promised my replacement at Bao Loc arrived on December 20th. I gave Lieutenant Frank Schmidt a two-day orientation with the area, the local inhabitants and the military. He seemed like a capable person although he was a new replacement for the 219th and I didn't know him previously. I wished him success and left with my belongings in my plane for Pleiku.

At Pleiku, Captain Leyda advised me that I would leave for Saigon immediately on the courier and supply plane and would be flying to Bangkok. I immediately hopped on board an Air Force C-130 and was walking across the airfield at Tan Son Nhut within an hour. Quarters had been arranged by my command for me to stay at the tent city until my flight departed on December 24th to begin my R & R.

I learned that the following day Bob Hope would be putting on a USO show at the airport and that anyone could attend. On the day of the show I walked over to where it was to be staged a good hour before the kickoff time. It was an extremely hot day and the show was set to be shown on an aircraft parking area in front of a large hanger that covered the stage. To my amazement there were thousands of military personnel already at the scene who were sitting on the pavement. The closest I could get to the stage was over 200 yards away. The performers look like extremely small dolls. The high ranking officers and important people had chairs set for them off to the side of the hanger. Their seats were covered and therefore out of the glare of the sun. Although Bob Hope was one of my favorite entertainers, I saw no purpose in sitting on the pavement under a hot sun to watch a show I could barely see at this distance. Consequently I walked to the nearby Officers' Club. It was virtually empty and I drank the afternoon away. I wondered whether all of Hope's shows were this crowded and also wondered why these thousands of military were all stationed in Saigon while so few military were in the field elsewhere in Vietnam.

The following morning I went to the small airport terminal. The personnel assigned to the terminal arranged for the R & R flights and showed the clerk my orders. The plane was another C-130 and would be leaving within an hour. To my surprise also sitting in the terminal awaiting his R & R flight to Bangkok was my good friend, Barry Taylor. The same Taylor that had attended OCS, Airborne Training and Flight School with me. Since we had not seen each other or communicated with each other in over eight months, our both going on R & R together was a stroke of pure luck. I knew that this trip was going to be great fun and I wasn't disappointed.

Only five other people were aboard the flight to begin R & R and when we arrived at Bangkok we were housed in a clean centrally located hotel in the downtown area. Taylor and I had rooms on the same floor and we immediately went out for a tour of the city. I was surprised that Bangkok was so westernized and most of the people spoke English. All the commercial establishments accepted American currency as though it was Thai money. The downtown area was unlike Saigon. The South Vietnam capital was characterized by thousands of bicycles, motor scooters, and rickshaws while Bangkok had primarily small cars. The bars and cafes were more like those in the states while those in Saigon were much more Oriental in character and looks.

Prior to settling in at a bar, I insisted on getting a drink that I had been dreaming about. A good old fashion vanilla milk shake made with real milk. After satisfying this thrust, Taylor and I decided to take a chance on one of the many massage establishments. I believe Taylor thought he would be able to locate a woman to satisfy his sexual appetite while I just wanted a good massage. I had never gotten a massage before this date. Unfortunately for Taylor the establishment just offered massages. We were told to undress and the massage would begin with a hot bath. I was a little bashful about coming into a large room in the nude with other patrons and a large number of female attendants but I gave in to the request. The baths were tall cement cylinders. They would accommodate one person in a standing position. When I went to enter the bath, I felt the water and immediately recoiled. It was extremely hot and I just couldn't put my body into that heat. It took four of the female attendants to literally pick me up and heave me into the bath. After a few minutes it felt great although the initial shock was bad. I am naturally dark and had a great tan from being in the sun most of the time yet my skin turned to a fairly bright reddish tint in the bath. After fifteen to twenty minutes of bathing with one attendant washing my back, I was told to get out of the bath and lay on a massage table. My body felt limp and relaxed from the heat. I didn't know what to expect other than my knowledge of seeing massages on television programs where a large man or woman pushes on your back with their hands to loosen the muscles. In this case a petit young woman began to walk barefooted on my back. This technique took me completely by surprise but it was certainly worth the effort. Her feet worked their way into my back and completely relaxed every back muscle and then she and another attendant worked on my arms and legs with their hands. When the massage was over, my body felt great but it felt drained of any strength and Taylor and I returned to our rooms to take a much-needed sleep. Consequently our first day of R & R was spent drinking a milkshake and having a massage. Not the first day of boisterous drinking I imagined we would have.

The following day was Christmas. It didn't seem to be as big a celebration of faith that is evident in the United States even thou I was told a large percentage of the Thai people our Christians. Taylor made it very clear that he wanted to look for a beautiful woman who would remain his companion and sexual partner during our stay in Bangkok. We went to the best looking bar and lounge we could locate and sat at a table and each ordered a beer.

The mama-san approached us and said, "You are GI's and looking for good company, yes?"

Taylor replied, "We want the very best women you've got."

The mama-san pointed at a large glass window and said, "You go pick the one you want. Remember, you must buy girl you pick drinks while she stay with you."

Taylor and I walked to the window. It separated the bar from another room filled with young, beautiful Thai women. Behind each woman was a large number with over twenty women sitting in front of a number. Taylor and I looked at the candidates. The Thai women behind the window were all quite good looking and had excellent figures. Like the Vietnamese women they had small waists and shapely hips but small busts. I thought they had very dissimilar faces from the Viets. Where the Viet women had elegant yet petit faces, the Thais had more round faces and less slant to their eyes. I was fairly certain I could easily distinguish a Vietnamese from a Thai woman although I wasn't that sure about the men.

I didn't see how having a young, beautiful woman having a drink with us would be harmful and I turned to mama-san and said, "I'll take number seven."

"You very wise man, Sara is an excellent choice."

I wondered how a Thai woman would get a name such as Sara but assumed the names were selected to make it easier for the American soldiers to feel at home and pronounce the names. Meanwhile Taylor was having a difficult time making a selection.

He said to me, "Which one do you think is better, four, ten or thirteen?"

"Barry, I think they're all great looking girls and it's only for a few hours."

Taylor turned to mama-san and pointed toward number ten, "I'll take that one."

"That is also a good choice. Michele is very nice girl. I will send choices to your table."

In a short time Sara and Michele joined us at a table and ordered drinks. It looked and smelled like tea although we were charged as thou they were whisky. Both women spoke English although Michele had a better command of the language. After about two hours I thanked Sara for her company and she returned to the showroom. Meanwhile Taylor was attempting to get Michele to join him outside the bar and remain with him for the night.

Michele responded, "So sorry Barry, mama-san would not allow me to leave with customer and we are not permitted to meet them outside of bar."

Taylor turned and motioned for mama-san to join us at the table. He said, "Mama-san I want Michele to join me for the rest of the day and night. How much would that cost?"

"No! Girls are not allowed to leave bar with customers. They are not prostitutes."

"Name a price," Taylor responded as though he had not heard her.

"No, my girls cannot leave bar especially with someone like you."

Both Taylor and I were stunned by her words. It seemed as though the mama-san was rejecting Taylor because he was black but I found that slightly impossible considering our location. Taylor asked, "Are you telling me that she can't join me because I'm black?"

She answered, "Thai girls very small compared to American girls and black men are known to be very large. You would hurt Michele if you had sex with her."

I roared with laughter and said, "God damn it Barry, even the Thais have heard how big black men are."

Taylor didn't respond to my comment but turned to mama-san and then started the most ridiculous argument I have heard as he attempted to explain that his penis was as small as any white man's penis. Taylor even offered to show mama-san his penis to prove his point. Evidently this offer had the effect that Taylor wanted and mama-san began the negotiation for Michele's services that would not include sex but merely a companion for the day. Taylor agreed but insisted on having Michele's services for the next three days. The eventual price was settled at $200 per day and only $100 for the remainder of the 25th. We finally left the bar with Michele and began a tour of the city. We hired a taxi from a driver whom Michele knew and drove around the city.

Taylor kept asking me when we were alone and out of earshot from Michele, "Do you think she will have sex with me?"

"Barry, I don't see why not, if you handle it discreetly. It may cost you a little more money paid directly to her but I think you can have her," I responded. "Just don't hurt her" and again I had a great laugh at Taylor's expense.

Latter that night after a light meal at a restaurant selected by Michele we went to a movie. The movie was American-made and in English with Thai subtitles. That night I said goodnight to Michele as Taylor led her to his room as he continued to negotiate for her services. The next morning I met Taylor and Michele who was wearing a different outfit. Her outfit meant she must have returned to her home at some point to get fresh clothes.

We toured a Buddhist temple on the outskirts of the city and then in the afternoon went to Bangkok's zoo. We had some good laughs and friendly conversation as Michele attempted to explain customs and habits of the Thai people. She didn't really have anything to offer regarding the Vietnamese war other than to say that it was a shame that the Americans had to come and fight. Taylor had fallen in love but he accepted the fact that he could only afford to pay for three days of Michele's services. I wanted to take a trip into the countryside outside of Bangkok to see how the people really lived. We were able to get a taxi driver to drive us about ten miles out of the city but he was unwilling to go any further especially with two Americans as passengers. He explained that there were some guerilla groups fighting for independence that were active in the area but usually not closer than twenty-five miles from the outskirts of the city. Even driving a short distance out from the city was fascinating as the people lived a life style very similar to what I saw in Vietnam.

The next four days were spent touring the city and drinking in the downtown bars. It was relaxing to stop worrying about death and trying to kill people.

We were expected back at the airfield on the morning of the 31st. Taylor and I went to the hanger were we were expected to rendezvous with the plane and met the pilots. The pilot in charge, Captain Merritt greeted us, "So how was your R & R Lieutenants?"

"We had a great time and sorry that it is coming to an end," I responded.

"It might not be as over as you think, guys. We're having a little trouble with one of our engines and I'm fairly sure that we will be stuck here over New Years Eve," Merritt said with a wink. "Oh, by the way, the American Ambassador to Thailand has decided to invite all servicemen in Thailand to the Embassy for a New Years Eve party. You wouldn't have to dress in anything special."

"Are you kidding, Captain," asked Taylor.

"No, it's an honest to God invitation. The party starts about twenty hundred."

"We'll be there," I said. "Oh' what time do we leave tomorrow?"

"Let's plan on a twelve noon departure so that we will have time to recuperate after the party."

"Are you sure the plane will be ready tomorrow," I asked?

"That depends on whether we're invited to any more parties," he said with a large grin.

"See you at tonight's party," I said, as Taylor and I departed the area to return to the city to reclaim our rooms.

That night dressed in shorts and polo shirts, Taylor and I arrived at the American Embassy. We had to show our ID's to the Marines on guard at the gate but there were no challenges to our arrival or entry. The Air Force pilots had been correct. We stayed well into the night drinking and eating. I even met the Ambassador although I cannot recall his name. I was amazed by the fact that he was willing to invite all the American servicemen to the embassy for a party although in reality I only counted about twenty-five obvious soldiers who were there. The food and drinks were great and I couldn't complain about the price.

The following day Taylor and I arrived at the hanger where we boarded the plane for our return to the war. Upon our return to Saigon, Taylor and I said our farewells. Baring some unfortunate incident with the enemy we knew that we would probably see each other again in six months back at Fort Rucker. Our former base was the location for most of the pilots being rotated back to the states.

By January 2nd I was back at Pleiku with the 219th. Captain Leyda was still my boss and briefed me on my duties. He told me, "Basically you will be given daily missions by Captain Sinclair who's the operations officer. Also you will assume additional duty as the unit's intelligence officer."

"Get the hell out," I responded.

"I'm serious. You are the 219th's intelligence officer. You will compile all the mission reports and present them at the weekly battalion intelligence meeting of all the units."

"Captain Leyda, this assignment is stupid. I don't know anything about intelligence gathering and reporting. Why me?"

"Vince, this assignment is not a reward. The CO is dumping it on you for that incident involving the unauthorized flight to Saigon a few months back. He hasn't forgotten that little episode."

I shrugged my shoulders and resigned myself to this additional duty. Being intelligence officer wasn't as bad as I thought since at least there was something to do in the time not flying. I was able to compile the day's intelligence data in about a half hour although the intelligence meeting did drag for a couple of hours.

Gathering all the intelligence data on the movements of the VC allowed me to have a fairly good idea as to their location and when the mission allowed, I would fly to those locations and either empty my load of explosives or call in air strikes. I was thrilled when we were notified that Air Vice Marshal and Prime Minister Nguyen Cao Ky would be visiting Pleiku and attending the intelligence meeting. I was notified by the 219th commanding officer, Major Lust that Captain Sinclair would be giving the briefing for the unit although I could attend the meeting.

The meeting was held in a large tent inside the air base. Ky was escorted by a number of high ranking Vietnamese officers including at least two generals, one of whom was an American. In addition to the officers, Ky had brought his wife. Both she and Ky were dressed in tight fitting tailor made black fatigues. Mrs. Ky boasted a great shape and reminded me of the Dragon Lady from the Terry and the Pirates cartoon that was still in syndication during the 1960's. Her long black hair made her look both beautiful but also gave her a tough, mysterious look. Ky walked with an air of confidence with his wife at his side and I thought that only in Vietnam would a high-ranking officer's wife attend an intelligence briefing.

The presentations by the various units including the 219th were full of exaggerated praise for the ARVN units and the effect of our air war in defeating the Vietcong. Finally Ky stood up and thanked those present for their sacrifice and courage and promised to let both the American and Vietnamese commands in Saigon know of our efforts and success.

I now realized why I was not allowed to give the briefing for the 219th. My report would have cautioned that while we have not received any significant casualties or defeats on the ground, there has also been little success. In addition, I would have been extremely critical of the efforts of the ARVN units They made no attempt to seek out the enemy in the jungle and were content, as were the Americans, to hold the populated areas and leave the VC to rule the jungle.

Chapter 21 – Heads & Senseless Death

I settled into one of the hooch's although I had no close friends at Pleiku. I got into the routine of flying once or twice a day, completing my intelligence gathering and then retiring to my hooch to listen to a tape of music on my Teac recorder. The one thing I disliked about the hooch was that within ten feet of my cot was a vat of acid that was cleaning at least one or two human heads at any time period. It seemed that the pilots began to take our call sign "Headhunter" literally. It began when Captain Kowalewski asked me to fly him to the Ia Drang Valley Special Forces camp where I was involved with the First Cavalry's fight against the NVA a few months previous.

I secured a couple of cases of beer and placed them in the rear of the plane behind Kowalewski and flew to the camp. I was greeted like a long lost son by the Special Forces team whom I had previously become acquainted. They thanked me for the beer and Kowalewski asked to borrow a jeep. They provided a jeep for him and after being assured the valley was quite safe at least during daylight hours he told me to accompany him. He drove into the valley about a mile away from the camp and stopped alongside a large field. He pulled an entrenching tool out of the back seat of the jeep and pulled a canvas bag from under his shirt.

Come on, I'm going to show you something," he said.

"What?"

I followed him across the field for about 100 yards when we approached a large earth mound. He pointed to the ground and said, "This is where they buried some of those North Vietnamese troops that were killed."

He then began to dig into the mound. I saw other obvious traces of someone digging into the mound and wondered what he was doing. In a short time he hit upon fragments of clothing, bones and decayed flesh. The smell was overpowering and I stepped back to get more fresh air. He kept digging and using gloves began to pull two corpses from the mound. Using the shovel like a large axe he severed the heads from the bodies. He then threw the bodies back into the mound and covered them with a few inches of dirt. Kowalewski placed the heads into the canvas bag and indicated for me to follow him. I was shocked by what I had seen but said nothing until we were in the jeep on the way back to the camp.

"What do you intend to do with those," as I pointed to the bag?

"One of the guys is leaving for the states in a few months and we decided to give him a memento of the war."

"You're going to give him a head?" I asked with disbelief.

"It's no big deal, we've gotten the heads before and never had a problem. A number of us are taking them home."

"You don't think that someone will get in trouble if they are found with them?"

"Why should they? Anyway they're NVA and we can disguise them easily. I'll show you later."

"Wait! What the hell do you or anyone else want with a head even a NVA head? I don't see the point and frankly it's a little grotesque."

"You'll feel different about this when you see how they are showcased."

"Showcased?"

"Wait a few weeks and I'll show you." With that response he walked back to the jeep where he placed the bag of heads behind his seat.

We returned in about an hour to the camp and I felt like a ghoul with the heads and wondered whether the Special Forces knew what Kowalewski had done. I wondered if they thought I also was involved with this stupid task but decided not to push the issue. Back at Pleiku, Kowalewski placed the heads in the vat of acid. Not much flesh was left on the skulls except for some bits of hair. The many insects and bacteria that reside in the humid jungle climate had done a very good job of cleaning the bodies in a short period. The heads remained in the vat for at least a week before Kowalewski and a couple of other pilots took them out and began to polish the bones. They joked about the teeth, which they removed and then placed back into their sockets.

In a few weeks I learned what Kowalewski had meant by camouflaging and showcasing the heads. They had hired a local Vietnamese carpenter to make a box of very nice wood of about 8"x12"x8" in which the head fit nicely. The box had a small door and for hours they would open the door and say, "hello" or "goodbye." A plaque was placed on the box dedicated to Major Lust for his leadership from the "Headhunters of the 219th." I wasn't present when the box was given to Lust and don't know if he had any objection to such a gift or whether he ever took the head home with him. I couldn't help wonder how such men as I arrived with to Vietnam could do such acts and not realize that something was very morally wrong with the actions. Unfortunately another four to six heads were secured in the following three months as other gifts and trophies to be taken home. The local carpenter was kept quite busy.

I did participate in at least one plan to ship something improper or illegal home. One of the officers wanted to ship a M-60 30 caliber machine gun home. The pilots sat around the hooch and discussed various ways to accomplish this trick without being caught by customs. Security precautions by the U.S. Customs were very relaxed but a M-60 was a big weapon with quite a few heavy machine metal components. Finally I suggested that the only way to do the job safely was to carry the weapon in plain view. It was decided to have the local Vietnamese carpenter make a wood board with a high finish and scroll. The pilot then had a local engraver prepare a plaque, which read, "Presented to Captain Smith for his Courage Against the Enemy, March 1965 thru February 1966". It was mounted below the gun on the wood. The firing pin on the M-60 was removed and a fake metal plug was inserted in the barrel of the gun. When it came time to leave Vietnam, I was told the pilot simply wrapped the weapon in a cloth and walked thru customs.

I never heard that our Customs Department was very vigilant during this period of the war although I can only assume that as the use of drugs increased, so did attempts to check for that contraband. It is interesting that although I disapproved of the use of marihuana or stronger drugs, their use was never an issue where I was stationed. I literally was never offered any marihuana or observed any use of that drug. Considering the extensive reports of marihuana use by U.S. forces later in the war, I would have thought that I would have observed some use of it. Perhaps my disapproval of drugs could have been the cause but I was never vocal about my opinion and I was simply never offered any drugs or even a puff on a marihuana joint. My drinking habits were similar to the other pilots in that we drank too much and too often. Therefore, if they were using drugs, they would have thought to include me. They didn't offer and I assume there was very little use of drugs by the Army pilots stationed at Pleiku. In addition, as a pilot that visited the many Special Forces camps and delivered alcohol that was not really authorized, I would have been asked to either secure or deliver drugs if their use was that widespread during that period of the war.

The lack of drugs could be explained that this was the beginning of the escalation of the war and the increase in deployment of U.S. forces. Also most of the troops in Vietnam were still volunteers and generally from the pool of career servicemen who were probably more disciplined in both their futures and the use of drugs. Secondly, there were few reluctant draftees serving in Vietnam who were more apt to use drugs as an escape from their situation. Eventually, however, the use of drugs, throughout all the ranks and regardless of whether the serviceman was a volunteer or draftee, would become common.

During my tour in Vietnam I observed two senseless killings of Vietnamese by our servicemen that could not be explained away by mistake or overzealousness. The first occurred while I was assigned to guard duty on the perimeter of the Pleiku defenses in January 1966. I was sitting on top of a sand bagged bunker facing to the north of the airfield looking over a large rice field. Off in the distance I could see a lone Vietnamese dressed in bright orange walking across the rice field parallel to our defense. The orange clothing signified the man was a Buddhist monk. I was told that Buddhist monks in Vietnam are not dedicated to this career for life but rather at some point in a young man's development, they will often dedicate a few years to this religious pursuit. One of the American servicemen sitting in the bunker was following the progress of the monk. On the top of the bunker was another pilot and we were discussing what we knew of the Buddhist religion when the serviceman who was a private in the Army announced, "Do you want to see something?"

The private then yelled, "Hey, asshole get away from the airfield."

The monk was obviously out of hearing range and it was doubtful that he could even understand English. The private yelled again and finally the monk turned and gave a friendly wave at our position. I never dreamed that the situation would result in any tragedy and just watched the events unfold.

Before we realize what was happening the private took his M-16 and shot once at the monk. He was approximately 100 yards from our position and was making no moves that could be considered a threat to the base. The monk was hit with the shot and went down immediately. He made no move and lay still, face down in the water of the rice field.

I yelled, "What the fuck are you doing?"

The private answered without any apparent emotion, "Just got me one of those slant eye holy rollers. Did you see that son-of-a-bitch go down?"

I could see the Officer-of-the-day and two other soldiers running down the security line toward our position. It was obvious that the private had lost his perspective on the war although I doubt anyone could argue that it was due to the stress of constant warfare. More likely it was simply a case of total boredom. Even the short periods that I was required to help man the defensive positions was very boring and in the daylight heat very difficult to stay awake. Regardless it was difficult to excuse his behavior simply because of boredom.

The Officer-of-the-day arrived and seeing me on top of the bunker asked, "What were you shooting at?"

I pointed inside the bunker and said, "The private just shot a monk walking across the rice field."

"Was he armed or making threatening gestures against the position?"

"No, he was just walking across the field."

"Then why did he shoot the monk?"

"You'll have to ask him, Sir."

The Officer-of-the-day then proceeded to question the private. He defended his action by the simple statement that the monk didn't belong there and deserved to be shot. The private was taken away and relieved of his weapons. A squad of Vietnamese soldiers went out into the rice field and examined the body of the monk. After a few minutes they came walking back and left the body where it lay. By the time my duty was over, two hours later, the body could still be seen lying face down in the field. Later I was questioned by a Major with the 52nd Aviation Battalion as to what happened and gave them my perspective as to what had taken place. I was never asked to testify at a court-martial and learned the private was quietly transferred back to the states and given a discharge. I thought that it was a terribly easy way of dealing with a murder and especially a murder of a religious figure in broad daylight.

The second murder was a little more humorous but just as deadly and cold-blooded. Because the Pleiku Air Base has almost devoid of vegetation and covered with red dust, those assigned to airfield duty such as pilots, crewmembers and crew chiefs were always covered with the dust the clung to their sweaty bodies. One of the primary pleasures at the end of the day was a refreshing shower. Unfortunately there was only one building for showers on the post although it had six showerheads. Fresh water was scarce at Pleiku although it rained every day and showers were tightly rationed. The water was supplied by a water tower located about 50 feet from the shower room.

The tower was guarded by a Vietnamese soldier and surrounded by barbed wire although there was path leading to the tower. It was the responsibility of the soldier to turn on the water for the showers every day from 5-5:15 pm.

The Americans would cluster into the shower room about ten minutes before the showers were turned on and await the welcomed streams of water. Usually there was about 30-50 of us waiting to shower. It meant that you really had time to only get wet, run out of the water and soap up and then a quick rinse. We had placed a large 50 gallon drum in the shower room that was filled with water. We used this water before the showers were turned on to get wet and to soap up. On one occasion a number of us were in the shower room and had gotten soaped when the water came on at 5pm but within five minutes was abruptly turned off. One of the helicopter pilots loss his composure and began to rant and rave.

He yelled, "That fucking Vietnamese bastard can't even turn on the water right. They can't fight and now they can't even do the simplest assignment." He went to a window that looked up at the water tower and yelled to the soldier at the tower, "Turn the fucking water on, asshole."

The soldier ignored the pilot and continued to sit near the turn-on valve. The pilot yelled again, "Hey asshole turn the water on."

The soldier continued to ignore the pilot although it was obvious that from this distance, he was aware of the pilot's tirade. The rest of us began to yell at the soldier but he continued to ignore our pleas to turn the water back on. Finally the pilot still covered in soap wrapped a towel around his waist, grabbed his pistol from the clothing he had brought to the shower room and announced, "I'll get that stupid son-of-a-bitch to put the water back on." A number of us gave him our blessing and encouragement thinking that he would simply scare the soldier to put the water back on. We watched out the window although some of the guys walked outside to observe the comedy.

The pilot walked at a brisk pace in his shower clogs toward the water tower yelling for the soldier to put the water on. The soldier continued to sit and made no move for the value or for his rifle they lay on the ground near him. The pilot walked up to the soldier and placed the gun to the soldier's head and fired one round. I could see part of his head blow away from his body as he lurched to the side from the impact. The pilot looked down at the private and merely turned on the water valve and began the walk to the shower room. Everyone in the shower room cheered as the pilot made his way back and received a number of congratulations from the men.

The pilot merely said, "We won't have any problems with the water now."

I recognized another young helicopter pilot who said, "That bastard deserved it."

While the killing shocked me, I had no remorse for the soldier's death. At the time it seemed like a logical move although much too violent. It was difficult until many years later for me to have any remorse about the killing. It seemed as though the water privileges were more important than a human life. The life of a Vietnamese soldier meant little since by now most of us who had been in Vietnam and observed the fighting spirit of the ARVN realized they were totally worthless in combat. Since this was a combat zone, the life of those who were worthless and did not contribute anything to win the war or to help protect our lives was not an important loss.

Perhaps the soldier had reasons for turning off the water although he made no attempt to explain his actions. His body language showed that he didn't care about our demands and was totally unconcerned. Perhaps he was as arrogant as the pilot but he suffered the penalty.

Meanwhile the pilot finished his shower as we allowed him the privilege of using the shower first. I don't think any of us were concerned about the pilot shooting someone else since he went about the killing as a job to do and he had done the job. By the time most of us had finished, two American security troops arrived and asked for the one responsible for the shooting to accompany them to headquarters. The pilot came forward and followed the soldiers toward headquarters. I noticed that he remained armed.

None of us were ever questioned about the shooting and in the days that followed I noticed that the tower guard was now an American and the path leading to the tower was closed with barbed wire. The water also became much more reliable in terms of time period. I heard that the pilot was quietly transferred back to the states and no charges were ever brought against him. I assume the Vietnamese soldier became a casualty of a VC sniper. The message that both these killings had was to reinforce our belief that Vietnamese life had little value and that to take a life would not result in any military justice action. It also sent a message that the taking of a Vietnamese life was a quick ticket home for one who was tired of the war.

In comparison, both of these killing had taken place within a short time period of each other and I had reacted differently to the killings. I was appalled at the killing of the monk although I felt no guilt at the killing of the Vietnamese soldier. Perhaps it was that the monk was merely a young man who was devoting a few years of his life in the pursuit of religious dedication. Yet I had no great respect for the Buddhist monks since it was common knowledge that young Vietnamese men often chose to dedicate a few years of their lives to avoid military duty in the ARVN army. I, as probably 95% of the Americans that served near or in support of the ARVN, had no respect for their soldiers or army. In my opinion we were better off if the ARVN army didn't exist. They did no fighting unless it was merely to escape to the rear and safety. They seldom ventured out of the cities and were reluctant to even accept posts in the outlining villages. They did manage to swagger around the cities bullying the civilian population or trying to impress young women.

Chapter 22 – Missions on the Coast

In late January 1966 the 219th's operations officer told me that I was to fly to Quin Nhon and rendezvous with a destroyer north of the city. The mission would require some fire adjustment for the destroyer's guns at a VC stronghold. I was also told that after completing the mission, I was to fly to Danang and assist Captain Danny Lee for a couple of days. He was reporting an increase in NVA activity in his area. The flight to Quin Nhon was uneventful and I located the destroyer about twenty miles north of the city and only about a mile off the coast.

On a prearranged frequency I contacted them, "Able Foxtrot this is Headhunter One One for fire mission."

"Headhunter One One we have a fire mission. Do you see the paved highway running north along the coast? There is a dense jungle slightly to the west of the highway near a bridge that spans a small river. Can you identify this location?"

"Able Foxtrot this is Headhunter One One, wait one." I flew along the road at about 500 feet and immediately spotted the location and again contacted the destroyer. "Able Foxtrot, I have the target in sight."

"Headhunter One One, your mission is to direct fire into that jungle and also at the bridge. A patrol was hit at that location yesterday and it is necessary to neutralize any enemy positions."

"Able Foxtrot, do I understand that you also want to destroy the bridge spanning the river?"

"That is correct Headhunter One One. We are turning you over to Fire Control with call sign Able Foxtrot Five."

I then placed myself to the west of the target at about two thousand feet and began to fly a horseshoe route. This location would keep the destroyer's shells, the destroyer and the target all to my east. "Able Foxtrot Five give me one smoke round at the target."

"Headhunter One One, smoke is on the way." As the control gave the message I could see off in the distance the destroyer fire a round from its forward turret.

"Wait one," I replied. I then began to look for the smoke and finally saw smoke rising to the west of me. The impact meant the round had cleared both the target and also my location by at least a half mile. Not the best of shooting but I said, "Splash one. Drop 2000 and fire one smoke."

"One, on the way," replied the Fire Control.

"I looked for the explosive and saw that it had missed the jungle target by at least 300 yards. "Drop three hundred and fire one HE."

"One on the way."

Again I looked for the explosion and saw that it was now short of the target by at least 200 yards. This miss should not have happened.

"Able Foxtrot Five, splash one, add one hundred and fire one."

The theory to fire control of artillery or naval gunfire is to always cut the corrections in half until the fire is within one hundred yards, then to correct the one hundred yards and to fire the necessary rounds to destroy the target. All corrects are based on a line running from the guns to the target and if the rounds are beyond the target, the adjuster orders a drop and if short of the target, an add. Unfortunately this fire mission was not going as it should and I wondered if the problem was due to the constant moving of the destroyer although their fire control should take the movement into account when computing their fire.

"On the way, wait."

I saw the explosion that was now 100 yards to the west of the target. "Able Foxtrot Five, splash one, drop one hundred yards and fire for effect."

"Headhunter One One, on the way."

I could see the destroyer fire four rounds from each of its three main guns. The jungle was ripped apart by the shells and knew if the enemy were in this jungle, they would suffer a good many casualties. The only problem was that I didn't see any signs of an enemy. There was no fire directed at my plane and I didn't see any indication that the enemy was leaving the area when they should have realized they would soon be under fire. However, the target selection was not my choosing and most probably the work of a CIA agent sitting somewhere in Saigon. I wondered why the destroyer was given this mission when it would have been far easier and more accurate to simply call a flight of three jets to handle the task. I guessed the destroyer needed a practice exercise.

After the strike against the jungle, I made the necessary correction to hit the bridge. After eight rounds, that were either too far or too close, the Fire Control gave up and said, "Headhunter One One, thank you for your support and the captain wants to pass on to you a 'well done'."

Although I believed the mission certainly lacked the effect that I expected, I accepted the compliment and flew to Danang and hoped that in the future I could use the more conventional means to destroy a target that I knew existed. I wondered how many of the enemy was reported dead although it was probably in excess of fifty. Amazing how many VC and NVA we reported killed.

Later that day I flew to Danang where I joined Captain Lee at the airfield. He ordered me to be ready at 0800 hours for a mission to locate a reported NVA unit to the west of Danang on the foothills of the mountain chain that separated the coast from the central highlands. At 0800 hours Captain Lee advised me to search slightly to the north of his position and to notify him of any enemy movement. We had three jet fighters available if we were successful.

At 0915 hours Captain Lee contacted me. "Headhunter One One this is Headhunter Eight, have over one hundred NVA in sight and have called for air support. I am ten miles due west of Danang."

"Headhunter Eight, will join you in ten minutes." I reached his position in about seven minutes and was shocked to see that Lee was flying at an altitude of no more than 500 feet above the terrain. Although I was flying at 1500 feet, I could clearly see numerous enemy troops in an open field who were firing at Lee with rifles and other small arms.

"Headhunter Eight do you realize that the target is firing at you?" I asked.

"Affirmative Headhunter One One but I want to make sure these bastards don't slip away."

I wondered how they could slip away since there was no cover for their unit for at least a mile. It was totally ridiculous for Lee to be flying that low since he could easily accomplish the mission with the same degree of success at a higher safer altitude.

"Headhunter One One, I've taken a couple of hits but don't consider them to be a threat to the plane."

"Headhunter Eight, do you want me to take over and mark the target for the fighters?"

"Negative, I've got this one and will complete mission."

In a minute the fighter commander contacted Lee who immediately marked the target with a WP rocket. The fighters attacked the NVA while Lee and I watched the slaughter. The attack was very successful and Lee probably accurately reported at least eighty enemy casualties. Back at the airfield I joined Lee at his plane. There were six small arms hits in the fuselage.

I asked, "Don't you think you could have completed the mission at fifteen hundred feet?"

"I probably could have but I like to put the fear of God in them. The lower the altitude the better."

I wondered how long the idiot was going to last with that attitude. When the 219th command heard about the success of the mission and also the rounds that Lee had received, they recommend him for a medal for bravery. I would have recommended him for a stupid medal and I began to question the reason for my presence. Was his show of bravery or stupidity depending upon your prospective merely for my benefit as a witness? I know that I was happy not to have to fly any more missions with him and was told by Lee to take the following day off from flying and to relax before returning to Pleiku.

I did fly one more mission that afternoon and had a very unusual experience. The flight was north of Danang along the coast and I heard a distress call from another plane. At first I didn't answer the call since it was very faint and I assumed there were more likely aircraft in the plane's vicinity that would hear the call. After the third call for assistance I began to climb in order to increase the reception of my radio in the event the plane was a long way off.

The plane made a fourth distress call, "This is Beachcomber Two One declaring an emergency. Does anybody read?"

"Beachcomber Two One this is Headhunter One One what is your situation?"

"This is Beachcomber Two One, I'm on fire and going down two miles out to sea."

Since he didn't use my call sign I couldn't determine if the pilot had heard my return call or merely omitted it out of panic or lack of time. The pilot also did not state where off the coast he was going to crash. I didn't know if the pilot was flying a jet, helicopter or small fixed wing plane or whether there were other people on board the plane. The signal indicated the plane was a long way off and he could be anywhere off the coast. I also wondered why no other planes were responding to the distress since there had to be at least a hundred planes and helicopters flying in Vietnam at that time of the day.

I called, "Beachcomber Two One, what is your position?"

My call did not initiate a response and I called the pilot at least six more times while I continued to climb to 10,000 feet. When I did not receive any additional distress calls, I contacted the Danang control This contact was mainly an airport control tower and I asked if they had picked up any distress calls. They had not heard any of the calls and by now I assumed the pilot had crashed into the sea. I told the control tower about the calls and could tell by their responses that they had no idea how to proceed without knowing the plane's location. After landing at Danang I went immediately to the Air Force operations command and notified them of the situation since I guessed the plane was a jet. The plane could be a jet flown by the Air Force, Navy or Marines and flying from any large airfield in Vietnam or from an aircraft carrier. The operations had no way of knowing whom to contact. Vietnam did not have a central command for control of aircraft and there was no one who monitored the location of planes or helicopters in Vietnam. It was literally a hit or miss situation. If a pilot got into difficulty, he had to hope there were other pilots in the area who could offer assistance or at least radio communication with someone who could offer assistance. All the pilots were aware of the situation and usually went out of their way to provide assistance. In this case, neither the Air Force operations nor I knew how to assist the pilot in distress since we had neither the location of the presumed crash or from what unit he was operating. There was no point in randomly flying along the entire Vietnam coast since he could easily have flown to land or further out to sea. There was also no way to mobilize the entire Vietnamese coastline to look for a downed pilot. I never learned the fate of the pilot and assume he became another casualty of the war.

Later that night I went to the Officer's Club for a few drinks and some conversation with other pilots. While sitting at the bar, I struck up a conversation with a man who identified himself as Gerald Jones. He was dressed in civilian attire and from his looks and conversation was probably another CIA agent. He showed me identification that indicated he was an employee of the United States. I discussed my mission at Pleiku to use small aircraft to locate and then destroy the enemy and he seemed impressed.

Finally he asked, "What do you plan to do after finishing your tour of duty in Nam?"

"I'm not sure if I will simply stay in the Army or try my luck with an airline as a pilot."

"How much longer do you have before your military commitment is over," he asked?

"I can leave the Army in a little over a year after getting home."

"You know that this war will continue for many years at the rate it is going. I also think you will be ordered back to Vietnam one or two more times before it is finished. Then what?"

I anticipated being ordered back to Vietnam one more time during the war but hadn't figured on perhaps coming back two more times. I responded, "Well, I guess I'll have to deal with that situation when it arrives."

"Listen, have you ever heard of Air America? I work for them and I have the authority to hire pilots for the airline. Would you be interested?"

"Sure! Can you give me some idea on the job, pay, location and type of planes?"

"The planes are primarily prop jobs similar to what the Army is already flying. You would be flying out of Thailand to different locations in Indochina. The tasks vary but you would be paid well. All the pilots must sign a three-year contract and will be paid $35,000 per year and Air America will pay for your food and lodging. The pay is tax-free, which means if someone saved most of their money; they could have close to $100,000 after the contract is over. How does that sound?"

"The money is good but I'm married and I can't see leaving my wife and daughter for another three years."

"Air America will pay for your wife and child to fly to Thailand and they can live there with you although the apartment you rent will be at your own expense or we will pay for a flight back to the states for a month each year you are away."

My mind was racing as I mulled over the offer. I knew immediately that Air America was merely a front for the CIA and I had no desire to work for them or to put my life in their hands. I gave him a diplomatic answer. "It sounds good Mr. Jones but I think I'll pass."

"If you change your mind you can contact Air America back in the states and I'm sure you will be received with open arms. I will mention your name in my next report so that they have a record of my offer. Good luck anyway." He then excused himself and left the club.

I knew very little about Air America other than seeing some of their planes flying into various locations in Vietnam. I also knew enough to know that the CIA supported their covert operations in the war with the airline and their planes also flew over Laos and Cambodia. There was no doubt in my mind that it was a dangerous assignment and I doubted if my wife would be overly enthusiastic about taking the job. Working for the CIA would also expose me to more of their shady deals.

In the morning I linked up with Lieutenant Danny Graves who was a Huey pilot flying out of Danang. We purchased a couple of six packs of beer and drove a jeep to the beach near the airfield. The beach was beautiful with clean white looking sand. There were at least twenty other people taking advantage of the sun and water. At about 2 pm I noticed a group of cameramen setting up motion picture cameras near us. Off shore there was a large Navy transport that seemed to be sitting about 500 yards out to sea.

At first I thought the cameramen were there to take film of servicemen relaxing from the war. I walked over to them and asked, "What's going on?"

One of them answered, "Were here to shoot the landing."

"What landing?"

"The Marines will be coming ashore in landing craft in a few minutes and we're here to shoot the taking of the beach and their deployment in Vietnam."

"Come on, they aren't really going to assault this beach, are they?" I asked.

Their response had me slightly concerned. I figured that if someone was crazy enough to order an assault upon a friendly beach already held by GI sunbathers then perhaps the Marines might come ashore shooting. The cameramen assured me that the Marines were aware the beach was not held by hostiles and they were under orders to simulate an actual hostile landing without shooting.

I went back to my beer and blanket to watch the fun. Shortly I could see three landing craft leave the ship and speed toward the beach directly where we were sunbathing. The landing craft kept perfect alignment and hit the beach at the same time. The cameramen were busy shooting the scene as the ramps of the landing crafts hit the shore or water. The Marines came screaming out of the craft just as I had seen in World War II movies. They ran for about fifty yards onto the beach were they hit the sand. Meanwhile those of us sitting on the beach were yelling encouragement and harassment at the poor Marines as we continued to drink our beer. A couple of beer cans were thrown at the poor Marines, one of whom yelled for a full can. The cameramen asked us to keep the noise down and to remain outside the camera views. It was all good fun and I enjoyed the event.

Unfortunately an hour later it was discovered that one of the Marines must have jumped over the side of the landing craft and was dragged down by the weight of his gear and the current. He died for merely propaganda purposes. Apparently, the folks back in the states were shown newsreels of the Marines landing on a hostile beach and securing it for the United Sates war effort. I couldn't imagine a more futile loss of life and the lies that the people back home were being fed to bolster their support of the war. I'm sure that the Marine's parents or wife were told that good old Joe was killed in the line of duty fighting for his country. It certainly wouldn't have been very acceptable to learn that Joe was drowned while a group of drunken soldiers sunbathed on a beach watching a fake amphibious landing.

I returned to Pleiku and continued my flying duties. I was finally relieved of the extra duty as intelligence officer. I flew only once each day for about three hours and spent the remainder of the day sitting around the hooch sunbathing and listening to music. Once in a while a pilot would begin the cleaning of a skull although eventually this practice was stopped by the beginning of May 1966.

Chapter 23 – The 25th Division

There was more and more evidence of the American build-up of manpower and Americans taking over more of the ground war against the VC and NVA. In Pleiku there was even a squadron of tanks that would venture out on operations as long as they were centered on main roads. The countryside was either jungle or rice paddies that did not support tank operations. Usually the tanks went out on these operations and were used at night for security like moveable bunkers. During the day they might be called upon as artillery pieces but generally the tanks were quite useless since they did not have the freedom of movement necessary to attack the enemy. The enemy was elusive enough to know that there was little point in attacking the tanks. Some of the American units began to go into the countryside to take on the enemy on its own turf. The main unit was the 1st Cavalry. This unit did much of the fighting in the central highlands. There were no Marine units in the area although Marine aircraft were usually available.

In the beginning of February 1966 I was ordered to the 219th's operations and advised that I was to lead a group of three planes including my own plane to Banmethuot and assist an American unit. The unit had recently arrived in Vietnam and was a brigade of the 25th Infantry Division. The brigade's aircraft had not yet arrived in Vietnam and the 219th was providing three Birddogs for observation and artillery adjustment purposes. The other pilots included Lieutenants Joe Lieber and Harold Crank. Crank had only recently arrived in Vietnam and consequently was a little green in terms of how to fly these types of missions. I was surprised to be placed in charge although I probably outranked both Lieber and Crank. Normally this type of mission would require the assignment of one of the captains. The next morning I was to fly to Banmethuot and put down on a landing stripe the 25th had constructed from the road passing through the region. I was to confer with a Colonel Lester Smith about the missions they needed.

Early the next morning I was airborne by 0700 hours and landed at Banmethuot by 0745 hours. Colonel Smith, who had been alerted of my arrival by the unit's radio command, met me. The 25th was concentrated along the highway. They were situated in a very thick jungle area. The only structure or sign of inhabitants was a huge log building adjacent to the road and being used by the 25th as their command center. The building looked like a lodge that might be found in the American northwest. It was square with a large wooden deck that surrounded the first floor. The roof peaked in the center of the building and had two floors with dormers extending at consistent intervals on the second floor. The building didn't seem to fit into the Vietnamese landscape and was unlike any building I had seen in Vietnam. Since there were no sign that the Vietnamese used the building for living quarters and no sign of farming, I was puzzled. I inquired as to the origin of the building from Colonel Smith and was told the building had been built in the early 1900's to accomodate President Theodore Roosevelt on one of his many hunting trips. I assumed the hunting trip was to kill a tiger and was planned after he left office since he was still a young man. Colonel Smith didn't know whether President Roosevelt ever came to Vietnam for the hunting.

I officially reported to Colonel Smith and told him that three of the 219th's aircraft would be assigned to the brigade until they had no further use for us or until their own aircraft and pilots came to Vietnam.

I asked Colonel Smith, "Sir, what type of operation will the brigade be running?"

"The brigade will be conducting a sweep of the area approximately ten miles to the west of this location. We will need your aircraft for observation and artillery adjustment purposes."

"No problem, Sir, our aircraft can be here at any time you signify."

"Excuse me Lieutenant, are you telling me that your aircraft will not be staying at our command post on a 24-hour basis?"

"Sir, there is no need for our planes to be parked here through the night. We can be on station at any time you specify and if we need to stay for a long period, I assumed we could refuel here. In addition we have no maintenance facilities here for the aircraft, no crew chiefs and no personal support facilities for the pilots."

"I'm sorry Lieutenant I want your planes here on a 24-hour basis anyway," Colonel Smith responded.

"Sir, unless there is a compelling reason for this request, the planes will return each night back to Pleiku unless they are needed for a night radio operation."

"In that case I'm ordering you to have the planes here for the full 24-hour per day. I don't think it would be good for the morale of the troops here on the ground if they knew that our pilots were returning each night for a warm meal and clean sheets on a bed."

I was beginning to doubt the sanity of Colonel Smith but kept my cool. "Sir, The pilots aren't asking the 25th to fly with us when we search for the enemy to keep up our morale. In terms of maintenance and care of our planes this location is unsuitable. In addition, you have operational control over our three planes but I have control over all other matters. We will be returning each night to Pleiku unless my unit orders something different."

I could see in his facial expression a look of disbelief but he also probably knew he had no choice but to accept my decision.

"Alright Lieutenant I shall contact your command and make the necessary changes to your orders. Now I want you to give me a flight orientation of the region to the west of here."

I took the Colonel for an hour flight during which we flew over the area where he said the brigade was to launch a search and destroy mission to pacify the area. The landscape was less jungle then that found near Banmethuot and with about 50% of the land open fields. There was no sign of buildings or inhabitants and there were no roads or paths visible. After returning Colonel Smith to the brigade headquarters he advised me to have one plane ready for missions beginning from 0700 to 2000 hours.

I took the first mission the following day and was met at the road that doubled as the landing strip by artillery major. He directed me to fly to an area about ten miles west of Banmethuot. He indicated his artillery unit would be flown into this open area two days prior to the airborne assault by the brigade via helicopters. The day prior to the assault the artillery unit would begin a barrage of the suspected enemy location to soften them up for the infantry. I thought it was strange to alert the enemy a full two days before the assault of the possible location of an attack. It was foolish to alert them even further with an artillery barrage a full 24 hours before the attack. They were thinking in terms of World War II and Korean War style of warfare but not warfare against a highly mobile enemy that did not recognize defensive lines. I gave the major my thoughts regarding the attack philosophy and was basically told to mind my own business and just fly. When I returned to the landing strip, the other two Birddogs flown by Lieutenants Lieber and Crank were parked along the road. Colonel Smith met the artillery major and they discussed the artillery's role in the assault.

When the Colonel finished I asked, "Colonel do you have any objections to our planes flying search missions when not needed by the brigade? I will make sure that there is a plane on the airstrip at all times ready for your use."

"That's a good idea Lieutenant. Do you need any personnel from us?"

"No Sir, I think we can handle the job. We will stay away from the area immediately to the west of Banmethuot where you intend to conduct your operation."

"Why is that Lieutenant," asked Colonel Smith.

"Too much aircraft activity above the target zone will alert the enemy of our intentions."

"I don't think that will be a problem, as far as I'm concerned you can fly anywhere you think you can locate the VC including our target area."

"Yes sir." Now I was really concerned about the success of the 25th's mission.

For the next four days our group flew at least one search mission each day. I usually took the missions in direct support of the 25th. They were all observation missions above the target area. There were two more missions for the artillery unit, four for the infantry units, one for the medical officer, one for the commander of the brigade, one for the brigade's executive officer and two more flights for Colonel Smith. If the enemy was at the target site and did not know the 25th planned to assault their position, then they weren't very bright.

When we returned to Pleiku after the first full day of support, I was greeted by Captain Leyda. "Have a good day, Vince?"

I could tell by the tone of his voice and his demeanor that he was about to chew my ass. "It was productive, Sir."

"The CO received a call from the commanding officer of the 25th's brigade who made a very strong point about you and your two comrades remaining at Banmethuot until you are no longer needed. Their CO said that you refused to remain overnight at the site. Is this correct," he asked?

I replied with a simple, "Yes Sir. I didn't see any logical reason to stay overnight other than to make them feel good about all of us roughing it with them."

"That may be true but Major Lust is ordering you and the other two pilots to take any gear you might need and stay on-site with the 25th. He is not a happy camper, do you get my drift?"

"Yes Sir," I replied. "Shall we take any crew chiefs with us and how about food and lodging?"

Leyda said, "The 25th will provide for your food and lodging and you will be provided with two crew chiefs for the three planes which should be sufficient." As he turned to walk away he added, "Listen try not to antagonize these guys, OK?"

With a somewhat sarcastic tone I said, "You've got my word, I will be obedient to the letter."

The following morning the group got together at the Pleiku airfield and departed for Banmethuot. After landing I reported to Colonel Smith and advised him that we would need food and quarters for the five personnel. He told us to use the brigade mess and that we would all be provided with cots to set up in the main hall of the hunting lodge. After the day's missions we all met at the lodge and after a meal at the chow hall settled into our beds quite early. Our planes were parked together about 50 yards from the hunting lodge pulled off to the side of the road. It was raining when we lay down.

In the same large room were a group of Americans and Vietnamese interrogating local villagers who they suspected of being VC sympathizers. There were two CIA agents and two Vietnamese officers who were translating the questions being but to the villagers and providing the punishment to obtain responses. The villagers were all tied to a high back chair and had their clothes ripped from their bodies. The CIA asked questions as to the location of the VC and whether there were any NVA units in the area. The villagers were also asked to identify other local people who may be VC sympathizers. None of the villagers admitted being associated with the VC and none knew of any local enemy units. Most gave a name or two of someone who may be a sympathizer. All the villagers were beaten after each question by one of the Vietnamese who used what looked like a good old American blackjack.

Two men had their genitals pulled and placed in a hole in the chair. The Vietnamese threatened to cut the man's genitals off if they did not confess. Other than hitting the person in the genitals there was no cutting. By the end of the interrogations that took about a half hour each, the villagers were all bleeding quite heavily and could not walk under their own power. There was a large pool of blood under the chair that obviously added to the effect of the interrogation. However for the six interrogations that I observed, the CIA did not obtain one confession or admission and only provided the names of perhaps other innocent people. Three of the villagers under intense beating finally agreed with the interrogators that the NVA were believed to hold ground to the west of the village. I had difficulty understanding the technique used by the CIA since any information obtained under torture would have been of questionable liability. Torture seemed to be the tool of an incompetent interrogator.

At about 2300 hours the interrogations were still being conducted. I was half asleep and half awake when I heard the unquestioned sound of incoming artillery or mortar rounds. Since neither the VC nor NVA had artillery in the area, I assumed the rounds were from a small caliber mortar. The rounds struck about 200-300 yards down the road in the vicinity of the main sleeping area of the infantry units.

I immediately came to full consciousness and jumped from the cot and listened near the door for additional rounds. They were still falling in the same location. I turned to Leiber and Crank who were still lying on their cots and said, "those are incoming mortar rounds. I think we should leave the building and get into one of those trenches that are just outside this door."

Leiber turned and responded, "If they get any closer, wake us up."

I was shocked by the response as Lieber, Crank and the two crew chiefs remained on their cots and were ready to go back to sleep. I was too embarrassed by my fear to say anything else and was intimated by the lack of fear by my comrades to take advantage of the safety of the trench. I noticed that the two CIA agents and their Vietnamese assistants had left the lodge although they left the last villager still tied to the interrogation chair. He began to yell in Vietnamese for what I assumed was a call for help. I went back to my cot and sat on the edge. Within a minute at least five or six more mortar rounds landed, the closest at least 50 yards away. When that round hit all five of us ran out the building and jumped into the trench. No additional rounds were sent against us and after ten to fifteen minutes we emerged from the trench. I could see a fire in the area where we had parked our Birddogs. I walked down the road and saw that one of the planes was a total loss and on fire while the other received serious damage in the wing. My luck remained since my plane did not seem to be touched.

In the morning I inspected my plane and radioed the good news to my command in Pleiku. Major Lust came on the radio and seemed quite agitated. "Where the hell did you park the planes?" He barked.

"I parked them along the road that doubles as a landing strip which was within fifty yards of where he were sleeping."

"I wasn't told the enemy was shelling the place when I gave the OK for you to remain overnight," he responded.

With a strong hint of sarcasm I said, "Yea, the enemy will do that sometimes without our permission."

Lust didn't respond to my statement but ordered me to send one of the other pilots back to Pleiku at the earliest time and to take all our gear with us since we would be staying at Pleiku at night for remainder of the mission. The two crew chiefs would await additional mechanics to attempt an emergency patch of the plane that was not destroyed. If made serviceable, it would then be flown back to Pleiku for more permanent repairs. I was also ordered to tell Colonel Smith that he would have to be content with only my plane for the next couple of days. I wanted to say something cute such as "I told you so" but refrained from any response that would further upset him. Happily I went to see Colonel Smith and gave him the news. He didn't make any comments but he could tell by my voice that I was pleased. The colonel merely asked if I was ready to fly him on another mission to the brigade's target site. We were airborne in fifteen minutes and were over the target site in a few minutes after takeoff. We flew a couple of passes over the area.

The colonel stated, "I haven't seen any sign of the enemy. Have you seen anything?"

"No sir. I haven't seen one indication that the VC or NVA are located anywhere near here."

"Could you fly a little lower?" He asked.

"Sir, I will fly you at this altitude or on the deck but I should warn you that continued flights over the area will certainly alerted any enemy of our interest if they are really here."

"Take me down Lieutenant."

I took the plane on a slow circle away from the area and made a rapid dive to treetop level. When we passed over an open field, I dropped to within twenty feet of the ground and covered a portion of the target area. There was no sign of any enemy personnel or defensive positions. There were no shots at the plane and as far as I could tell, there was no enemy within miles of the site. As I climbed, I asked, "Have you seen enough colonel?"

"Fine Lieutenant, take me back home." After we landed the colonel politely thanked me and I sat on the ground for another five hours before returning to Pleiku. The following day Lieber and I were both at Banmethuot and I watched from the air as the artillery unit had three 105 mm artillery pieces flown into the area by Chinook helicopters. A company of infantry accompanied the artillery. The following day I picked up a 25th artillery officer at Banmethuot and flew back to the target area where we began to fire at suspected enemy locations in the landing zone scheduled for the next day. There was still no sign of any enemy and I marveled at the brigade's willingness to expend ordinance at empty hills.

The following day was a busy one for the 25th as they airlifted a large portion of the brigade's infantry units to the target site. I had radio relay responsibility if it was needed. The brigade encountered no resistance and in fact did not have a shot fired at them. After three days in the field the artillery and infantry had amassed an enemy body county of zero. The 219th's enemy killed or wounded for the time period prior to and during the 25th's mission was eight. The cost of the operation for the 25th and the 219th had to be greatly different and yet despite the brigade's manpower they had nothing to show for their activities.

The problem was the lack of understanding of the type of fighting being waged in Vietnam. The 25th had probably trained in combating conventional fighting forces of an enemy rather than small unit guerilla tactics. A brigade was simply too big and required far too much preparation to trap small guerilla units. The brigade failed to realize that the constant observation flights were an indication to the enemy that something would soon be happening and to leave the area. It would have been far easier for a plane to take a photographic mission over the area and commanders of the interested units could have studied the photos and maps to make decisions regarding their actions. Each of the commanders wanted to get into the act with some active participation and therefore jeopardized the security of the mission. The brigade commander should have controlled this activity.

Although I was a mere 1st Lieutenant, I had given various brigade officers advice about the enemy that they disregarded probably because of my rank and duties. I had learned very quickly in Vietnam to never refuse advice from those who had experience in the country. If they had been here long enough and were still alive, they had to know some good information regardless of their rank or position. Some officers and administrators learned this lesson while other continued to show arrogance. This arrogance cost the 25th a great deal of time and money with no benefit.

Finally, the brigade relied upon the advice of the CIA who gave them concrete intelligence information that the NVA was at the target site. This information was obtained through torture of villagers who were basically forced to admit the questions about the enemy were true or face more punishment. This type of intelligence gathering was quite common for the CIA who taught their pupils, the ARVN the same techniques.

By this time Colonel Smith notified me that the brigade's aircraft had arrived in Vietnam and our services were no longer needed. I was pleased to be leaving the control of the 25th.

"By rights colonel, the eight enemy our planes have claimed can be the 25th's since we were detached to the brigade during the mission."

"No thank you Lieutenant, I'm sure we will have greater success next time. You will need them to bolster your own kill ratios."

"Your right sir. After all that's why were out here." I saluted him and departed and never heard from him again. I returned to Pleiku and the CO never discussed the mission with me or the loss of the aircraft. What bothered me was the fact that our commanding officer did not have the guts or perhaps the authority to tell the 25th that our pilots could remain at Pleiku and still give them all the support they needed without having to 'rough it' with them. As I indirectly told Colonel Smith, our pilots had no qualms or bad feelings about the fact that we usually flew alone over the enemy and didn't require company to keep up our morale. I resented the fact that Major Lust gave the 25th permission to put our lives in additional jeopardy for morale appearances.

I celebrated my return to Pleiku by getting completely drunk that night. Unfortunately the Pleiku bar did not have any beer, champagne or liquor other than a few bottles of liqueurs. I got drunk on Drambuie, which I like but is basically an after dinner drink used in small quantities. After leaving the bar I 'borrowed' a three quarter ton truck parked near the club. It had been raining all night and there were numerous puddles of water. I drove through what appeared to be a small puddle only to discover the water pool must have been over two feet deep. The left front tire hit the water pool and sank with a jolt to the axle. The hole caused something to break and left the vehicle without power to move. I merely walked away from the truck. It remained with its wheel in the hole for over three days without drawing anybody's attention to its condition although I returned two days later with a friend who took my picture in front of the vehicle. I wondered why the unit that owned the vehicle did not discover it was missing for over three days.

Chapter 24 – Flying for God and New Ways to Kill

At the beginning of April, I was given the added assignment of flying a catholic priest on Saturdays and Sundays to the small Special Forces camps and detachments for religious services that did not have a minister. The priest was a full colonel named Father John Callahan. He was a burly man in his late 40's but with a quick wit and pleasant manner. When we met prior to our first Saturday mission, he extended his hand and said, "Call me Father John or plain John if you prefer."

"Nice to meet you Father."

"I assume Lieutenant Capozzella that with a name like that you are a Catholic and of Italian decent?"

"Yes sir or rather, yes Father."

"Good, then we shall get along great together. I also hope that you will attend at least one mass that I give over the course of the weekend?"

"I will be attending mass but I was wondering how many stops we will be making?"

"I will select camps in the general vicinity of each other and I try to fly to a camp at least once a month, if possible. By the way, what is your first name?"

"Vince," I answered.

"Proper name, Vince. Let's get this show on the road and we'll hit Kontum and Dakto today."

"Hop in Father," as I led him to my plane. I couldn't help but notice that Father John was wearing a .45 caliber Browning semi-automatic much like my own sidearm, which was in his shoulder holster. "Father John, I didn't think that priest were allowed to be armed in Vietnam?"

"Vince, besides being a priest, I'm also in the military and I doubt if the Viet Cong would recognize my religious vocation. If I have to use the weapon to protect you, or myself, I will. I'm wearing the same uniform as you."

"That's fine with me Father." The flights to Kontum and Dakto were uneventful. I attended the first mass and enjoyed Father John's service. It was very down-to-earth much like the man. The following day, I flew him to Quin Nhon. We parted company back in Pleiku and I promised to meet him at the airstrip on the following Saturday at 2 pm. From Monday thru Friday I flew one or two missions a day to locate and kill the enemy while waiting for my weekend mission to help spread the gospel of the Lord.

We met the following Saturday at 2 pm as I promised. Father John got into the back of the Birddog and we flew to Nha Trang. Again I attended his mass and even went to confession with Father John. When we got into the plane for the return trip to Pleiku, it was already a little past 1700 hours. I noticed high clouds over the mountains and some lower clouds to our east over the ocean. I decided to fly north along the coast until I hit Quin Nhon and then to turn west to Pleiku and assumed I would fly beneath the cloud cover. As I flew north, the clouds over the mountain chain seemed to go from a few feet above the terrain to an altitude that I would not be able to fly over. To make matters worst there appeared to be a weather front behind us and now to our front. Although I would not have flown toward the sea to avoid the weather, another front was moving from that direction also. I was completely surrounded by massive clouds from a few feet above the terrain to an unknown altitude.

The Birddog is capable of flying to about 11,000 feet although pilots are warned to not fly above 10,000 feet because of the lack of adequate oxygen to maintain alertness. I knew I had two choices: first, to fly above the clouds if the plane could fly that high and second, to land somewhere within the area surrounded by the clouds. There were no airfields near this area and no known friendly American or ARVN forces in this area. As far as I knew the area was hostile country controlled by the VC. As I began to circle I noticed another Birddog in the same area who was also circling.

I attempted to contact the plane, "Birddog aircraft north of Nha Trang, this is Headhunter One One."

"Headhunter One One this Raven Four, we seem to be in a tight fix here."

"Raven Four, the weather looks very bad and I believe this will be a major storm. If we can't get out of here, we will be in a world of hurt."

"Headhunter One One, do you know of any friendly fields in the area?"

"Negative Raven Four. I'm thinking of trying to get over the clouds and head inland and hope the weather is better."

"Headhunter One One, that seems very risky. I'm going to continue to fly in this open pocket and if it gets too bad will land on the beach and take my chances."

"Good luck Raven Four. I will let you know if it is safe to climb over. Hope to see you later."

I turned and looked at Father John who seemed very relaxed and undisturbed. "Father, I'm going to try and climb over this mess."

"Do what you think is best, Vince."

I then began a slow circling climb. I went through 10,000 feet and still could not see over the clouds. When I hit 11,000 feet I was beginning to get very concerned. At 11,500 feet the Birddog refused to climb any higher and I lower the flaps by 15 degrees to keep the plane from stalling and to maintain this extreme height. The plane was flying at a very nose high attitude and although the front of the plane was above the clouds the plane's tail and rear seat were in the clouds. My airspeed was a mere 65 MPH although my ground speed was probably far less but at least I still could see the sun. I knew that if I lost control of the plane it would fall toward the earth in a spin. I might not be able to recover without seeing the ground and being, by now, above the 8,000 foot mountains. I looked at Father John who was sound asleep.

I called Raven Four. I was not able to make contact until I faintly heard him radio for help. "This is Raven Four, declaring an emergency. I am approximately thirty mile north of Nha Trang and I am landing on a sandy beach next to the ocean." Again I attempted unsuccessfully to contact him.

Father John and I continued our flight to the west at a painfully slow speed after about 30 minutes of very stressful flying I noticed the clouds had dropped about 500 feet. I was able to raise my flaps and slightly lower my altitude and pick up some airspeed. In another 15 minutes the cloud cover had dropped an additional 1000 feet and I began to feel some relief. Soon the clouds began to dissipate and I occasionally saw some of the ground about three thousand feet below my plane. I knew that we would be safe and I turned the plane for a heading that I hoped would take me to Pleiku. In another hour we were over Pleiku and I landed. Only after my wheels touched the ground did I notice that Father John had awaked from his sleep.

"Well Father we made it back. I can't believe you slept through that storm. I had my doubts we would make it."

"Vince I wasn't worried. I knew that God was with you."

"I wish you had told me that we were safe. I sweated like a stuff pig." I laughed.

I remembered Raven Four and went to the operations building and reported his position and predicament. They promised to take care of the situation although I never bothered to follow up on the final disposition of my fellow pilot. As for Father John, I flew him on another religious flight the next day and my duties were assumed by another pilot. I tried to attend mass whenever he was scheduled and we became good friends while I remained in Vietnam.

The remaining months that I had to serve in Vietnam became something of a blur. While I continued to fly missions from Pleiku, I started to look forward to leaving. Once the time period remaining to serve a one-year tour gets to be less than sixty or ninety days, personnel get a short timers attitude. This attitude is often characterized by lackluster effort and an effort to avoid any dangerous assignments. While I certainly began to count the days remaining, I don't believe I acquired those other unfavorable traits. Each day was characterized by basically the same regiment. After finishing my flying for the day, I would shower, eat and then hit the gambling scene. By now there was always somebody leaving the country to return to the states and the departing pilot would host a party. These parties meant that the guys attending would generally become quite drunk and as long as there were no incidents, the command ignored them.

I continued my habit of eating a majority of my meals at one of the Vietnamese restaurants in Pleiku. However the heat, lack of truly good food and my loss of appetite were beginning to take their toll on my body. When I arrived in Vietnam I weighed just about 150 pounds but by April 1966 or ten months in country I was down to 125 pounds. When I first arrived in Vietnam, I visited Saigon in September and had gone to one of the many tailor shops that specialized in serving the Americans. I ordered two hand-made suits made of Italian silk. When they were finally delivered in April, I discovered the suits were much too large for my now shrunken frame. I packed the suits away and accepted the fact that I would probably put on weight when I returned home and then the suits would fit.

My missions started to take a different twist beginning in April. While on a typical search mission, I was flying with an observer assigned to one of the Huey gun ships as a gunner. He had taken an M-60 machine gun with him. He had the weapon hanging from the observer's open window. As I passed over a very small village of about five huts within five miles of the Laos border, a number of enemy personnel began to shoot at my plane. I didn't see any village people or children around the five huts and decided to attack the three or four people doing the shooting. I came in at the enemy in a dive from my usual 1500 feet altitude above the terrain and unleashed my rockets in four salvos of two rockets on two attacks at an altitude of about 300 feet. I continued my descent until I was only thirty to forty feet above the village. Meanwhile the gunner was firing his M-60. The only concern was that I ordered him to make sure that the gun was extended far enough out the window to prevent the spent cartridges from coming into the plane and perhaps jamming my steering mechanism. After the first two attacks that consumed my rockets, I made two more attacks with both the M-60 and my own grease gun continuing the fire. By the time we were finished the five huts were either destroyed or on fire, there were three confirmed VC lying on the ground and the fire directed at my plane had stopped. When I returned to Pleiku and advised my command about the attack, I was called into Captain Kowalewski's office.

He asked, "How effective was your attack this afternoon?"

"I think we completely neutralized and destroyed the position," I proudly announced.

"Do you think you could take on a bigger target if you had three planes in the attack?"

"Theoretically three planes should mean three times the punch. Yes, I think it would make sense with three planes. They could then cover each other."

"Fine, tomorrow I want you to lead Lieutenants Crank and Finley on the same type of mission. Are you familiar with a small village about ten miles north of the village you attacked today that sits between the Special Forces camp at Dakto and Laos?" He asked.

"Sure I've seen the village a number of times."

Kowalewski continued. "A couple of days ago two Hueys were fired upon from the village as they flew into Dakto and they reported at least a platoon of VC stationed there. Tomorrow morning, I want the three of you to attack the place. It's the feeling of our command that our planes can be more offensive minded and this type of attack may be what is needed. You will coordinate the attack with Crank and Finley."

"Yes sir," I said as I left the office. I immediately called together the two pilots and told them about the mission. I told them to make sure that their rockets were either HP or WP explosives and not smoke. They were told to either enlist the services of a Huey gunner or one of our unit's crew chiefs as the second man in the plane but that I didn't want the position taken by another pilot from the 219th. I didn't want to take the chance on losing two pilots in the same plane. They were advised the gunner in the back seat could use either an M-60 or a M-16 with automatic fire and to make sure they had adequate ammunition for at least three passes against the target. I then contacted my own Huey gunner and enlisted him for the next days' mission. We also decided that he should bring about six hand grenades and that he could throw them out the window as long as the pin on the grenade was pulled outside the plane and there were no other planes close behind my own plane.

We left at 0700 hours the next morning and were approaching the village within 45 minutes. We attacked the village with three planes abreast of each other and finished the first attack about twenty feet above the buildings. The planes then attacked individually three times each. I was very pleased by the effect of the grenades. They added to the mayhem on the ground. The enemy had been taken by surprise on the first attack but had begun to return fire on the second attack and then either stopped or was eliminated by the third and fourth attacks. I was somewhat dismayed to see what appeared to be a few women and children running from the village and silently hoped they were clear of the onslaught. I told the other pilots and gunners to resist shooting at them if possible.

The mission was a complete success and from that time I was ordered, at least once a week, to continue this type of mission. We were very lucky in that none of the planes I led on these missions were ever shot down although it was obvious we were violating our altitude restriction that was in place since our arrival in Vietnam.

It seemed somewhat ridiculous that we were violating our own safety precautions to attack targets that could easily have been destroyed with jet aircraft. It was equally ridiculous that we had turned some of our planes into attack craft even though they were much to slow for combat and used techniques that would have been laughed about at the Army's War College. The only compensation in using our planes instead of jet fighters was perhaps more innocent people were able to escape the attack although this meant that more of the enemy also escaped the attack. In addition, all the pilots enjoyed the opportunity to become more offensive.

The war was taking on a more sinister approach to the destruction of the enemy. Any idea that resulted in the death of the enemy was acceptable. I recall the first time I saw 'Puff the Magic Dragon' that was a converted C-47 World War II cargo plane. The plane was stripped of all loose weight including its side door and windows. At least three gatling guns were mounted on the door side of the plane. The pilot would locate a target and then do a circle around the enemy in a right wing low attitude. When the plane was in the right configuration to the target, the pilot or co-pilot would press the fire button. The gatling guns then expended their ordinance with devastating results. The guns could fire for only a short period of time before expending thousands of rounds of ammunition. It was said that a bullet would hit the target area every three or four inches. This power ensured that if the pilot had the plane in the right position, the enemy could not escape its weapons.

I began to be more aggressive in the air and attacked targets that I would have allowed other more suitable airplanes to accomplish. On one mission I made a mistake that made me realize how careless I was becoming. I was flying at tree top level over a 'kill zone' area when I saw a rope bridge that spanned a deep gorge separating the 'kill zone' from a friendly area. I didn't see any logic in allowing a bridge to this area to remain in tact and decided to attack it with a HP rocket. It was a small target and I seriously doubted I would be able to hit it but lined up on the target. I had my small black mark on the windshield targeted on the bridge and let the rocket fly at about five hundred feet. Either I was lined up improperly on the target or the rocket was defective since it veered sharply to the right over the friendly area and struck a rather long hut. The hut was a little unusual in that it was larger than what I was use to seeing. The rocket penetrated the grass wall of the hut and struck it in the middle of the building. Immediately there was a huge explosion. I hoped this meant that it had struck either gasoline or explosives. However I was not authorized to attack the building and had not seen any indication it was being used by the enemy other than the larger than normal explosion. I was worried that perhaps there were innocent people that had become casualties and immediately flew away from the location. I didn't report the attack and tried to block it from my mind.

The attacks stimulated me in my final months in Vietnam. I was somewhat worried that my fear of the enemy and crashing was diminishing to the point that I really didn't think about it anymore. I can only assume that one cannot be frightened for a long period without eventually developing a "I don't care' attitude. I hoped that my lack of fear would not result in a catastrophe before I was rotated back to the states.

Chapter 25 – Home and Lessons

The time period for my return home grew shorter and I tried not to think about anything except flying my missions. The last two months seemed almost to be lost from my memory although perhaps it was just that I had settled into a groove where I did the same thing each day without any unusual or humorous incidents. I didn't have any doubts as to my safe return to the states since I felt I truly wasn't meant by God to be killed or seriously wounded in Vietnam. I still believed I had some kind of mystical ability to escape death or hurt. I decided to test my invincibility in a safer environment two weeks before my return to the states. I was eating at a Vietnamese restaurant in Pleiku when the waiter brought me a glass of water. The water probably contained the same parasites that had given me diarrhea during my first week here in July 1965. I reasoned that I had eaten so many unusual foods and eaten primarily in Vietnamese restaurants that my body was now immune to these parasites. I took a drink of water from the glass. The next day I was scheduled to be the security officer for the airbase. This assignment meant I had to ensure the guards were on duty and at their assigned locations. After assuming my duties at about 1800 hours I developed the most severe cramps I had ever experienced in my life. The pain was so bad I could only lie on the ground in a curled position to help relieve the pain. The officer-of-the-day refused to allow me to get off duty due to sickness, as there was no one to relieve me. I stayed the night, unable to sleep and unable to perform my duties since I could not walk. By morning the pain had subsided and although I did not develop any diarrhea I had a renewed respect for the Vietnamese parasite. It continued to defeat me when I tested its strength. Another lesson learned.

My command notified me that I would be returning to the states on June 3rd and I was to be at Tan Son Nhut Airport by 12 noon. On June 2nd I threw my going home party for any of the men of the 219th. Captain Leyda had already departed for the states and was not available and Charlie Kellum would be leaving for Saigon and then the states from his base at Quin Nhon. I had a good time and for once made a special effort to limit my drinking to ensure I was on the flight to Saigon the next morning without mishap. When I arrived at Saigon, I reported to a duty office and was advised that I would be returning home via commercial flight by way of Alaska and then New York City where I could then arrange for a flight to Saranac Lake to reunite with my family. The flight was flawless and I arrived at New York City the next day. I was wearing my dress uniform when I exited the plane and was surprised that no one seemed interested in me. It was as if I was a nothing. This lack of response burst my ego since I was so proud that I had endured a year of combat in the most trying circumstances and no one cared enough to even notice me.

I was proud of my record. My command gave me a copy of my efficiency rating that surprised me by the high marks. Captain Leyda had rated me in the top 87 % bracket while Major Lust rated me in the 90 % bracket. Captain Leyda wrote:

> Lt. Capozzella has performed his duties as an aviator in a superior manner during the rated period. His duties were to fly visual reconnaissance missions in Iam Dong Province, Republic of Vietnam, an area of extensive enemy activity. Prior to Lt. Capozzella's arrival in Iam Dong Province, there was no visual reconnaissance capability available to the Sector Advisor. During the short period covered by this report he has been instrumental in the organizing of an efficient, systematic visual reconnaissance program which continuously supports the combined efforts of US and ARVN forces. Lt. Capozzella's personal observations and reports of hostile activities within the Province have contributed a major portion of intelligence used by ground forces in planning combat operations. As one of two officers in a flight section supporting a large Province, he is often required to solve difficult problems not usually encountered by officers with his grade and experience. He has used good judgment and made timely decisions in every instance. Much of the flight activity in Iam Dong Province is over dense jungles and mountainous terrain. He has demonstrated courage in coping with the stresses arising from these conditions and refused to abort missions even when hostile fired was encountered.

Major Lust was even more complimentary and wrote:

> Lt. Capozzella's performance of duty as an aviator and often the only aviation officer in Iam Dong Province, Republic of Vietnam has been exceptional overall. He has conducted missions over long periods of time which required hazardous flight at low levels and caused him to be exposed to hostile fire on many occasions. Every flight was successfully concluded and the intelligence gained from his aerial reconnaissance was of much value to the ground commander. Because he was the only aviator in the sector for extended periods of time, he was often required to make decisions not normally associated with one of his grade. The soundness of his decisions has been reflected by the many favorable comments received from the Sector Advisor and the ground commanders he has supported. He has become quite adept at directing artillery fire and in marking targets with rockets for fighter aircraft. His efforts have resulted in many casualties being inflicted on the Viet Cong forces during counter-insurgency operations conducted in his sector of operations.

Naturally I was quite pleased with these reports although I assumed I was more of a pain-in-the-ass than the reports indicated. At least it was reassuring to know that I had been appreciated. I was also awarded the Army Commendation Medal for my time in Vietnam and twelve Air Medals. These Air Medals are based primarily on fifty missions for each medal. I therefore had completed over 600 combat missions. My only regret was my belief that I had not accomplished much in terms of the larger picture. The goal was to bring the war closer to a conclusion. I had long ago stopped counting the casualties for which I was given credit and had no use for a personal body count. For each of the enemy I killed or wounded I believed there was more than one taking his place. My primary personal accomplishment was not killing anyone who could be considered innocent of fighting for the enemy. I felt that I had redeemed my military record and that I was truly worthy of being a soldier for my country.

I continued to support the principles of the war although I did not believe we could win the war. I also continued to support both President Johnson and then President Nixon in continuing the fight with the hope that the military and the administration would correct the method the war was being waged. It was not until after the United States had pulled out of Vietnam and then a few more years after when the truth about our activities became public that I turned against the war. I was totally disillusioned by the deceit of our leaders who either lied or mislead the American people regarding the need for the confrontation or its progress.

When I returned to the United States to continue my life with my wife and one year old daughter, I was still supporting the war. I was assigned like most of the returning pilots to the home of the Army Aviation School in Fort Rucker, Alabama. I was surprised to be given a job as an instructor of instructors but was able to cope with the tasks. In January 1967 I contacted my career advisor at the Pentagon in Washington, D.C. Basically I asked him to give me an idea as to my career options. He stated that I would probably be receiving orders to attend helicopter training at Fort Rucker within five to six months. After completing the training by January 1968 I would be returning to Vietnam as a platoon leader of a groups of Cobra Attack Helicopters with a group of young newly commissioned warrant officers fresh out of helicopter training.

The advisor said, "I'm think that this second tour of duty in Vietnam will be your last tour although naturally I can't speak for the Army. It is possible the war will continue for a few more years. This fact could force the Army to send pilots back for a third tour."

I had not thought of a third tour of duty in Vietnam and already was concerned about surviving my second tour. However, for the advisor to mention a third tour brought memories before my first tour of being promised to having to endure only one tour. I was convinced that a third tour was not only a possibility but also a sure thing especially when one studied the way the war was progressing. I thanked the advisor and now studied the possibilities. My obligation to the Army was through April 1968 and it was unlikely that I would be sent back to Vietnam if I submitted my papers to leave the military. Yet I truly loved the Army and flying. Another fact was obvious. In my unit at Fort Rucker, I was one of nineteen other officers assigned to the Instructor's School. All nineteen of the instructors were pilots and as a Captain I outranked only one other officer. I realized the Army was becoming top heavy with officers, especially pilots. When the war finally ended, I didn't think the Army would have use for so many pilots especially those in the higher ranks and they would either be dismissed from the service or be allowed to remain with a rank of sergeant. I decided immediately that the only way I would remain in the Army was with a Regular Army commission. This situation would ensure that I would remain in the Army after the war and at the rank I was holding. I prepared my application for the commission and was pleased when I was scheduled for the board in March 1967. My command believed I had an excellent chance to be successful based on my efficiency reports in Vietnam and my performance as an instructor. I had high hopes. Unfortunately neither my current commanders nor I had anticipated that I would be stricken by an honest conscience and my deep disappointment as to the direction of the war.

As I stood outside the room where I had just mismanaged the interview to secure my standing in the Army and receive my regular army commission, I knew my future no longer would be with the military. In anticipation of the worst-case scenario, I had already prepared a request for release from the Army to take effect in April 1968. I had job applications for all the airlines and had scheduled a Civil Service test for positions in the government. I also decided to apply for a position as a Special Agent with the FBI since it sound like a different thing to do.

I knew that in the event I left the Army I would need to complete my college education. A month after my return from Vietnam I had contacted Troy State College to discuss continuing my education since the college has an extension course at Fort Rucker. I enrolled in the college and computed that at the rate I was progressing, I would receive my BA degree in Business Administration in January 1968. The future was uncertain but bright in terms of many different occupations that were available. I also wouldn't have to return to Vietnam for a second and third tour and then to be discarded as useless.

I was still numb from the interview and sat down on a bench in the hallway outside the interview room. I began to think about the twelve months in Vietnam and realized that there were a number of lessons to be learned from my experience.

First, I no longer felt as if I was a loser. I had been successful in one of the most demanding assignments given to me and I had excelled. The down side of this good feeling was that I had excelled in locating and killing people although it was an enemy of my country. This achievement wasn't a marketable commodity in the civilian world.

In combat there is only one absolute truth and that is the ability to do your job correctly with some degree of courage or at least willingness to risk your life occasionally. Those people who cannot handle combat in a satisfactory manner are expendable or at the very least those people to keep at arms length since their incompetence or cowardness could cost the lives of others. This truth is a hard lesson and perhaps overly cynical since not everyone can be competent. However, when your life and those of your comrades are on the line, failure is unthinkable.

Regardless of your position and job, one can always learn from the experience of others. It is not important what position the individual may have or his physical looks, advice should always be sought and at least listened. The advice can certainly be ignored or determined to be unacceptable for the task or problem on hand but it does not hurt your decision-making ability. Seeking advice and even accepting the advice for overcoming a task is not a sign of weakness but rather a sign of strength. Not everyone in Vietnam was willing to seek advice even when they were faced with problems and assignments for which they were not prepared to handle. It seemed as though the higher in rank the individual, the less the individual would accept or invite advice. I believe the individuals believed this process would indicate a weakness and yet their stubbornness was the sign of weakness.

The CIA was not as effective or competent as most Americans are lead to believe by the press coverage they receive. While the CIA agent that came to BaoLoc was thoroughly incompetent and lacked the courage and integrity to tell the truth, he was probably representative of many of their agents. Not embarrassing the ARVN may be a consideration; the bottom line was that the truth concerned a military situation upon which lives were dependent. The agent then compounded his failure by hiring a Vietnamese national to spy on me because I refused to play the game of deception and deceit. In addition to this agent, I had witnessed the interrogation of Vietnamese peasants by the CIA and the ARVN. The primary method to secure information was through the use of torture. Eventually the peasants gave the CIA the information they were seeking to confirm what they had already decided was fact. Unfortunately for the 25th Infantry this information based on torture and wishful thinking was incorrect and cost millions of dollars and wasted military effort. The 25th would have been far more productive to plan an operation against the enemy based upon the intelligence obtained from the troops on the ground and the pilots who flew over the enemy on a daily basis. I also believe torture only instills in the victims a deep hatred of the interrogators and the country they represent. If the people who are being tortured are innocent of the charges, they and family members will turn against those who condone this type of activity. In essence the CIA was creating more of the enemy that the military would have to face in the future.

The public cannot accept everything that the government tells them as being the truth. The body count issue was a typical attempt to convince the American people that the military was winning the war. Obviously from my own experience it was often impossible to give an accurate body count and it would be fabricated because a count was required in all action. Also the body count philosophy encourages our military to provide bodies to show success. It was not necessary to prove the bodies were those of the enemy and some military personnel were more than willing to kill any Vietnamese to raise body counts. Besides being immoral, the killing of innocent Vietnamese only increased the number of enemy to be faced. I always believed that the Vietnamese and every human have similar family values as Americans. If one of my family members were killed by an enemy and especially if the family member was innocent and considered "collateral damage," I would become an active opponent of the enemy. For each innocent Vietnamese killed, seriously wounded or tortured by United States forces, at least two new Vietnamese enemies took their place. It is easy then to mathematically conclude that as the war progressed the number of enemy continued to rise although the body count number suggested the enemy had to be getting weaker. Americans simply do not credit our enemies with having the same sense of patriotism and family ties as we do. This opinion often leads us to conclusions that are incorrect and hinder success.

In Vietnam the American Army as a whole simply did not bring the war to the enemy. In order to keep our casualties to a minimum, the administration and the American high command in Vietnam attempted to win the war primarily with air power while holding the major population centers. This philosophy simply did not work since, while airpower can inflict casualties on the enemy with a minimum of American losses, it cannot destroy the enemy nor occupy ground the enemy holds. The enemy's ground forces must be defeated and the ground taken from them. Perhaps the number of American troops was not sufficient to hold the population centers and to take the fight to the enemy. If this was the case, then our leaders had two possible choices. Increase the number of troops on the ground or to admit our failure and to get out of the battle. Our government chose to do neither until public sentiment forced our withdraw.

Our government placed their hopes of a successful conclusion of the war or at least our withdraw from the fighting on the training and involvement of the ARVN. In fact the ARVN were never prepared to take on greater responsibility in the war and were more of a liability than an asset. Our leaders could not understand how the ARVN could not match the military ability of the NVA or the Vietcong even though they had been trained by our military and were equipped with the same weapons as our own forces. The answer is fairly obvious. There was no reason for the average ARVN soldier to risk his life. The United States assumed the ARVN were committed to defend their country much like the American soldier was committed to defending his country. Yet the ARVN never considered South Vietnam to be his country. True, the ARVN lived in South Vietnam, were paid by this government and wore the uniform of this country, yet the country was believed to be merely a puppet of the United States in its fight against communism. The ARVN soldier had no desire to fight and die for America's fight against communism. Consequently the average soldier did as little as possible to serve his army and certainly did not go out of his way to put his life on the line. The higher ranking ARVN officers had the same philosophy although many of them prepared for the eventual withdraw of US forces by lining their pocked with American aid or by selling American supplies on the black market. As a country, the United States simply assumed our allies had the same motivation as our own troops without studying the reason for the ARVN's failure. Our government knew the ARVN were not reliable and assumed the problem was with their training and numbers. Simply put, no amount of training, numbers or equipment can overcome dedication to a cause or belief. Consequently the basic principles, by which this war was fought, were serious flawed and could only lead to defeat regardless of the number of casualties the United States was willing to accept. It took me a year of my life in Vietnam and then four or five additional years to acknowledge this fact.

Epilogue

I did leave the Army in April 1968 and was hired by United Airlines in their pilot training program. While receiving my training, I also received an appointment as a Special Agent in the FBI. I choose the FBI primarily because my assignment with United Airlines was to be at Kennedy Airport in New York City. This location to me was not the most desirable place to raise a family. I remained with the FBI until 1980 in the field of Foreign Counterintelligence and then accepted a position as a college professor at Jefferson Community College, State University of New York at Watertown, New York. From a college dropout I was now teaching college. It was surprising to say the least.

My fellow pilots faired much worst then expected. Most served three one-year tours in Vietnam. Those that survived were generally told they could accept a rank as a sergeant or leave the service without any severance compensation. Essentially they were told their services were no longer needed regardless of the sacrifice they had made. Their treatment was shameful although I must admit they received exactly what I expected.

While with the FBI, I often was required to arrest military deserters and men who refused to be drafted. I still remained a strong supporter of the war and didn't have difficulty arresting those that opposed the war. As the war continued and I observed our government's attempts to destroy the reputations of those that opposed the war, I became more cynical. As a FBI agent I was often directly involved with programs designed to convince the American public that the antiwar protestors were not loyal to America and were linked to the Soviet Union and China. These attempts were not realistic and although condoned by the Nixon administration, they were the inspiration and fabrication of FBI Director J. Edgar Hoover. It is generally a simple task to discredit and immobilize a minority opposition by the government. Once the opposition becomes a significant majority as during the Vietnam War, the government can not successfully discredit them.

On a personal level, I began to discover the truth about the war by the end of the 1970's and upon examination of my accomplishments, failures and deeds, realized that war was not always the easiest or more intelligent way to accomplish one's objectives. This story is a testament of a wasted year in a young man's life in terms of reaching my country's objectives. Perhaps we can all learn that war is the absolute last resort and even when that time materializes that our leaders should pause once more before sending their citizens out to die.

Glossary

ARVN: Army of the Republic of Vietnam.
Birddog: Cessna Army observation plane also called the L-19 and the OV-1
CIA: Central Intelligence Agency
Charlie: Name use by US forces to describe both Vietcong and NVA
Fragging: Act of killing a fellow soldier, usually an officer, with a grenade
Huey: Main Army helicopter used to both transport troops to battlefield and medical evacuation. Designated the UH-1.
L-19: Cessna Army observation plane also called the Birddog and redesignated as the OV-1 in Vietnam
MACV: Military Assistance Command, Vietnam (US forces)
NVA: North Vietnamese Army
OV-1: Army observation plane also called the Birddog and the OV-1
RVN: Republic of Vietnam (South Vietnam)
Special Forces: US troops trained for small unit operations to assist and train the Vietnamese people. Often called the Green Berets
Vietcong or Viet Cong: Communist South Vietnamese forces fighting the US and the ARVN
Vietminh or Viet Minh: Nationalist and Communist forces that fought the French primarily under the leadership of Ho Chi Minh

ABOUT THE AUTHOR

Vincent J. Capozzella was born and raised in Utica, New York, and served as an Army officer from 1962-68. After receiving his pilot training at Fort Rucker, Alabama, he served in Vietnam in 1965-66. He became a Special Agent in the Federal Bureau of Investigation in the field of Foreign Counter-intelligence for twelve years at Allentown, Pennsylvania, and then as a professor at Jefferson Community College, SUNY, Watertown, New York, for fifteen years where he researched the history of the Vietnam War. The author was also elected to five two-year terms as mayor of Sackets Harbor, New York. He has recently completed a novel, *The Alaskan Protocol*, concerning the purchase of Alaska from Russia in 1867 and a modern-day conflict between the intelligence services of the United States and Russia. The author currently lives in Canon City, Colorado near Colorado Springs.

www.ingramcontent.com/pod-product-compliance
Lightning Source LLC
Chambersburg PA
CBHW071417160426
43195CB00013B/1726